Barbara

Dancing through Life!

The fascinating story of Barbara Stewart

Barbara
Dancing through life!
ISBN 9780954723675

First published in 2007 by TwigBooks.
Copyright © Barbara (Stewart) Vanner 2007.
Edited by Terry Gasking at TwigBooks

For their kind permission our thanks go to –
  James Clevett, Littlehampton for the Cover Photograph
  Sylvia Hayes, Bognor Regis for many of the text photographs.

Enquiries concerning film or media rights or reproduction outside these terms or the purchase of copies of this book should be sent to the publishers –

TwigBooks
1-2 Biggs Lane
DINTON, Aylesbury
Buckinghamshire, HP17 8UH
England, U.K.
http://twigbooks.com

Dedicated with grateful thanks to
MUM and DAD
for their care and loving support
as I followed my dancing 'STAR'.

Special thanks to my husband Wally
for his love, encouragement and untiring help,
and to Terry Gasking
who made me into an author.

Contents -

Barbara
1923 to the start of the WAR - 1939

3

Barbara 1939 - 1943

Barbara
1943 - 1945 War Service with ENSA

Barbara~
Back to civilian life 1945~

Photographs

Barbara 1980 - to date - The Extra

<u>*Barbara - Dancing through Life!*</u>

My life on stage has been a fascinating journey for any girl! Beginning as a tèenage dancer prior to the Second World War; I danced through the 'Blitz', and during my E.N.S.A. service, struggled to make a living after 'demob'; I had triumphs and tragedies; until the excitement of appearing as a 'Extra' in a whole series of TV shows and serials since 1982. It has been full of interest and excitement that I share with you.

This book is a collection of my many journals, photographs, show billings, and other memorabilia up to the present day - with recollections of almost 70 years appearing in London and provincial theatres up and down the land in musical productions, both professional and amateur

There have been tragedies as well as triumphs and I have recorded those that had the greatest influence on my life. These recollections make nostalgic reading as I consult diaries and the 'filing system' of thoughts since I first saw the light of day in West Hampstead, London, on 22nd November, 1923

I give thanks to James Clevett and Sylvia Hayes for allowing us to use the photographs taken by them, to my dear husband Wally Vanner for his help in typing the manuscript and his work on the text photos, to Bertha Peek, Tony Alexander & Jill Gasking for their kind words, to Colin Gillert for his design of the picture pages, to Terry Gasking for his editing, endless encouragement, and for putting this whole project together, and to all my friends who have helped and encouraged me to write

'Barbara - Dancing through Life!'

I hope you share my enjoyment of my lifetime as a dancer!

Barbara

2007

The Barbara we know!

We first met Barbara in 1959 when, after a fabulous professional career as a dancer, she came to dance in an amateur operatic show for B.E.L.R.A. (British European Leprosy Relief Association).

Bertha was choreographer and Tony and Jill danced in the show. That was the start of many shows together and nearly 50 years of friendship, companionship, and joy.

If Bertha ever needed help with a dance or a show, socially or personally, she had only to contact Barbara and it was taken care of with wonderful spirit and kindness.

Tony danced with Barbara in the early 1960's in an amateur production of 'Love from Judy'. "My partner and I needed a break but had my mother and elderly aunt staying with us so it seemed impossible. Barbara offered to be in touch with mother and aunt every day so that we could have a holiday and every single day she was in touch. Little did I realise then that some 40 years later she would still be one of my dearest friends – and still an excellent dancer!"

Jill has shared many a dressing room with Barbara and a friendship that has lasted long beyond their dancing days.

Jill actually wore one of the beautiful costumes that Barbara so delightfully describes in 'A look into the Past'. – 'A beautiful Edwardian Dress in pale turquoise and white with tiny pleats. Every pleat was hand sewn with the tiniest of stitches that covered the whole of the dress.

"In all the years I have known Barbara I cannot remember a disagreement or argument. Barbara is always most supportive of all her friends and acquaintances".

We are all thrilled that Barbara has written this book that so delightfully tells of her experiences when *'Dancing through Life'*. It is a fascinating life and we hope you enjoy reading about it. This book is full of interest and has been written by a lovely, genuine and kind person.

Bertha Peek,
Tony Alexander, Jill Gasking

10

Barbara - 1923 - 1939

Destined to be a DANCER!

I think that I was always destined to be a dancer!
When I started to walk it was always on my toes.

A visiting aunt said *"Look how that child is walking"*-
my big brother, all of five and a half years old, sprang
to my defence with *"All babies walk like that!"*

When I was 4 years old my mother took me to
dancing lessons at the church hall at the end of our
road. I treated it just as a game and were it not for
mummy I may not have become a dancer.

I can still remember her holding my hand and
counting out the steps as we danced across our living
room floor. She made sure I remembered the
sequences as we were to do a concert. Something
must have entered my head and feet for when the day
of the concert arrived I made my debut as a fairy.

In my fairy dress and wrapped in a shawl I was
pushed to the hall in our big pram – that was then in
use for my baby brother. I don't recall if it was the
dress, the fuss, or the applause, but from then on I
took dancing lessons more seriously.

By the time I was 5 years old I did a solo dance on
pointe! It was at **Foresters Hall** in Kilburn High Road,
London. The hall is still there but known today more
famously as the **Tricycle Theatre**.

I don't remember the dance or the dress but I will
never forget the cream roses of my very first bouquet
presented to me after my dance. Many years later I
found out I should not have been allowed to dance on
pointe until I was about 12 years of age.

When my first dancing teacher gave up teaching to get married I was very sad I used to give great sighs as I longed to dance again, and it wasn't done out of a sense of drama or childish pique, I just couldn't seem to help it . It was quite some time before a new dance school was found for me.

Anna Pavlova

When **Anna Pavlova**, the great ballerina, appeared at the **Golders' Green Hippodrome**, I was still only 5 years of age but I was taken to see her, my very first visit to a theatre.

It was all very exciting and I still remember it especially Pavlova's dancing.

Flavia Galli Dancing School

My new teacher's name was **Flavia Galli**. She had an Italian father, English mother and a brother Lewis and they lived in a basement flat in Kilburn Square, London.

When we had our lessons the furniture would be pushed aside in the living room and her mother played the piano for the many songs and dances for the annual concert she put on.

Flavia was young and we all loved her. She designed all our costumes and I recall her cutting yards of net into circles for ballet skirts while counting out our steps for us.

On Saturday mornings we rehearsed in a hall - a luxury after the confines of a living room. These were some of the happiest days of my life and my whole family became involved.

Mummy made my costumes, Daddy made my hats and worked the 'lights' for the shows and my elder brother **Jimmy** played the piano and Flavia's brother **Lewis** played the drums.

My younger brother **Roy** refused to act on stage but he acted as our call-boy. I loved every minute of the fuss, the music - but above all the dancing. Soon I was walking the mile to Flavia's house every evening whether I had a lesson or not.

The more affluent parents paid for their children to have private lessons - something that could not be managed on my father's pay as a policeman. I would curl up in a corner on the floor and watch and learn.

It is only now as I'm writing this that I realise I was getting second hand 'private' lessons. When Flavia started an adult dancing class I helped them learn the basic steps and in return I was allowed to join the acrobatic class for free.

Flavia later married, had a son - **Mike Hurst** who became famous with Dusty Springfield in the

'Springfield's' group and also as a top record producer.

Mike appeared in November, 1946, at the Metropolitan Theatre of Varieties, Edgware Road, London, in Flavia's "Twinkle Little Star", in one sketch as "Big Mike Pickworth and his Girlfriends", and in "Miser Miser".

I had come home from E.N.S.A. by then and Flavia 'wrote' me into the show as **'Queen of Fiesta'** and as a Solo Dance act.

Mike as a young 'speciality' act appeared with Max Miller, Tessie O'Shea, Leon Cortez and Sid Fields among others. He also went on performing and touring in America

In the early 1960's unknown to Mike, Flavia arranged for him to have an audition which resulted in him replacing Tim Field as guitarist with Tom and Dusty Springfield in the 'Springfield's' group.

They immediately had 'hit' records in the top 10, but when the Beatles' phenomenon came on the 'scene' they disbanded after appearing in their last TV show, Bruce Forsyth's 'Sunday Night at the London Palladium'.

Mike went on to discover and produce the likes of Marc Bolan of T-Rex, Shakin' Stevens and Cat Stevens, producing albums with many other 'greats' including Cilla Black, The Four Tops and Showaddywaddy.

My husband **Wally** and I went to see Flavia at Henley's 'Kenton' Theatre in December '78 where her children's theatre group were putting on 'Aladdin' in which her grandchildren **Muffin Hurst** and **Bryony Hurst** appeared as Aladdin and Princess Mimosa and which made her and Mike very proud.

The programme, which I have, is a constant reminder of what Flavia did for my career

Pennies
not quite from Heaven

Among the highlights of our childhood was a football international at Wembley Stadium;
Scotland versus England.
We didn't go to the match but the coaches taking the teams away from Wembley passed the top of our road going along Kilburn High Road, London.

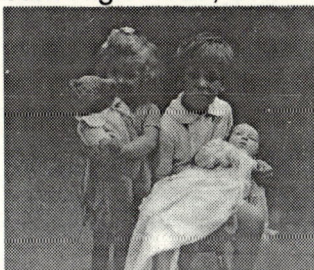

It didn't matter which team had won, the Scots were in party mood and when they saw us and several other children waving to them they threw money out of the windows.
Only pennies and halfpennies but at 12 toffees for one penny - yes that was the cost - they would buy a lot of sweets in those far off days between the two World Wars.

Madame Andreyeva

When I was 13 years of age I was accepted for three months 'free' special training by **Madame Andreyeva** who had been a pupil of **Anna Pavlova**.
She had a studio in Bond Street, London where we went for lessons on Saturdays.
I began to be put in the front row as I learned so quickly but unlike the other girls I had only been told the names of some ballet steps and had to watch the

others interpret the spoken instructions before I could perform them.

We worked very hard before taking a break – when Madame would cut thick pieces bread and spread them generously with butter, honey and cream – for energy we were told. Of course we loved it.

Some times she would trip us along to Lyons Tea Shop and buy us those long iced buns.

One day Madame gave me a pair of green satin pointe shoes. Mine had always been canvas and I had only ever seen them in pink.

I adored those green satin shoes and treasured them long after I had worn them to a pulp.

My bus fare home from Bond Street was 2 pennies (old pence). I used to walk halfway, about a mile - and this was after a really hard dancing class - and spend the penny I saved on chocolate!

Madame Andreyeva had planned to form a troupe to do some professional work but sadly that never came to pass.

When I was just 14....!

(My first professional job!)

In 1937 when I was nearing my 14th Birthday, **Flavia,** my dancing teacher, took me to auditions for juvenile dancers in pantomime in London.

'Babes in the Wood',
- 2 weeks at **Hackney Empire**
- 2 weeks at **Shepherd's Bush Empire**.

Having failed the secondary school entrance exam when I was 11 years old, I was at a senior elementary school and due to leave at Christmas. To attend rehearsals for the pantomime I needed to leave earlier. My mother was interviewed by a board of what I presume were governors,

"Did she realise she was setting my feet on the road to ruin?" they asked,

"Did she know the sort of people I would meet on the stage?"

Mummy answered crossly! *"Don't talk to me about stage people "I could tell you plenty about the so called 'Gentleman' of the House when I was a young girl in service."*

"I trust my daughter to behave well, I know how I have brought her up - and anyway her brains are all in her feet".

At this it was agreed I should be allowed to leave three weeks early, two weeks after my 14th birthday.

I hadn't seen a pantomime before. It was an exciting new world and I loved it. I don't remember having any 'nerves' or trouble learning what I had to do.

One day another girl asked me what Grade I was? I had no idea what she was talking about. Flavia taught what I now call 'instant dancing'. Apart from a little barre work for ballet dancing, we did not do any preparation exercises just learnt the steps and dances. We had never heard of exams.

I was never again asked what grade I was and I danced alongside girls who had been to the 'top' schools in the Country, so Flavia did a good job even if she didn't teach me the names of all the steps.

Sixty years or so later, I went back to the Hackney Empire to see some friends in a show.

The theatre had been restored, all the gilt was as bright as anything in the auditorium and it looked just beautiful.

After the show I went back-stage to see my friends, I walked on to the stage and looked down at my feet and thought *"This is where it all began, the very first stage I danced on professionally".*

Well, who'd have thought it?

In those 60 intervening years I danced on so many stages it is difficult to recount them all.

I survived years of the 'blitz' and danced whilst bombs were falling.

I helped entertain the troops in –

- **Great Britain**;
- **Africa**;
- **Italy**;
- **Holland**;
- **Belgium**;
- and into **Germany**
- often with the 'enemy' only a few miles away.

I appeared in numerous television dramas as an extra and when approaching my 80th year I was one of the dancers in the '**All New Harry Hill Show'** on mainstream television.

All of this was unimaginable in 1937 to a 14 year-old girl when Baird was still experimenting with TV and his first trial broadcasts were being made from Alexandra Palace in London.

It was impossible to believe that I would be 'on-screen' in the nation's living rooms time after time as an extra in some of the major TV series and that I would again appear as a dancer long after many of my friends had 'hung up their dancing shoes'.

But more of this later in the Book.

For now it was back to **Flavia** as a 14 year-old at the end of my spell at the -

Hackney Empire
and **Shepherd Bush Empire.**

State Cinema, Kilburn

I went back to **Flavia** and did a little unpaid teaching for her. Then she landed an engagement to provide the live entertainment between films at the –

Gaumont State Cinema, Kilburn High Road, London, which was at the time the largest cinema in Britain and still may be.

We did this for a week, I did solo dances on the lovely big stage and it was only a short walk from home.

I was in my first Pantomime when I was 14 years old

'Babes in the Wood'

When it was over my mother struck a bargain with me. She said if I would learn a trade that I could fall back on if I needed to, then I could go on *'The Stage'*

I realised this was the sensible thing to do so I allowed myself to be marched into our local Departmental Store, in Kilburn High Road, London, - B. B. Evans & Co.

I was duly accepted as an apprentice for 2 years training, it was then February, 1938.

Needles, Pins & Knicker Elastic

It's hard to imagine now, that Shop Assistants did 2 years training in those days. My pay was 12 shillings and sixpence a week, (62.5 new pence in today's sterling – US$1.18 – or in Euros = €0.93).

It was arranged I would have lunch in the Canteen for which I was charged 2 shillings and six pence a week, leaving me with 10 shillings pay, (50 new pence – US 94c - €0.74) for the rest of the week.

I gave this to my mother and she gave me 2 shillings 'pocket money', (10 whole new pence - £0.10). Believe it or not, I spent half and 'saved' half towards Christmas Presents.

Unfortunately I was put on the haberdashery counter, selling **needles, pins and knicker elastic**.

It was all terribly boring. The counter itself was about 6 metres long and it was manned by two other apprentices as well as me and 1st, 2nd and 3rd 'Sales' (Sales Assistants).

Order was strictly observed! When a customer approached 1st 'Sales' would step forward to serve and only if she was busy with a customer would 2nd 'Sales' take over, and so on, right down to us apprentices - which meant I was the last in line.

We were on commission and if by chance an apprentice had a customer interested in a larger item, such as a Sewing Kit or a Needlework Basket, 1st, 2nd or 3rd 'Sales' would swiftly take over even if it meant serving 2 customers at the same time.

We had to wear black, which I hated. As I hadn't started to use 'make-up' and being very pale-faced, I always looked ill in black and soon I wore a large white collar. I had my mother make me a black overdress; I wore pretty dresses under it and always managed to have a bit of colour peeping out at the neck, very frowned on but I got away with it. When work was over I whipped off the offending 'black', hung it in the cloakroom and 'skipped' home in a bright dress.

When I look back it's like watching a 'Period Film'.

The 'Buyer' was a lady and she was the Head of the whole Section, which included the Jewellery counter. Her white hair was beautifully coiffured and she wore a long black velvet dress with a 'train'. All the men wore black jacket and pin-striped trousers.

I soon earned a name for being willing to go on any errand at the drop of a hat but truth to tell I was only too happy to escape from behind the counter. If I was sent down to the stock room I would often lock myself in and do a quick tap-dance before completing my errand.

I could buy a 2oz (60 gm) bar of chocolate for 2 old pennies (1p). Most days I would eat half a bar, breaking each of the four squares into 4 pieces and surreptitiously eat 1 piece every half hour. How's that for boredom relief or clock-watching?

Although I was only 14, customers would often ask me if I thought there would be a War, for in 1938 War was continually being talked about. I always cheerily answered *"No, of course not "*.

The nearest counter to ours was the Jewellery, part of our Section, which was presided over by just 1 Assistant. How I envied her surrounded by all those beautiful things. What's more she was allowed to perch on a small stool between customers, a luxury not possible or allowed behind our counter although it was twice as long but there were 6 of us moving about. Somehow my interest in the Jewellery counter was noticed and although I was the junior apprentice I was appointed to 'cover' it during the Assistant's lunch hour. She was a lovely attractive lady and kindness itself to this very 'green' and very young girl. I lived for that 1 hour away from the very mundane things that made up the Haberdashery counter and the chance to wallow in the things of beauty.

I must have acquitted myself well for when holidays came round I was entrusted to manage the Jewellery counter for 2 whole weeks. This included setting out a display of my own choosing every morning and packing it all away every evening.

'Gretna Green'

Brothers **Jimmy** and **Roy**, I and our parents travelled on holiday every other year (we couldn't afford every year) from West Hampstead, London, to **Carluke**, Lanarkshire, home of our Scottish father's family. It was not unknown for me, considered somewhat a bit of a tom-boy, to frequently sport grazed knees, elbows etc.

Leading up to these holiday visits however, mother was continually entreating me not to run too fast, or other activities that could attract scabs and bruises or worse - *"You must look your best for Granny and Grandpa"*. I was quietly in awe of them for the first day or two as a result.

We usually travelled overnight from Euston station by rail. For a change in 1938, without elder brother Jimmy – now at work – we made the journey by coach.

On the way home we had an engaged couple on board and knowing that we were to stop at **Gretna Green** (famous for elopements, 'instant marriages' and marriages without requiring parental consent!); the co-driver persuaded them to get married!

All the passengers trouped excitedly into the famous Blacksmith's Forge and with the loan of the driver's signet ring and all of us passengers as 'guests' the pair were married over the anvil. We all added our names to the white washed walls as was the custom. I have often wondered how they fared!

Would they find two angry mothers at home, cross at having been done out of a wedding? Did the two fathers come to blows with the father of the bride accusing his counterpart's son of leading his daughter astray?

Are they still married with children, grandchildren, or even great-grand children having celebrated their diamond wedding anniversary?

I would like to think so!

November 1938

November (1938) two events are still vivid in my memory –

- *First: Armistice Day,*

Everyone in the store suddenly going quiet and standing perfectly still. Seeing through the windows all the traffic in the road outside at a standstill. I could almost 'feel' the silence, it was that dramatic.

I don't suppose I noticed it that much when we stood in the Hall in school for our 2 minutes silence.

- *The Second event was a miracle to me!*

I was sent a contract from the dancing school that had taught us the dances for the pantomime 'Babes in the Wood' the year before.

It was for a 4 week 'Tour' in –

'Robinson Crusoe'

1 week in each town,

Ramsgate; Dover; Bedford and **Luton.**

What a relief to get away from the haberdashery counter, trying to sell **needles, pins** and **knicker elastic.**

If I could convince my parents to agree then I would be going back on the stage as a dancer. My father was easy to convince I should go but it took 3 weeks to get Mummy to sign the contract on my behalf.

Looking back it is not surprising - it meant the end of my apprenticeship and my first time away from home – and I would not be 15 years old until 22nd November!

Robinson Crusoe

The dancing school where we were to rehearse Robinson Crusoe was at Wimbledon and the first weeks of rehearsals were held in the evenings so I continued to work at B B Evans that week.

My brother **Jimmy** now working for a Shipping Company in town met me after work and whisked me from BB Evans at Kilburn to Wimbledon on the back of his motor-bike. I used to feed us both chocolate as we went along.

This good natured brother of mine used to hang about looking in the window of a model train shop until it was time to take me home. We did this every evening – Monday to Friday.

On Saturday I completed my notice at the shop and was given a gold bangle as a leaving present.

I remember very little of the rest of rehearsals – only the joy of going to them and not being behind the Haberdashery counter – selling **needles, pins and knicker elastic** any more.

When I had started in the shop my long 'ringlets' had been cut shorter and this time on stage I would not be a 'juvenile'.

The company arranged 'digs' for us in advance of each week's show and several of us shared.

In one place four of us had to share one bedroom and in it was a double bed and against it a single bed, a few inches from the single bed was a built in cupboard and its door wouldn't quite close.

Late at night after two performances of the 'pantomime', this took on a sinister feel.

We four young girls began frightening each other about *who* or *what* was in the cupboard and no one would dare to open it to see.

We had to decide who would have to sleep next to the cupboard and the slightly open door and who would sleep in the middle of the big bed.

At length we worked out a routine, one, two and three in the double bed and number four in the single bed on the first night. Second night it was four, one and two in the big bed and number three in the single and so on, moving up a place each night. As there were only seven nights number one got off with only one night next to the cupboard.

The show was well received and on the Friday night after one of our dances we had boxes of chocolates thrown on to the stage from men sitting in the Side Boxes. They were waiting outside the stage door after the show but we were whisked away by our chaperon; I can say however, that I started my stage career in the days of **Stage Door Johnnies.**

When our week in Ramsgate and then Dover finished we had to journey to Bedford. Arriving in London at Waterloo station we young dancers were met by our parents eager to see how we had survived two weeks away from home; I was just 15.

They met us at our arrival station and then came with us to the other station. We had all washed our hair on the Saturday night in order to look our best.

My mother had always washed my hair putting it into rags to set the ringlets, so I did my best but come the Sunday morning I could not understand why my ringlets fell into place on one side but were all over the place on the other.

When my mother saw me she laughed. I had set my hair correctly on one side but when I turned to do the other side I had wound the hair round the rags the wrong way.

In those days we thought nothing of going to bed with wet hair. I must have corrected the error for Monday night's show as I don't remember being told my hair was untidy.

The four weeks soon passed and I was home again. What next?

That was the question.

I had burnt my boats with my apprenticeship to learn a trade and we had no idea how to go about finding another dancing job.

Principal Dancer

While still wondering how I was going to get my next job I received a phone call asking if I could join a show at once!

It was 'on tour'; the next stop was **Weston-super-Mare, Somerset.**

A friend of mine had given them my number.

26

They were looking for someone who could do toe-taps, tap dancing on pointe, to replace their principal dancer who had broken her ankle.

It was arranged for my mother and I to meet this lady at the railway station and she would take me to join the company. I packed my toe-tap shoes etc., and off I went.

Next day I started to learn the dance.

Normally I would rehearse off pointe to save my toes but this was not allowed and I slogged on until all my toes were bleeding in two places. I still have the marks where they bled until this very day.

All day Sunday and most of Monday I spent learning the dance and then went on for the two performances on Monday evening.

The rest of the dancers were behind me off pointe dressed as soldiers and I was the Captain. At the end of the dance we saluted and then I was supposed to say *"One, Two,"* as a signal to march off. I opened my mouth but nothing would come out, I imagine the trauma of it all happening so quickly overcame me, but fortunately one of the dancers, realising I was having a problem came to my rescue and said *"One, Two"* for me.

I was alright after this first time and spoke for myself.

The other main dance I had to do was a pointe ballet! There had been no time to rehearse this and I had to make it up as I went along. The other dancers were also on stage and at times I had to be in a certain position with them, I relied on whispered directions for the first two nights.

The finale of the dance had me in the middle and the others each pulled a flower from around the waist of my dress to each of which was a coloured ribbon and they stretched them out making a decorative final picture.

After the curtain fell I had to scoop up the ribbons as they were still attached to my dress and carry them back to the dressing room. Then I had to carefully fold each one into its tiny pocket around the waist of my dress leaving just the little flower showing.

I don't know how long I was with this show but once I had settled in I remember being quite happy with my new found friends and certainly enjoyed my dancing.

Searchlight! - from where?

In 1938 I was attending a dancing school in Kilburn, North West London and my brother **Jimmy** often played the piano for our lessons.

One evening when we were walking home after the class we saw a searchlight shining up to the sky. It was an unusual sight and seemed quite near.

"Let's go and find it", Jimmy said.

We were walking along Kilburn High Road and instead of turning into Iverson Road where we lived we continued up towards Cricklewood. We kept expecting the light to be round the next corner until we reluctantly had to give up. It was only then we realised how far we had strayed.

Arriving home at last we were greeted by a 'telling off 'from our anxious parents. Relief that we were home safely soon took over and we were forgiven.

'THE LONDON PALLADIUM'

I auditioned for **J. SHERMAN FISHER,** who led the field for dancing troupes at that time

Quite unbelievably I landed a job as one of the famous 'Palladium Girls', dancing at the **London Palladium.** The show was -

'Band Waggon'
with
- **Arthur Askey** and **Richard Murdoch,**
- **Tommy Trinder** and
- **Jack Hylton's Orchestra**
- conducted by **Billy Ternent.**

The ringlets had gone by now and I had a more grown up curly hair-do. *I was still not 16!*

I was somewhat dismayed to be given 3 inch heels to wear with a long evening dress.

During a tap dance we lined up across the front of the stage where metal pieces were screwed into the stage floor and we had slots in the front of our heels that slipped over them enabling us to lean forward right out over the footlights and we always got very good applause for this dance.

Another dance involved one girl lying on her back with a second girl kneeling across her sitting on her tummy; her full skirt hid her legs and the first girl's body so the audience saw a girl doing incredible things with her legs. After a while we jumped up and all was revealed.

Rehearsing this dance over and over again produced bruised knees on the no. 2 girl, and I, a no. 1 had a bruise the size of a tea plate on my back.

The song '**Hands, Knees and Boomps'a'Daisy**' had it's first airing in this show and we girls were dressed in the most beautiful bustle dresses and little hats.

Some girls had to go out into the audience and try and persuade men to get up and do the dance with them. I was still very young and rather shy but luckily didn't have to do this as I was the one who was chosen to dance with Billy Ternent on the stage in front of the orchestra.

During the time I was dancing at the London Palladium. In a break I was sitting outside the dressing room writing a letter to brother Roy who had been evacuated to Rutland.

Tommy Trinder breezed by and called out *"Give him my love"*,

I hurriedly put him straight *"It's to my brother"* I replied.

My younger brother Roy had already been evacuated to Rutland and by December my elder brother Jimmy, 20, had been 'called-up' and was in the Army.

During the next 6 years Jimmy was saved from Dunkirk and went on to serve in South Africa, Egypt, Palestine, Cyprus, Jordan, Lebanon, Syria, Iraq, Libya, Tunisia, Italy, Sicily, France, Belgium, Holland and Norway

One evening at the Palladium two men came into our dressing room and painted the inside of the windows black. A blackout rehearsal we were told.

Going home that evening was an eerie experience! Waiting for a bus in Oxford Street in complete darkness was really scary. I am very glad I didn't know it would be 1945 before the lights would be switched on again.

Very soon War was declared and theatres were closed. They did gradually open up again but a new show was put on at the London Palladium and I wasn't in that one.

Later on Tommy Trinder used to joke that he started at the London Palladium and worked his way down.

Well I can say the same thing, for although I worked in several other London theatres I never appeared at The London Palladium again.

Barbara ~ 1939 ~ 1943

On the day war broke out........!

There had been talk of war for a long time, many families had Anderson air-raid shelters in their back gardens built by themselves, the components delivered by local Councils, but we didn't believe war would really happen.

Even when the black-out regulations were put into effect people dutifully bought the dark heavy material and tarred paper sheeting for their house to make curtains and covers on frames from the paper that would not let any light escape and be seen from the street.

For our living room my father cut pieces of left over linoleum to exactly fit the window frame which could be removed during the day so we could keep our cheerful curtains in that room.

A.R.P. (Air Raid Protection) Wardens patrolled the streets making sure no chink of light could be seen at night, accompanied when necessary with the shout *"PUT THAT RUDDY LIGHT OUT!""*.

Children in London and elsewhere had been evacuated to various points in the country from the 1st of September 1939.

I learned many years later when I met my future husband **Wally** that he had been sent with his school from Canning Town, East London, to Shepton Mallett, Somerset.

Brother **Roy** went to Oakham, Rutland, billeted with a Church of England Canon. The first Air Raid sirens were in place and had been demonstrated.
The Air-raid Sirens –

- The awful wavering wailing sound of the siren meant **'Air Raid'** take cover.
- The long one note unbroken sound was the **'All Clear'**.

Young men of 20 were being 'called up' into the armed forces. Still we couldn't believe War would come, hanging on to the hope that all would be sorted

Neville Chamberlain, Britain's Prime Minister, flew to Germany to see Adolph Hitler – at that time - Dictator of Germany - and returned thinking he had achieved peace.

Then on Saturday 2nd September we were told he would speak on the wireless, (radio) the next day,

Germany had invaded Poland!

Britain had given an ultimatum to Germany to agree to start to withdraw by 11.00 am on Sunday 3rd September 1939 or consider our two countries –

'**AT WAR!**

No reply had been received so consequently,
"We are At War with Germany!"

WAR!
but the show must go on!

On 2nd September 1939 I was dancing at the London Palladium.

On the 3rd September 1939 WAR was declared and all the theatres (apart from 'The Windmill') were shut down only to open gradually over the weeks ahead.

The London Palladium re-opened with a different show and I was not included amongst the dancers.

Shortly after war had been declared the Air Raid Siren sounded! It was the terrible wail we were to hear so many times after that.

Mum, **Dad**, brother **Jimmy** and I stood in the hall by the staircase, thought to be the safest place in the house. We stood in silence listening for the sound of German planes.

My poor mother was trembling with fear remembering her experience of the 1st World War in 1914/18. Dad, who had been years in the trenches in France as a Scots Guard, earning the Military Medal, didn't show what he must have been feeling.

The **'All Clear'** sounded quite quickly. This time it was a false alarm!

We got on with the rest of our day, lunch of Roast Beef and Yorkshire pudding as usual on a Sunday. I think the kettle was on for cups of tea several times as we wondered what life 'At War' would be like.

Then I went to Bradford to dance in
'Mother Goose' at the Alhambra Theatre.

It must have been so hard for our parents but I was never made to feel I should have found a non-dancing job and stayed at home with them.

It was nearly six years before we siblings were together again.

The Black-Out

For me the 'black-out' started when I was dancing in
'Band Waggon' at the **London Palladium**,
At the end of August 1939 two men came into our dressing room and painted the inside of the windows black. There was to be no light showing from any building or vehicle for fear of showing German Bombers that they were over London and could now drop their bombs.

After the show I made my way from the stage door of the Palladium to my bus stop in Oxford Street.

I remember waiting for my number 60 bus.

I was aged 15 and all on my own!
There were no lights in the shops and no street lights. Traffic lights were covered with only a small cross of light showing.

The few cars had covers with slots over their headlights only allowing light to point downwards on to the road.

My bus, when it came also had hoods on its lights and no lights inside. The bus windows had thick mesh stuck on them to prevent glass flying about if caught in an air raid. There was a small triangle left clear in the middle of each window helping passengers to look out for their stop.

With everywhere in complete darkness it was difficult to recognise anywhere. We relied on help from the conductor. There was one on every bus in those days.

I travelled along Oxford Street, past Marble Arch into Edgware Road, through Maida Vale to Kilburn High Road.

Alighting at Brondesbury Station I nervously crossed the road and turned into Iverson Road where I lived. It was completely black, no chink of light showing from any house window.

Half way along were three train bridges all together, always gloomy to walk under, by now I was really frightened

Out of the blackness I heard a strange noise coming towards me, a sort of a c- plop! c- plop! c-plop! , I was terrified. I carried on walking; - home was on the other side of the bridges.

The apparition that emerged out of the blackness was an A.R.P. Warden in boiler suit and Wellington boots.

I ran the last 50 yards home and shutting the front door behind me with a great sigh of relief, at last I felt safe.

Evacuation

In 1939 people had no idea what war time conditions would be like apart from Newsreels that had shown the German Blitzkrieg on Poland and Czechoslovakia. It was feared something similar would follow on London and South East England and perhaps other big cities.

No one expected the war to last long, but never-the-less the Government decided that as many children as possible should be moved away from the danger of air-raids.

In late August and Early September an estimated 1,800,000, children, teachers and some mothers, were moved out of London to safer places together with hospital patients, invalids, blind people and expectant mothers.

Children who were to be evacuated, (not all children were, it was not compulsory) met at their schools. Then they and their teachers, with some mothers, marched off to underground stations or bus stops to be taken to Main Line stations. Virtually all tube trains, buses and main line trains were monopolized for the evacuation.

Each child had a label pinned or tied on their coat with their name, address and school written on. They carried a gas mask, bags or knapsacks even small cases for clothes, toilet things, etc., plus maybe a game or a toy. They also had a food bag, sandwich, apple or orange, bar of chocolate for the journey until they arrived at their billets.

Most children were excited at going off on such an adventure but the mothers, not knowing what sort of home they were going to, and when, if ever they were going to see them again, often had tears rolling down their cheeks as they pinned on a smile and waved their children off.

Meanwhile, in the 'safe' areas homes were surveyed, anyone with a spare room (excluding pensioners and the sick), had to take in evacuees, although the WVS (Women's Voluntary Service) had organized some schemes themselves.

Often households had children of their own but to people without children it was to be a whole new way of life. There were those who simply did not want to share their home and in these children were not made welcome and in some cases were very unhappy.

Friends have told me how on arrival at their destination as evacuees they were assembled in a school or village hall and the people who were to be hosts, sometimes very unwillingly, walked round and picked out a child or children to take home with them.

It must have been a horrible experience as children waited for someone to like the look of them

Sometimes siblings were split up.

Evacuees were sent in all directions.

My Editor **Terry** was first evacuated with his family (his father was blind), West to Hertfordshire and later to Wales. My brother **Roy** went to Rutland (North) and my future husband **Wally** (West) to Somerset first and then to Cornwall.

A friend of mine **Ray Scudder,** (who, incidentally, after the war appeared at the London Palladium in

The Norman Wisdom Show) was evacuated with his school North to Derbyshire.

In August 1939 brother Roy's school was preparing for evacuation. He was 13 and didn't want to go: Mum and Dad agreed he could stay with them in London.

As Roy watched his friends excitedly preparing for the adventure he felt left out, changed his mind and went with them.

Arriving in Oakham. Rutland. Roy, six other boys and two masters, were billeted in Ashwell Rectory.

One of the teachers was Roy's form master, a young man who before long was 'called up' into the army.

The Rectory was a lovely big country house, **Canon Roberts** and his family made their visitors comfortable and happy. I recall Roy saying he waited at table when the family had guests.

I recently said to him "*I believe you liked doing it*". "*Oh yes*" he said, "*I got paid for it*" adding "*We all had jobs*".

When Canon Roberts suddenly died the boys had to move. Roy went to a family called Neal. **Mrs Neal** had been cook at the Rectory and **Mr. Neal** had been the gardener.

When Mum and Dad managed a visit to Roy two years later, at 15 he decided he wanted to go home. Although it meant him leaving school before he was 16 he was allowed to. Roy was apprenticed to carpentry spending most of his time repairing bomb damaged houses. There was a plentiful supply.

Some 50 years later, Roy and his wife **Marie** went back to Ashwell, asked directions to the Rectory from a local man who said he was just going there and would introduce them to the new owners.

The house was no longer a Rectory and had seen many changes since 1941. A lot of modernization as one would expect. The present owners were happy to show Roy and Marie round.

Roy remembered there had been a cellar, it had no lighting and had an old toad as a tenant. The boys had delighted in shutting the trap door, giving any boy down there a fright. On hearing this the present owner said *"Come and see it now"*.

What a difference; lighting, central heating, a wine rack and no sign of the toad.

On 1st September 1939, my future husband Wally and his mother and other friends and their mothers, walked round to West Ham Underground Station. Farewells were said and then away pulled the underground trains with the children and some mothers aboard.

The underground trains linked up with the railway at Paddington. The children were loaded into the train's carriages. Eventually the engine's steam roared, the whistle blew, and the train set off with the children still unaware of their destination.

They arrived at Shepton Mallet, Somerset and were herded, the only word for it really, into the Drill Hall, an Army building.

He with his friend **Johnny Purdie** were picked out very early on by very kindly families. Both lived in Victoria Road almost opposite one another.

Wally claims to have had many adventures and was evacuated for 5½ years first in Somerset and then in Newquay, Cornwall.

1,800,000 children left London in little more than a week-end leaving behind a huge number of broken-hearted parents!

It was a great adventure for many of the children but what a trauma it must have been for their parents, not knowing if they were ever to see their child again, or indeed what sort of home they were going into!

I left school before the war started and was not eligible for evacuation.

In September 1939, I was appearing at the London Palladium and my dancing life had begun. My next show was -

Mother Goose

at -
The **Alhambra Theatre** in **Bradford**
was a **Francis Laidler** production.

We were still **J. Sherman Fisher** dancers and we learned our special dances in his rehearsal rooms in Newport Street, off Charing Cross Road, London.

One I remember called for us to wear face masks on the backs of our heads. We danced with our backs to the audience, appearing to be able to do really weird contortions with our arms and our legs.

Once again it was costume fitting, long hours of rehearsals and back to the excitement of it all.

As well as our troupe of 12 dancers there were 20 chorus girls and 12 juveniles. The latter were called Sunbeams. We soon learned that each dancer was expected to 'adopt' a Sunbeam for the duration of the show.

We watched over and helped them and brought them little treats, it was a very good tradition making the 'Sunbeams' feel special and spoilt and made us feel important and grown up.

While everybody was wishing everyone else *'Good Luck'* as we waited for the curtain to go 'up' on Opening Night I suddenly got very nervous, I thought *'What if I should go wrong?'* Thankfully none of us did.

We spent 10 weeks in **Bradford** and it was 6 weeks before we saw it without snow on the ground.

At first we had a matinee every day, but this lessened to only three a week after the first 2 or 3 weeks. It was hard work but we thoroughly enjoyed it.

One night a stagehand asked us if we would like to see an underground theatre that had another one built over it. His name was **Seth** and we thought he was very old; he was probably only about 40.

An empty theatre is always a bit spooky but an underground one no longer in use is especially so.

At 16 I was not really steeped in theatre lore but I realised how lucky we were to have this chance to look into the past.

It was very small and I stood in the middle of the stage trying to imagine performing there. I felt so near to the audience, not a bit like the bigger theatres we worked in. I tried hard to 'drink' it all in and tried hard to never forget it.

Sadly I never made a note of the details of the playbills on the walls.

Albert Modley - was the comedian in
'Mother Goose' and towards the end of the 'run' he asked some of the dancers –

Joyce Tench and I included to join him in his own show on tour.

This was arranged with **Sherman Fisher**.

'Mother Goose' closed and we travelled back to London by train, back to rehearsals for the tour.

I don't recall how many dances in total there were but I do recall –

- a tap dance; dancing on drums;
- a Half and Half dance; (costumes designed one half man and the other lady);
- a dance dressed as waitresses carrying silver trays whilst carrying out complicated manoeuvres with them.

It was nerve-wracking at first but it was only when we were getting confident that one was occasionally dropped with a resounding and embarrassing crash.

Albert Modley and his wife were lovely people. They looked after we youngsters and fixed up 'digs' for us.

The tour was for only a few weeks and we were very sorry when it ended

Arthur Askey & Stinker!

Summer was just around the corner and of course the start of the Summer Season Shows.

Joyce and I and our friends from the Albert Modley Tour landed a Summer Season at the -
Blackpool Opera House.

We realised how lucky we were as it was the premier theatre outside London.

The programme of 1940 states –

**'This is Britain's newest and most beautiful theatre'.
The new Opera House is not only Britain's most modern and largest theatre but its stage and auditorium are the finest in Europe.**

This time we did not learn any **J. Sherman Fisher's** routines, we went straight to Blackpool and rehearsed mainly in the theatre.

Joan Davis was our choreographer and all our costumes were individually made to measure and all our shoes were new, quite a luxury. We usually had to fit into costumes and shoes that had been used before.

We eight joined 16 other dancers making a troupe of 24. We did two shows a night and three on Wednesday when we had a matinee, and another luxury we had was 2 dressers to help us with our costumes.

The show was -

'Band Waggon'
with
- **Arthur Askey** and
- **Richard Murdoch** (Stinker)
- **Albert Sandler and his trio**,
- **Norman Evans** 'Over the Garden Wall' and
- **Syd Seymour** and his **'Mad Hatters'** band.

A lot of the show was the same as the one I was in at the London Palladium but all our dances were different.

The producer was **Jack Taylor** but when we came to Dress Rehearsal it was an absolute nightmare.

One item in particular caused a lot of trouble.

The scene started at the entrance to a big church, people in Victorian dress hurried along and entered the church, then the whole set turned round to reveal the inside of the church. As the stage had no built-in turntable one was assembled during the scene change.

It was on casters and many stagehands were required to pull on the ropes to make it revolve.

The assembling and revolving was a very difficult operation and had to be done over and over again and again.

Some of the dancers were dressed as Saints and we were perched on the platforms along the sides of the church at different heights. I was one of the two highest Saints, one each side and we had to hold a replica trumpet up to our mouths. It was getting very late and we were getting very hungry but Jack Taylor would not give us a break even when **Joyce** fainted and fell face down off the pedestal she was on, he would not stop.

Syd Seymour was very concerned about us dancers and he went out and bought some pies and biscuits for us to eat and we were at last allowed to get down.

It was quite a spectacle for the audience who came to see the show and this particular scene was a highlight. As usual as we got used to the show we would put off getting on our perches until the last minute.

One night I shot up and hurriedly picked up my trumpet put in place by the props people and put it to my lips only to find a big blob of Vaseline on the end of it. Nothing for it but to hold the trumpet there throughout the scene watching the grins on the stagehands faces out of the corner of my eye. Another time they put the Vaseline where I held the trumpet making it almost impossible to grip and hold steady. I could have killed them.

We had very good audiences and enjoyed our summer by the sea.

I'm not sure exactly how long it lasted but I remember how sad we were when the two weeks 'notice' to finish was posted on the board by the stage door.

What was next, we wondered?

My first experience of 'the Blitz'

The outbreak of the Second World War closed the theatres! Shows were disbanded; by the time the Palladium re-opened I had signed up for a 10 week Pantomime run in Bradford.

Tours followed and 3 glorious Summer Seasons at the **Opera House** in **Blackpool**, the summertime 'home' for many of the 'stars'.

Touring was extremely hard, the War was in full spate, food severely rationed - especially for travellers like us, (my 'Cook Book' diary of the time shows the rations of the week and the majority of the allocation), and 'digs' very hard to find.

When the producer of the Summer Show, **Jack Taylor**, offered to put another girl and I in one of his tours we thought it would be of a similar standard to the Opera House extravaganza and 'jumped' at it. We travelled home from Blackpool on Sunday arriving in London at tea-time.

The **'Blitz'** had started and when the siren sounded at about 6.30 pm, my family calmly assured me it was the 'usual' time. This was my first taste of the excitement and terror of an air-raid.

I watched my family settle themselves in a ground floor living room, prepared to sit it out.

In the early days Londoners had felt it best to keep their clothes on and stay awake during raids, by my next visit home - fatigue and familiarity had set in and folk either spent the night in a shelter or, as in the case of my family, went to bed.

It was a very long night and most of it was spent sitting on a hard chair. I tried to put a brave face on but when I attempted to join in a game of cards I couldn't keep my hands from shaking.

At dawn the 'All Clear' sounded on the siren and we grabbed a short rest before starting the day.

I had to unpack and re-pack and with my friend **Dorina** be on a 10 am train bound for Peterborough.

'Eve on Parade'

We found the theatre and reported to the 'Head Girl' dancer Our reception was 'very cool' and later we learned that these girls had vainly hoped to be put in the resident Summer Show to give them a rest from touring. Some of them were openly hostile and this period was a nightmare of bad 'digs', little food and 3rd rate theatres.

They started teaching us the dances at once for we were due to appear in as many as we could that evening. During a break for lunch Dorina and I scoured the town for 'digs', we found a very 'doubtful' room and rushed back to the theatre buying some buns to keep us going.

More rehearsing followed, dresses were tried on and make-up unpacked.

When the show opened we were about fit to drop, we hoped the audience wouldn't realise how tired and confused we were. I was not yet 17 years old! Thankfully the manager seemed satisfied. Most of the evening is a blur to me but one memory remains.

A scene in which they wore long gowns covered in silver sequins, silver headdresses over ½ metre high with a cascade of fringed cellophane coming from the top and carrying poles taller than themselves with more cellophane cascades. The effect was like water and they walked about forming various patterns to resemble fountains and a waterfall.

A dress was found to fit me without alteration so I was put in this scene the first evening. There had been no time to learn the sequence so they gave me a pole and shoved me on in the right place telling me to follow the girl in front of me and stand still shaking my pole when she did.

It was at this point real fatigue overtook me; there had been the closing on Saturday night of the Summer Show, the packing and the farewells, the long journey home on Sunday, a night in the 'blitz' without sleep, another journey followed by rehearsals and fittings, a sea of new faces and very little food.

Following the 'silver clad figure' things took on a dream like quality, what with tiredness and the lights on the silver cellophane. I felt utterly confused; it was like walking in the sea. All the girls looked alike and I could only hope I was still following the right one.

The show over we found our way back to our 'digs' and room longing for bed. It was not to be however!

Bugged!

At last that evening's show was over and back to our 'digs' and oh, how we were longing for some sleep. Twin beds had not made an appearance at this time, bed-sits had not been coined. They called ours a 'combined' room and we shared a double bed.

When the bedspread was flung back, there nestling on the pillow was a gathering of bed bugs!

We were horrified; we were scared they would get on our things or us. Everything was pushed back into our cases and we spent the night sitting back to back on an upright chair keeping watch.

It sounds very silly now in the telling but at *16 years old* and used to nice clean homes it really did upset us

Neither of us had ever seen them before but we knew without doubt what they were. There was no alternative other than spending another night sitting on a hard chair and again 'no sleep'.

The next day we rehearsed hard and had no time to look for new 'digs' - so that night and the rest of the week we slept on the floor in our basement dressing room. At first I feared there would be no sleep again as we thought we heard the squeaking of mice in the room and rats scurrying across the stage above us but we were too exhausted to be frightened and sleep we did.

Breakfast presented a problem. There had been no supper or drink the night before and we were ravenous.

We bought a loaf of bread; some of our ration of butter and jam would do, and then remembered we had no knife. Cutting bread with a nail file and spreading butter and jam with a toothbrush is doing things the hard way!

After little or no food and little or no sleep our bread and jam truly tasted like that overworked cliché 'Nectar of the Gods'! It tasted wonderful and well worth the effort.

As the week wore on my body ached from sleeping on the hard floor. This was my first encounter with real hardship but although we had some short air-raids I was not in danger as my family in London was; - for them the blitz continued with daily raids and a continuous one each night from dusk to dawn.

We learned all the dances and settled into the 'Show' but our companions never softened their attitude to us and we suffered in dozens of petty ways. Always getting the worst place in the dressing room and even having to make-up on a skip in the corridor on one occasion.

It seems they had been on tour all the previous winter and they had hoped Jack Taylor would give them the 'plum' Blackpool job come the summer. It was a forlorn hope. The Opera House job went to 24 girls in their teens all a uniform 5'6" tall. The ladies we were now dancing with did not fit into that category. Imagine how they felt when two of us from that Blackpool Show joined them? They were not happy bunnies, but neither were we!

Dorina and I had not done this sort of tour before and had no' magic' address book of likely 'digs' collected from past tours.

The war-time 'blackout' and air-raids completed our misery.

We arrived in towns after dark with nowhere to stay.

I shiver even now when I think of two young 17 year old girls traipsing 'blacked-out' streets in strange towns knocking on doors looking for someone with a room to let.

On one occasion at Barnsley the air-raid siren went as we came out of the railway station before we had started looking for 'digs'. We made our way to the police station and asked if there was any hope of a cell for the night.

In true story-book style the sergeant was a kindly man and due to go off duty, he took us home and his wife agreed to have us stay with them. That was a lovely week.

This warm-hearted couple made us so welcome - looking after us as if we were members of the family.

In contrast at one other town we slept on couches in the foyer of the theatre where our show was appearing for a week.

We wore our dressing gowns over our clothes and covered ourselves with our top coats. It was fairly comfortable despite the cold and the fright we got when the ice-cream fridge suddenly switched on.

The night-watchman brought us tea in the mornings making us feel a shade less unwanted.

A kindness when it was most needed!

In all the miles I have travelled with their attendant trials and misfortunes there has invariably been someone, often the most un-likeliest, who has shown me such a kindness.

Again there was the occasion on a pouring wet night when Dorina and I were on our usual hunt for 'digs' joined by another policeman trekking from street to street and door to door and it seeming hopeless. At one house a lady we had never seen before lent us an umbrella, *"How trusting can that be"* I thought.

We became sad and rain sodden, despair mounting as we faced the prospect of losing our policeman escort due to go off duty, not to mention the hunger pangs nagging at our stomachs.

Suddenly the owner of the umbrella came running after us, all her rooms had been let to long distance lorry drivers but on hearing of our plight 2 of them offered to share a room together so we could have the other. It was fantastic walking from the drenching blackout into the light and warmth of that house.

It was full of activity, belongings being transferred from one room to another, clean sheets being hastily put on the bed we were to have. The marvellous 'glow' of being able to sit and feel life returning to frozen feet and fingers. Hot soup then a cup of tea and our heaven was complete, the battle was over for another week.

Unexpected kindness again prevailing - it went further. The lorry drivers collectively took it upon themselves to be chaperones escorting us to and from the theatre like big brothers. Yes, before you speculate, very like big brothers!

There are many instances and individual stories I relate later in this book -

- the dog that would not get off our bed, the landlady saying "He always sleeps there",

- a daughter who worked in the Mill, going off to work with her clogs 'clacking' away down the hall.

- saving a chocolate bar to put on a bought cake for my 17th birthday.

Seasoned professionals accumulate a magical 'book' of 'theatrical digs' where they or friends have stayed in the past and therefore simply write in advance to book a room and meal. This meant they could be swept off in a taxi at the end of the train journey, settled and dining in no time. These books were jealously guarded especially from us two innocents, - how they loved seeing us suffer.

Sometimes we pretended to be booked up, only to find that one of the houses we knocked at contained some of our tormentors. They would come to the door and gloat, purposely leaving the room door open to give us a glimpse of the fire.

This very hard way of life lasted for 30 weeks! Keeping a small week-end case with us, our big cases travelled with the scenery and had to be packed ready for collection on Saturday morning - we didn't see them again until the following Monday afternoon. The time between unpacking on Monday and packing again on Friday seemed very short, unless the 'digs' were particularly bad.

The theatres were very depressing places in a number of the smaller towns, with very small dressing rooms and endless flights of stairs. I couldn't say there was anything 'glamorous' or exciting about it, quite the reverse of the image the term 'Show Business' conjures up nowadays.

Suddenly, despite enjoying the actual dancing in quite a good show, our ghastly conditions were too much.

Feeling very brave and reckless we gave in our 'notice' once the 31st week was over and we returned to our homes in London.

As it was May by this time we decided to try and see if a summer show in **Blackpool** was available.

We found that **George Black** was putting one on without the same producer we had left last year.

We applied; went through the audition and were 'in'!

Ration Books

People living at a permanent address were required to register with a particular grocer or butcher where they would obtain their *'rations'* of food, meat etc. and the occasional 'extras'! Eggs, special pieces of meat at the butchers were kept for registered customers only.

We had what were called Traveller's' Ration Books and we didn't get any of these little 'extras'.

Our Ration Books would be handed to our Landlady on our arrival and she would do our shopping and prepare our meals which we ate in our own rooms not with the family.

I only remember having toast for breakfast and toast for supper, made on an open fire and our meagre butter ration and jam skilfully spread to eke it out.

Every so often our mouths would get sore from chomping on toast so we ate the bread untoasted for a few days.

In today's world if we need any food we just walk into a grocers shop or a Supermarket and purchase it.

In 1940 our farmers did not grow enough food to feed the nation – Great Britain needed to import food.

German U-Boats were blockading the seas around the U.K. and stopping vital food supplies from getting through. The Government rationed the food and controlled what the ordinary person could buy through Ration Books.

Tokens were taken out of the Ration Book to cover the food purchased by the holder of the book.

MY COOK BOOK
War time rations per person

2ozs Bacon   per 2 weeks
2ozs Cheese   per2 weeks
1 oz Lard   per 2 weeks
4ozs Margarine   per 2 weeks
2ozs Butter   per 2 weeks
1 jar of jam   per month
  ½ lb tea or ¾ lb tea   alternate months
1s1d worth of meat   per week
  ¾ lb Sweets or chocolate   per month

POINTS RATIONS 16 points per week
You can buy from the following list a combination of
foods up to a total of 16 points –

1lb tin Golden Syrup	10 points
large tin Baked Beans	8 points
small tin of Baked Beans	4 points
Sardines	2 points
Peas	3 points
1 lb unsweetened biscuits	8 points
1lb sweet biscuits	12 points
1lb chocolate biscuits	20 points
1 lb Sultanas	8 points
1lb Currants	12 points
1lb Dates	6 points

Meat and Veg, tin	I point
Steak and Kidney	8 points
Egg powder (dried egg) box	10 points
Egg	I per week

Sausages, occasionally, only for 'registered'
customers, not given on 'travellers' ration book.

All the above might sound quite reasonable but if you set all that out on a table top and realize that it was *all you were allowed to buy to feed an adult for one or two weeks* then perhaps it was not surprising that some 'landladies' fed us toast for breakfast and toast for supper whilst saving the rest of our 'ration' to help feed their own family.

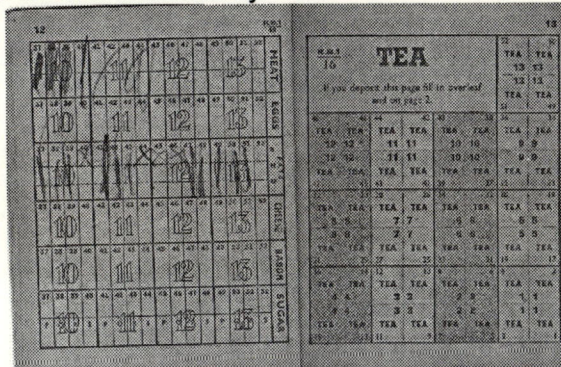

Finding 'digs'

We continued to have a tough time finding 'digs', they were scarce because the forces were billeted in private houses.

Factory and other essential workers who moved into the towns to do war work were also billeted at houses that might otherwise have been available to us as 'digs' for the week.

Most Sundays we would arrive in a town strange to us, traipsing around knocking on doors trying to find places to stay.

'Digs' varied so much.

At one house we had to sleep in the living room, forced to share our bed with a large shaggy dog that we tried to push off but failed.

When we told the landlady she said *"Oh he always sleeps there'.*

Her young daughter worked in the mill and she got up at the crack of dawn coming through the living room past our bed to get to the kitchen, and yes, she did wear clogs.

Another time we found rather good 'digs', some of the other people from the show were in other rooms and we all shared a sitting room.

One night Dorina and I went upstairs and there in our bed was a figure the face turned towards us and the eyes staring. The light was dim and we were terrified and we raced downstairs shouting *"there's a 'thing' in our bed"* One of the company asked *"what sort of thing?"* all I could say was *"it has eyes".*

He went up to investigate saying afterwards he had no idea what it could be that had frightened us so much. It turned out to be a shop dummy; the father, mother and son of the house thought it was a huge joke to put it in people's beds and frighten them.

I did not note at the time which town was which as we travelled about so much.

Travelling from town to town

Every Sunday would find us on a train to the next town the show was booked into.

During the War trains were very over-crowded with servicemen and women and civilians all crammed into corridors with every seat in the compartment full.

Several compartments were reserved for the theatre company so we were assured of a seat but we used to get black looks from those travellers without seats.

The scenery, costumes and props would also be on the train but the journeys took hours.

We were once shunted off to a siding in **Crewe** and had to wait hours until we were back on our route.

Every Monday we made our way to the town's theatre after getting directions from our landlady, picking out landmarks to help us find our way back as we walked *'home'* in the blackout.

We would have band-call. In each town it would be a different orchestra - but we did have the same musical director who travelled with us.

We had to unpack our costumes and carry them up to our dressing rooms and dancers were always at the top in the smallest dressing rooms.

As we were not expected to stay in our 'digs' during the day - fires were allowed to die out and be relaid for the evening, so we spent nearly every afternoon at the cinema, - the warmth was very welcome especially in the winter.

Most towns had two or three cinemas and some of them changed their programmes mid-week. We had printed cards - **Barbara Stewart, Dancer** - and would hand one in at the Box Office and were allowed in free or half price, usually best seats in the circle.

One of the snags was the big film always finished too late for us to get to the theatre so we always missed the last 10 minutes or so. Another snag was seeing 'trailers' of films and never catching up with them as we travelled around.

Auditions

Summer 1941 was approaching and when we saw an audition advertised in 'The Stage', the trade paper, for a Summer Season in Blackpool, **Dorina** and I whispered a silent prayer and went along to try our luck.

We wore bathing costumes for auditions in those days, me in a green and white elasticised one, 5 shillings and 11 pence, from Marks & Spencers.

A line of us at a time across the stage were looked at, the lucky ones being picked out and asked to wait.

It was 'The girl in green' or 'The girl 3rd from the left etc.' Only after passing this test did we get a chance to dance. Those unfortunate not to be picked out were thanked and sent away.

One at a time we then gave our music to the pianist, said our name and did our dance.

Dorina and I both passed and were overjoyed to hear we would be in this year's (1941) **Summer Season Show** in the **Opera House** at **Blackpool**.

The show was called

HULLABALOO

Nervo & Knox of the **Crazy Gang**
headed the cast with
- **Teddy Brown,** the great xylophone player comic,
- **Anne Zeigler** & **Webster Booth** and
- **Albert Sandler.**

Again we were fitted with new costumes, among them beautiful crinolines which cost £150 each so we were told, and another set £50 each. Bearing in mind there were 24 of us and several other outfits with matching shoes the total bill must have run into thousands of pounds at a time. This was when a salary of £1,000 per year was considered to be a luxury wage!

Rehearsals were very hard work. For a start we were unused to getting up and out to the theatre by 9.00 a.m. For these big shows we had 3 weeks of rehearsals and during the last week we would never know when we would finish for the day.

Then there would be the excitement of 'Opening Night', the few teething problems, and we would settle into our costumes changes and dances.

We also had words and music to learn as we sang in the background behind the 'Star'.

Nervo & Knox were terrible pranksters and often left the manager frantic. They thought nothing of cutting somebody's tie off and once when the manager was standing holding a newspaper in each hand they set light to it and it went up in flames.

The opening scene of 'Hullabaloo' was an airport, with people bustling about and a big stage aeroplane out of which the leading people arrived on stage except Nervo and Knox who came down on parachutes. To do this they had to be hoisted up behind the proscenium before the show started, sitting on their little seats dangling as if on parachutes. On more than one occasion we would all be assembled waiting for the curtain to go 'up' and they would throw down 'stink-bombs'. Not very nice but they were just like naughty school-boys. We dancers had to be on a constant 'look-out' as we were fair game.

Teddy Brown was almost as bad! For one of our 'entrances' the stage was set with flounces of white silk. The back was of single doorways spaced out.

Before the curtain went 'up' on the scene the girls would be standing concealed by the silk between the doorways. At the musical cue we would take one step into the doorways where we would pause for our lovely dresses to make an impact before walking forward.

It was during this pause, Teddy Knox, Jimmy Nervo or Teddy Brown would sneak up to the end girls, of whom I was one, and put a foot out just as we went forward causing us to trip on, not very elegantly.

During a tap dance I couldn't seem to move one of my feet. When I looked down it was a broomstick which Teddy Knox, standing in the wings, had hooked around my ankle making tap-dancing somewhat difficult to say the least.

As I said there was never a dull moment with that lot. Webster Booth entered into the spirit of things when - during a very lavish scene with us wearing the crinolines - he looked into Anne Zeigler's eyes while tenderly singing "Only a Rose" to her, and gently slid down the zip in the back of her dress. How on earth Anne continued to look lovingly at Webster and then sing her part I just do not know.

It was easy for us for we were supposed to be smiling anyway. Webster did the zip up again just in time for their bows. They were a lovely couple and had a very happy show-biz marriage. She was always beautiful and elegant on and off the stage.

This time in Blackpool I shared 'digs' with **Mary** and **Pat** as well as **Dorina,** they were comfortable and we all enjoyed being in Blackpool for a second year.

My Season was marred when my mother was in a car accident in a friend's car. She dislocated a hip among other things and it was awful for me not being at home to cheer her days in hospital and look after my father and brother Roy.

My brother by this time had come home from being evacuated. Isn't it strange the way so many youngsters were 'evacuated' away from their families and into safety in the country at a time before bombs were falling on their homes but so many returned home to live often when the bombing was at its worst!

I wrote to my mother every day carrying my pad with me wherever I went, scribbling away whether on a bus or tram, in the park or in the swimming pool or sunbathing. I began to be called 'the girl with the writing pad'.

I was desperate to see Mummy so I resorted to subterfuge and asked my Father to send me a telegram to say her condition has worsened, naughty me. When I showed it to the Manager he agreed to let me have the Saturday off.

I travelled down to London but had to wait until the Sunday to go into the hospital: visiting hours were rigidly kept in those days.

When I went in on the Sunday I was told they would have let me in on the Saturday under the circumstances especially as they were keen to see the writer of all those letters.

My Mother was a brilliant knitter and during her three months stay in hospital knitted jumpers for all the nurses.

It was back to Blackpool for me on the Monday morning in time for the show but I felt so much better for my visit and my conscience did not 'prick' me too much about the telegram.

We were enjoying our summer by the sea, swimming and sun-bathing, but we had to be very careful. Our hair had to be kept dry in order to look nice for the show. We had no hair dryers or heated rollers in those days. I still give that as the excuse for only ever doing a lady-like breast stroke with my head held high out of the water.

We also had to guard against having marks where the sun tan stopped, sleeves and neck-lines as they would show up in our theatre costumes.

The Stars come to our Midnight Show

We were excited when we were told we were to do a midnight show for charity.

So many 'stars' converged on Blackpool for the event;

-   the rest of the **Crazy Gang,**
-   **Anna Neagle,**
-   **Laurence Olivier** and **Vivian Leigh,**
-   **Frances Day** and many others, all a great thrill to us dancers.

Both **Kay** and **Kim Kendall** were in the show,

Kay was a dancer with us, a friendly, lively and very lovely girl. **Kim** had grown too tall for the line-up and was given some solo 'spots'.

Gas Masks

We all had identity cards in World War II and everyone was given a gas mask. They came in small square cardboard boxes and we carried them on our shoulders or around our necks on a long string.

Special gas protection for babies were boxes for them to lay sealed up in and it was very distressing for mother and baby. We all prayed we would never have to use them.

We were supposed to carry the masks with us every where we went but as time went on we didn't always bother.

In 1942 while in 'digs' in Blackpool and appearing in "Hullabaloo" at the Opera House Theatre, a friend and I were watching a film one afternoon when our eyes started to sting and water. Puzzled we looked around and everyone was dabbing at their eyes except a few people who had their gas masks on. As the air cleared we were told it was tear gas but if it had been enemy gas we would have all been dead!

We always carried our gas masks after this experience.

Three of our 'boys' are missing

During a Summer Season in Blackpool, one of our dancers heard a close friend had been killed in action. The only way she could handle her grief was to be left quite alone, no one even speaking to her.

I have never forgotten seeing her looking lovely in her make-up and costume pacing up and down on the side of the stage with tears streaming down her face.

A quick dab of a handkerchief and there she was on stage a smile in place on her face doing her stuff.

Playing the 'Empires' in wartime London

For a short while I was in – **Variety,**
-    working around the '**Empires**' in London.
This meant we had just 4 dances to do. We opened the show, closed the first half, opened the second half and then there was the finale. In between there were a variety of acts.

One of them was a comedy duo called '**Murray & Mooney'** - and one evening just before the show one of them, I can't recall which, heard that his son had been killed in action but they went on stage as usual.

I stood in the 'wings' watching and thinking the audience don't realise they are watching a truly 'Broken-hearted Clown'.

In a pantomime '**Jack & Jill**' we were all upset when one of the dancers heard her friend serving in the R.A.F. was missing.

He had been a friend since childhood but when he went missing she realised how much he meant to her.

This time there was a happy ending for he turned up safely and they fell into each others arms newly aware that they were in love.

Stepping over the crowd in the Underground

The Underground Stations were used as air-raid shelters by a lot of people. By the time we went home from the theatre most people had already settled for the night on the platforms. They lay on their blankets etc. hoping to get some sleep and praying their houses would still be in one piece in the morning.

Little children had their toys with them and played quite happily but children do quickly accept things as the norm.

There was even a trolley going round with food and drink. I'm not certain who ran it - but guess it would be the W.V.S. (Womens Voluntary Service).

The trolley on the platform which **Dorina** and I got our train from was usually stocked with packets of "Butterkist" (honey coated popcorn). This was not on 'Sweet Ration' and we were allowed to buy two packets each.

Dorina used to eat one of hers on the way home and gave me the other one as her parents didn't like it, so I arrived home triumphantly with 3, one each for my mother, my brother Roy, and me.

Daddy fortunately also didn't like 'Butterkist'.

'Safe' from the Blitz

Although London was badly hit with air-raids at first - the government did not allow Underground rail stations to be used as shelters However people took matters into their own hands and opened up the chained entrances to the tube stations.

Each day by 4.00 pm all the platforms and passages were 'staked out'. Family members, mostly women and children, arranged folded blankets on the ground near the walls, saving places for the rest of the family who came later after work.

A white line was painted the length of the platforms about a metre from the edge. The space between this line and the edge of the platform had to be kept clear as the trains were still running. The rest of the platform could be used by those sheltering for safety.

Sleeping on Underground railway stations people felt safe from large bombs and the incendiary bombs that set fire to their targets and were falling on London.

It seems incredible today but I never remember a single incident of any adult or child crossing the white line and into danger. They stayed, slept or played the 'safe' side of the white line.

They soon adapted to this nightly routine bringing flasks, food and toys for the children. Some people played cards and others just read or chatted and many women brought their knitting. Passengers walked between the white line and platform edge. In the passages leading to the platforms we often had to step over a sleeping form and to others we would give a cheery *'Goodnight'* as we passed by.

Come morning, after the 'all clear' sounded on the sirens, people went home or directly to work, hoping their homes and places of work would still be standing undamaged by bombs.

I well recall seeing children snuggled down asleep with a doll or teddy bear at **Piccadilly Station** when I was going home from His Majesty's Theatre where I was dancing in the pantomime '**Jack and Jill'**.

If the Siren warned of an air-raid during a performance at His Majesty's the Manager went on stage to inform the audience; not many left when this happened and the show continued with 'noises off' – the odd dull thump of a bomb

Wartime Shelters

The London 'Underground' Railway Stations provided a lot of people with shelter from bombs dropped during the nightly air-raids but only a few of those living in the metropolis lived close enough to an underground station to take advantage of their cover.

There were some 'public air-raid shelters' dotted around but again they were not close to everyone and access was not very prompt when enemy Bombers were rapidly approaching.

Many people chose to have an air-raid shelter in their homes or their garden.

- The Anderson shelter, was built in back gardens and distributed in spring or early summer in 1939 to poorer people, or sold for £7 to those earning over £5 per week (Most working men only earned £2.10s.0d - £3.00).

- The earth was dug out and piled on top of the shelter and some built 'blast walls' of bricks and earth around it for added protection.

Some fathers personalised their shelters for comfort.

Wally's father made 2 bunk beds fitted in his shelter, steps down and a floor which was carpeted. A paraffin oil heater and warm blankets gave a little comfort

People regularly slept in their shelter as a matter of course, air-raid or no air-raid. I have heard of occasions when some shelters were flooded after rain but this was rare.

Wally recounts a story when he and some friends came back from where they had been evacuated to London on a 'holiday'.

His father was by this time in the Home Guard, (the civilian corps made famous by "Dad's Army", on TV), operating 'Rocket Guns', devices set out in a grid formation on the ground which when fired were fused to explode at different heights. This devastated any aircraft unlucky enough to be inside the 'cube' it formed.

Wally was then 12 and the first time he experienced an air-raid he rushed out, climbed on to the shelter and was calling out *'Go on Dad give 'em hell'* or some such even more colourful expression!

Then later the Morrison shelter was introduced for inside assembly. These were approximately the size of a double bed and table height. One side was usually left open for people to 'dive' in if necessary then the side pulled up and fixed in place. Many people used this shelter to replace their ordinary table especially if their rooms were small.

Mr. Speight was one of the other fathers building shelters. His son Richard was a school friend of Wally, and they lived opposite with elder son Johnny. **Johnny Speight** later wrote the 'Alf Garnett' series "Till Death Us Do Part".

A bomb did demolish two houses about 50 metres away but no one was hurt.

My friend **Tony Alexander's** cousin **Joan Franks** had a different experience in Ravensdale Road,

Stamford Hill. They were in their shelter when a terrific explosion shook them all up. When she and her family emerged from their shelter their house and others around were completely demolished.

My editor was a babe in a 'Public Shelter' in Tottenham in 1942 with his family when a bomb hit the shelter! The Shelter was badly damaged but thankfully the bomb failed to explode else we would have been robbed of **Terry's** company for the past 40+ years we have known him and this book may never have got off the ground!

The shelters did their job.

JACK & JILL

In 1941 I was at home for my 18th birthday. 18th birthdays didn't have the significance that they have today but it did mean that I had to register for War Work as we all did.

I registered but my itchy feet and the need to earn soon had me looking for work again.

Now four of us who had shared 'digs' in Blackpool scouted around going to the agents and auditions.

Luckily again we landed a pantomime –
'**Jack & Jill**'
at the **Palace Theatre** in **London**.
The line-up included
- **Arthur Askey,**
- **Eddie Gray,**
- **Florence Desmond**
- there were just 24 dancers.

As usual our dressing rooms were at the top of the theatre. The lowest ones were for the 'Stars', next up the lesser acts and so on. It didn't matter that we had the most changes of costume and some of them were very 'quick'. I can still hear the pounding of tap shoes on the stone steps as we raced up to get changed and then down again.

Half of us were given a 'Pointe' ballet to do; happily I was one of those as I loved pointe work but rarely had a chance to do it. The other half were called upon to do a high boot dance.

Dressed as penguins they wore boots with foot-long wooden soles and at certain points in the dance the girls had to jump up on the points of their toes. It took them a long time to get the knack which made me even more pleased to be in the ballet dance.

Because of the black-out and air-raids, theatres gave an afternoon performance and an early evening one finishing at 9.00 p.m. We did have a few children come to the afternoon performance.

A clause in our contract stated if the theatre was closed because of an air-raid or an air-raid warning no salary would be paid for any performances missed. Luckily although there were warnings - the performances continued and none missed.

Life was good! Living at home and appearing in a London Theatre was bliss.

We were getting used to wartime rationing etc., and though some landladies had looked after us as well as our 'Ration Books' allowed - it was generally a better diet at home than was available in many of our 'digs'.

'**Jack & Jill**' was a very successful pantomime and had a long 'run'.

ROYAL VISIT

There were children at every matinee performance even though this was our second War-Time Christmas. We could always hear the excited buzz from the audience as we took our places for the opening scene behind the curtain.

It was our turn to be excited when the word went round that the Queen –
Queen Elizabeth had brought her daughters, **Princess Elizabeth** and **Princess Margaret Rose**, (she was always given her full name in those days), to see our pantomime.

We were told not to look up at the box that held the Royal Party but I couldn't resist a few quick glances as I danced, it was such a thrill to have them there.

Princess Margaret Rose was 10 years old and Princess Elizabeth, **our present Queen**, was 14, fairly grown up by to-days standards. The two girls in public always dressed similarly and it was some time before Princess Elizabeth seemed to wear more grown up styles

I found a spot in the 'wings' where I could see the Royal Party. They obviously enjoyed themselves, clapping and laughing at every 'turn'. Princess Margaret Rose jumped up and down with excitement and they all joined in the audience participation song.

Sadly for us they didn't come back-stage after the show, understandably with the threat of air-raids ever present.

The Knitting Brigade

Florence Desmond arranged to have wool and knitting patterns delivered to her dressing room. She recruited a band of knitters from the company and we were all busy turning out sea-boot socks made with oiled wool, ordinary socks for the troops plus balaclava helmets and other things.

I was a fast knitter but my mother was much faster. Between us we got through endless amounts of wool and made piles of garments. I was always in and out of Dessie's dressing room to get more wool.

Knitting is not allowed back-stage in a theatre except in the dressing room. This time however the rule was waived and during a longish wait and not possible to return to the dressing-room, due to cumbersome crinolines, the stage manager arranged benches behind the stage and we were allowed to continue our war effort.

'Get a load of This'

The **London Hippodrome**
in **Leicester Square**, London.
I joined in 1942 following pantomime.

It was in a different mould, put together under the auspices of the impresario **George Black**, described by him as a 'Surprise Musical'.

Another description was a 'Melodrama with Cabaret".

The underlying story was a dramatic one of drug-running in New York, and written by thriller writer **James Hadley Chase** who also wrote the acclaimed *'No Orchids for Miss Blandish'*.

It was staged on a specially built set that embraced not only the stage but also the orchestra pit and parts of the stalls.

With no stage curtains the audience felt they were in a night club -
'The Orchid Room'.
with- **Chappie D'Amato** a leading band leader
- and the **Hatchett's Swingtette** played on stage,
- taking turns with **Sam Bennie**, the blind pianist of radio fame.

The Hippodrome was turned into one big night-club. At the back of the stage, raised up, were 2 office sets behind gauze. Unseen by the audience until they were lit up, sometimes singly sometimes together.

The skullduggery took place in them in between performances on the stage.

Drama in one performance was heightened when **Albert Lieven**, the well known film actor, whose forte was playing a stereotype blonde German, fell out of the set on to the stage below, during a realistic, simulated 'fight'.

He was not noticeably injured and the set gauze was obviously repaired while it was subsequently unlit, for the 'Show went on' as if nothing had happened in the best tradition of 'theatre'.

Famous band leader Sydney Lipton's daughter, **Celia Lipton** sang in the show. One memorable song I recall was 'Button Up Your Overcoat'.

Rumour had it that Celia's father had not wanted her to work as a singer so she, still very young, ran off and got herself a job. She is of course, after her successful career and all these years later, known mainly in American society as 'The Queen of Palm Beach',

Vic Oliver, who was for some time Winston Churchill's son-in-law, was the star of the show. He was very popular with audiences but I'm sorry to say not with me! I didn't like the way he encroached on other performers' acts.

These included **Jack and Daphne Barker**, well known for their rather naughty songs, very mild by to-day's standards, and the **Cairoli Brothers**, international clowns.

When the young and lovely Celia Lipton was singing, Vic Oliver often went into the audience and sat on a lady's knee, making everyone laugh with chit-chat. You could say it may have been scripted but I personally was not impressed!

I was not in this show very long and for once not dancing. I was in a couple of guises, first seated on a balcony, part of the set, with another girl.

During whispered conversations between the two of us she suddenly told me of her heart-break. Her fiancée was in hospital dying!

He didn't realise this and during her hospital visits he would talk of their wedding plans. She kept up the pretence while knowing they would never realise their dreams. It was terribly sad for her but we 'smiled' when on stage and played our parts.

The second scene scintillating and dressed in a stunning long evening dress, partnered with a young man we 'swanned' about, 'guests' at the club sitting at a table or moving to the bar drinking 'champagne', (ginger ale really). It was easier than rushing about dancing and frantically changing costumes but I would much rather have been dancing.

I was actually 'filling in', waiting to join George Black's next Summer Show at the Opera House Theatre in Blackpool, "Black Vanities", where I met up with the Cairoli Brothers again, but under tragic circumstances, told in the "Black Vanities" storyline.

The Hippodrome Theatre became the "Talk of the Town" later, 1957, the audience sitting at tables for dining and refreshments. It staged some of the top acts from around the world. It has also flourished under Peter Stringfellow, since 1983.

Recently it is "Cirque" and claims to be the 'ultimate' super night-club. 'Cirque', French for circus, reflects its original name 'Hippodrome'.

BLACK VANITIES

After resting for a while from the long run of 'Jack & Jill' pantomime it was time to think of possibly getting a Summer Show again and for the third time we were booked for the season at the **Blackpool Opera House**. This time we didn't even have to audition.

We got the same 'digs' we had shared before, **Pat, Mary, Dorina** and **me** - and we looked forward to another happy summer season together.

The show was called –

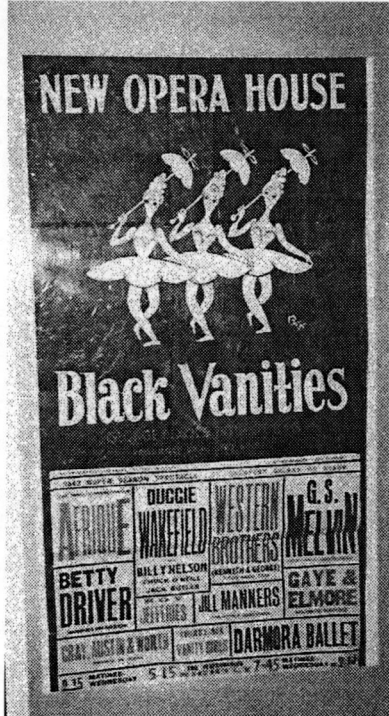

It was put on by the impresario **George Black** who was a big name in show business at that time and also responsible for shows at the London Palladium. Black Vanities was first shown there.

George also gave his name to 'Black Velvet' a previous Palladium show. This production of Black Vanities was not a lucky one.

The cast was headed by comedian **Billy Bennett.**

We opened to a great reception, but that very night Billy went back to his hotel after the performance but then suddenly collapsed and died. What a shock for his family, and all of us the following day when we heard of the tragedy.

Performers of quality were not free for a whole season so from then on we had a succession of 'stars' topping the bill; -
- **George Formby,**
- the **Caroli Brothers,** the famous clowns, and
- the **Western Brothers, Kenneth & George**

Also on that bill was a young singer, **Betty Driver** - Lancashire's own Radio Star. Many years later to be known as 'Coronation Street's' **Betty Turpin.**

The Elsie Carlisle Show

When we heard **Jack and Jill** was to be put on again at **His Majesty's Theatre** in **the Haymarket** this time we begged the agent to let us be in it.

He struck a bargain with us; -
- we could have **Jack and Jill**
- if we would go into the **'Elsie Carlisle Show'** for the last few weeks of it's run.

We were not thrilled at the prospect - it not being a 'top' show, but the carrot worked and we signed up.

How they came to need 4 replacement dancers I don't know. Again only one dance remains in my memory. A top hat and tails routine with walking sticks. One of us had to go on that night.

At Flavia Galli's Dancing School I had sat watching others have their private lessons; learning their routines just by watching meant that I was very good at picking up dances just by watching. Thus - I would be the one to go on that night.

There was also tricks to learn, swizzling the canes round my fingers etc. The other girls in the show were really nice and helped me all they could. They were so worried in case I dropped my cane that one of them dropped hers. We soon settled in and it was a happy company.

I can't recall where we got to with the tour but the last week was at **Wimbledon Theatre** in London.

Our week at Wimbledon Theatre coincided with the first week of rehearsals for Jack and Jill.

We rehearsed **Jack & Jill** all day and then went to the theatre and did two **Elsie Carlisle** shows in the evening.

It was all worth it to be in a good London show and living at home again.

Happy Feet as a Penguin!

The penguin dance and the ballet were still in the show and *I had to be a penguin!*

I found it quite scary and hard work jumping up on the tips of my long boots. It took me a while to learn it. I likened it to jumping backwards on to a chair. The music chosen for this number was **'Happy Feet'**.

We had to be right on the tips of the boots otherwise they slid away and we fell. This actually happened to me during one show, my feet sliding out in front of me and I sat down 'bang' on my seat. Trying to scramble up having foot long planks on my feet was not easy.

There is an old superstition that if you fall and sit on a stage you will have a return date to that theatre.

It didn't work for me there and then; all I got was a bruised bottom and hurt pride. However some 25 years later I did go back to
Wimbledon Theatre
playing **Kissie Fitzgarter**
in the musical **'Belle of New York'.**

Strange to reflect that more than 60 years later a film called **'Happy Feet'** and starring **Penguins** was to become a worldwide hit!

Fun on the last night

Although it is traditional to have a bit of fun in the very last show of a run, the only time I remember doing this was in **'JACK AND JILL'**. At one point in the story we dancers were in two diagonal lines each side of the stage leaning on one knee and at the back of the stage was a well.

Florence Desmond was 'Jack' and walked between our lines up to the well. She held up the talisman and dipped it in then bringing it out and holding it up explained '*Look, it's turned to gold* '.

We moved our 'down stage' arm to our upstage shoulders and said '*Gold?*'

On the last night we all said '*So What?*'

In another scene we were soldiers with white trousers, red tunics and black hats. We carried replica rifles with which we had been drilled at rehearsals by an army sergeant-major. We learnt how to present arms, slope arms and stand at ease. The routine was very impressive and done with great precision. At one point we stood still while Florence Desmond did her "*This Jewel set in a Silver Sea, this England* "speech with tremendous emotion and drama.

It was a high point in the show bearing in mind we were in the middle of War.

She particularly asked us not to do anything in this scene to make her laugh because of the very serious nature of the speech. So we drew little curly moustaches on ourselves with our eyebrow pencils and kept completely straight faces as we marched on. **Dessie** had to smile but we had arranged that we would not look at her in case we made her giggle. She had time to compose herself and the 'speech' went off without a hitch.

77

Air Raid Shock!
"Iverson Road has caught it".

After a rehearsal in town (London), I travelled home on the London Underground to my home station, Kilburn.

I knew there had been an Air Raid and when I arrived at Kilburn Station I heard people talking about it in a way that had a terrifying effect on me –

"Iverson Road has caught it!"

I lived in Iverson Road and Mummy would have been in the house at the time of the air raid.

Houses were flattened or torched in air-raids every day with their inhabitants killed or maimed – now this was my own road hit and possibly – my own house!

In a panic I raced there - fearful for my parents and home.

Outside each house was the tell-tale pile of debris from fallen ceilings and broken windows.

As I ran down the road the piles were getting bigger! Would our house still be there I wondered.

Then I noticed the piles suddenly becoming smaller and I found ours had scarcely been damaged.

My mother had been blown across the room but though shocked was otherwise unhurt.

Dad had come home from work and was repairing the front door that had been blown off.

The fanlight over the front door had been blown out and had hit the floor but was unbroken and my mother still in shock from being blown across the room kept saying

"And it still has the number 67 on it",

(The '67' was painted on!).

Much later on we found a piece of glass inside the lid on top of the piano.

The blast must have blown the lid up and the piece of glass inside before it banged down again.

The nightly Air-Raids

At home we didn't go into an air-raid shelter but four of us did sleep in the same room. My mother felt that whatever happened we at least would all be together. The exception being when my father, a policeman, would be on night duty.

It was a shock when a land-mine fell at the top of our road with an almighty explosion!

We checked to see if we had had any damage but when we found all the windows were intact, we went back to bed again.

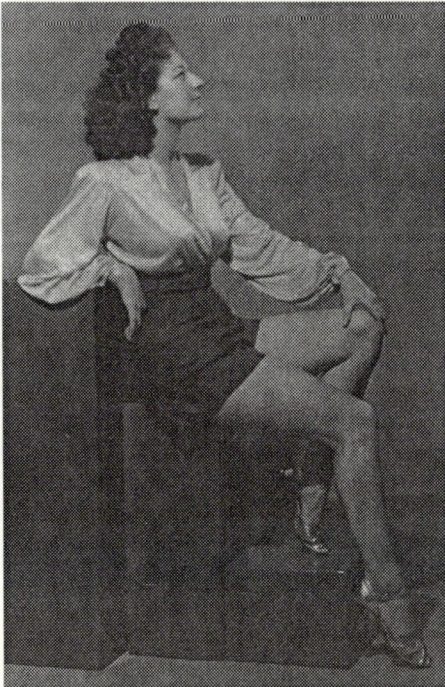

'Barbara 1943'

Barbara!

My parents - May Clements and James
Stewart - when they first met in 1915

Off to school with brother Roy
Aged 5 and 7

Hitching a ride with brother Jimmy
Aged 7 and 3

Barbara!

Flavia Galli - my dancing teacher

An early sister act at age 10
with Marion Seagrave

Backstage preparing for a dancing school concert

A scene from a Flavia Galli dancing school concert

Barbara!

Aged 13

Aged 14

Aged 16

Barbara!

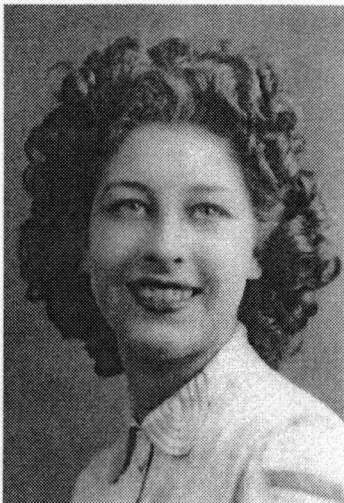

As I was in the 1940's

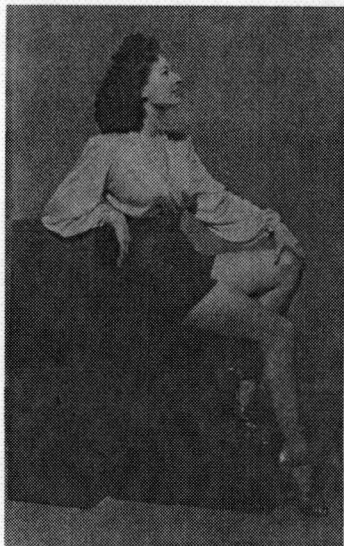

Dancers and show girls in rehearsal for "Mother Goose" (1939/40)
(There were four sets of twins among the show girls)

Dress fitting for "Mother Goose" (1939/40)

The finale scene in "Mother Goose" (1939/40)
(There are 12 dancers and 20 show girls.
The 12 Sunbeams had been sent home to bed!)

Barbara!

On Blackpool Beach with Dorina and, on the right, Kay Kendall

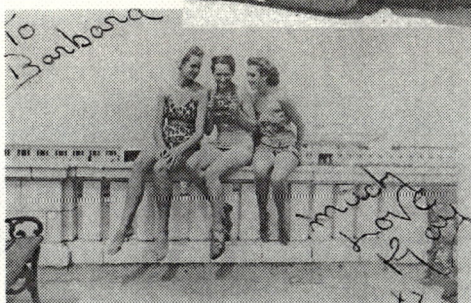

To Barbara

much love Kay

Kim and Kay Kendall (Their mother is in the middle)

Nellie - my Sunbeam in "Mother Goose" Alhambra, Bradford (1939/40)

Norman Evans -famous for his "Over the garden wall" sketch while dressed as a woman

Phylis Ward - she played the Fairy Queen in "Robinson Crusoe" (1938/39)

Albert Modley - comedian in "Mother Goose" (1939/40) and on tour with his own show (1940)

Two dresses from "Hullabaloo" -
Opera House, Blackpool (1941)
(The crinoline cost £100,
and the dress below cost £50)

Dress from "Black Vanities" -
Opera House, Blackpool (1942)
(Worn as Betty Driver sang "Blue Skies".
Note the blue bird on the hat)

Barbara!

Anne Ziegler and husband
Webster Booth - singers in
"Hullabaloo" (1941)

Florence Desmond - famous impressionist
and Principal Boy in "Jack and Jill"
Palace Theatre (1941/42) and
His Majesty's Theatre (1942/43)

JACK HYLTON
presents by courtesy of the B.B.C.
an enlarged edition of the Radio Feature

"BAND WAGGON"

(Adapted for the stage from the original production produced by Harry S. Pepper
and Gordon Crier)
This Trip Scheduled by Roy Rich

OVERTURE
" Beer Barrel Polka "

1. **THE BAND WAGGON ARRIVES**
   The Palladium Girls welcome BILLY TERNENT and the
   Band Waggoners, introducing " STINKER " MURDOCH,
   "Big-Hearted" ARTHUR ASKEY & TOMMY TRINDER

2. **CHESTNUT CORNER**
   " STINKER " and " BIG-HEARTED "

At the London Palladium (1939)

Opening scene of "No No Nanette" - on tour (1943)

Barbara - 1943 - 1945
- Entertaining the troops!

CALLED-UP FOR WAR SERVICE

When I was nearly 20 years old I was touring with - **'No, No, Nannette'**.

I had registered for War-Work in 1941 when I was 18. I was nearly 20 when 'the call' came we were appearing in Dewsbury, when I was summoned to the Labour Exchange. We only spent one week in each place but the 'powers that be' had my progress logged and all my papers were to hand.

Of the three Services I had chosen the Women's Auxiliary Air Force but on the way to the Labour Exchange I met one of our dancers and he told me, as a professional dancer I could request to do my War Service entertaining the troops with **E.N.S.A.** (Entertainments National Service Association). I hadn't known this and later wondered what I would have ended up doing if I had joined the W.A.A.F.'s.

I contacted E.N.S.A. and arranged to go to their HQ in the '**Theatre Royal', Drury Lane**, in London.

E.N.S.A.
Entertainments National Service Association.

I was immediately given a contract and was asked if I was prepared to go overseas. They needed a fourth dancer for a show already in rehearsal.

Overseas work was voluntary and as I was under 21 I needed written permission from both my mother and father. What they must have felt like writing the necessary letters I can only imagine.

Then followed a busy time, with rehearsals, vaccination and seven inoculations to fit into our schedule.

We had to put in a big envelope any writing thing that we wished to take with us - address book, reading book, knitting pattern etc. and hand it in. I seem to remember it was handed to the War Office. We were to have it returned when we were three miles out to sea.

At that time there was no E.N.S.A. uniform and we were given some clothing coupons to buy tropical kit as we were bound for the Middle East.

Without government issued clothing coupons you could not buy clothes, shoes, sheets, pillow cases, curtains, underwear or anything else made of fabrics, wool or cottons. The enemy blockade of the seas around Britain meant that no cotton was getting through from the U.S.A. or the Far East and most of the available wool was being used in making uniforms for the forces. Clothing rationing lasted a number of years after World War II.

In those days we ordinary folk never went abroad for holidays and we didn't know exactly what tropical kit was.

I bought a nice warm dressing gown with some of my coupons, which surprisingly proved to be a good idea although at the time drawing some amusing comments.

We were instructed to pack all toilet things we would need for our six months tour as we would not be able to buy them while we were away.

There were 11 of us in the show -

- singer **Joan Lane**,
- comedienne **Evelyn Eckcott**,
- soubrette **Madelayne Arnold**,
- comedian **Chip Saunders**,
- pianist **Terrence Kellaway**,
- manager entertainer **Cyril Wakefield**,
- baritone **Duggie Dalton**
- four dancing girls **Mona, Betty, Mary** and **me**.

After a few days on stand-by with strict instructions not to tell anyone we were waiting to go overseas! The call came and we reported to the '**Theatre Royal**', nicknamed '**The Lane**'.

It looked very different in those days to the way it does now. Temporary offices had been built all across the back of the stage and at the sides; most of the dressing rooms had also been turned into offices.

It was where everything happened; auditions, rehearsals, costume fitting, and of course we had to fill in a great many forms, - nothing changes much does it?

We had our photographs taken there for the special identity cards we would need now that we were going into military places.

All of us - and another show's cast - sat in the canteen for nearly two hours and then we were put on a coach and driven to a small railway station.

It was dark and in the 'blackout' - we didn't know where we were. After collecting boxes of eats we boarded a train. We slept, and ate, until we arrived at another small station.

We had our smaller luggage with us as we left the train and hoped the larger stuff was being 'looked after'.

We were allowed to take a small week-end case with us, a large case and a trunk. We still had no idea where we were but after a further short ride we found ourselves at the Customs point in Liverpool.

It took ages going through the Customs procedure and it was mid-day before we assembled on the quay, and waited.

There were several formations of troops waiting as well; each with an officer in front of them. They all looked very fed up and I wondered how long it would be before they would be coming home again.

A cheer broke into my thoughts, and I found it was for us few girls. There were about twelve of us and of course we had no uniforms and were in civilian clothes.

I hoped they would always be cheered up by us.

Dying to 'spend a penny'!

After a very long time waiting on the quay at Liverpool we girls wanted to 'spend a penny' so we asked our manager to find out where the 'Ladies' was.

He went along to the officer at the front of the first formation of troops and we could see them talking and we saw the officer shake his head. That officer went on to the next one, a shake of the head, then he went on to the next one, same result. He came back, more shakings of heads, then our manager came back and said there is no 'Ladies'.

Well we were completely embarrassed by now for we felt that everybody knew. We were not so open about such things in those days as we are now but after another uncomfortable wait we were eventually allowed to board the ship.

We found a soldier posted to direct us to the nearest loo.

What tact.

Full marks to the army.

H.M.T.S. Maloja to Algiers

The ship was a big 3 funneled liner. A cabin that in peacetime would have only 2 occupants now had 10 girls in it.

There were 5 double bunks and when you add 10 small cases and 10 big ones you can imagine the squash. Thankfully our trunks were in the hold.

There were 3 girls from another show and the 7 of us. It was all very exciting and we reveled in the food. Fresh white rolls with breakfast - no butter rationing.

We soon began to feel bored however and looking at Liverpool offered no relief. I tried to write a letter home but nothing I wanted to say would pass the censor; weather, type of ship and other passengers for instance. Mustn't even put the date; I gave up and went on deck and back to gazing at the docks.

Mummy gave me a lovely iced cake with 'Bon Voyage' piped in pink on it. My friends said I mustn't cut it until we are under way.

We were issued with life- jackets, they had lights attached to them, we were told they would stay alight for 24 hours so that we could be seen in the water if we were torpedoed!

We took this news quite calmly. The life-jackets had to be carried with us at all times. There were sentries posted on all gangways and they sent anyone back if they had no life-jacket.

On the 4th day on board we woke up to find we were moving. I rushed up on deck and of course all I could see was the sea but I had never realized how beautiful it is.

I wrote in my diary - *'The ship churned the sea up as it went along and made it all creamy, it looked good enough to eat. Then as it sinks down the foam goes a wonderful light blue'.*

Next day I wrote – *'We have stopped again. As usual we don't know where we are but it was thought to be Belfast, Ireland. Another boring stationary day'.*

We started making friends with the officers on board and some Queen Alexandra nurses but were not allowed to do more than wave to the troops. When we saw how crowded they were we realised what luxury our tiny cabin was.

Next day we were on the move at last and already 7 of my friends were seasick and the people in the dining room got fewer at each meal. It was pretty rough. Soon all 9 of my mates were in bed sick.

I washed their hands and faces each morning and left; it was not very nice in there!

Later I managed to bring them tea and dry toast, - not easy with the rolling of the ship. I couldn't wait any longer to have a piece of Mummy's cake but with all my friends seasick they didn't want to even look at it.

I waited until everyone seemed asleep and quietly cut the cake with the knife my thoughtful mother had provided. Yum, Yum! I repeated this each night until all the cake was gone. It was a small one, by the time they were all well my cake was forgotten and no one ever mentioned it. Phew!

With everyone recovered we were asked to put a show on but then it was found out that theatre costumes were on one of the other ships in the convoy. We couldn't see the other ships only the destroyers escorting us; they were smaller and seemed to disappear when the waves were high and then they would pop up again. We shuddered at the thought of what it would be like on board them.

By now there were budding romances and there were some red faces when we realised the officers we were friendly with were censoring our letters home. One girl had written a loving letter to the boy she left behind only to have it read by the one she was flirting with.

We kept expecting it to get warmer but it never did. When Christmas Eve came it felt strange having no cards or presents and not to know where we were. On Christmas Day we woke up to find we had arrived in Algiers.

We listened to King George VI make his Christmas Day speech. When he said *"Some of you will be listening on our ships"* I thought *'Yes, I am'* and felt really proud.

We were taken to a lovely Arabian house. Snag was marble floors and no heating and it was bitterly cold.

The army sergeant running the hostel with local staff, for that was what it was, had lemonade bottles filled with hot water for us to take to bed. That night we all slept in a room together on camp beds.

ALGIERS 1943

We arrived in Algiers on Christmas Day 1943!

We were driven to a lovely white Arabian house and learned that was 1 mile from a little village called –

El Biar, 8 miles from **Algiers.**

The house at El Biar was now an E.N.S.A. hostel, run by an army sergeant with a staff of local people - none of whom could speak English.

My first trip overseas and the next day we were keen to get out and visit **Algiers.**

The shops had all looked so wonderful and colourful there when we came through in the truck.

Mary, Joan and I put our town suits on, (at that time EN.S.A. did not have a uniform). We walked the mile to **El Biar** and with the help of a Canadian soldier we bought tickets and boarded a tram to **Algiers.**

We loved the town! It was bright and bustling.

It was only when we began to feel hungry that we got a little nervous as we spoke not a word of the local language. When we came across a **Y.M.C.A.** we went in.

We were not sure whether or not we would be accepted as we had no uniforms but we need not have worried - we had a lovely warm welcome and they said we must join their Christmas Party - everything free and *"you can eat as much as you like"*.

We sat in a daze. We were warm and had a wonderful feed, mince pies, sausage rolls, cream cakes, - the lot.

Thanking them we left, time to go 'home' we thought.

It was then we found it impossible to get on a tram. We assumed it must have been rush hour; people were hanging around the sides of each tram and they were jammed packed inside. We did not have a clue how to get back to **El Biar** and we were unable to ask.

On top of all this it was suddenly dark and there *we were completely lost on our first day in North Africa in the middle of a war!*

When an army truck went by **Joan** shouted *"Please stop!"*

The effect was great! They stopped dead in their tracks amazed at hearing an English girl's voice.

We explained what had happened to us and the driver said they were going our way and to hop aboard.

It was no easy feat clambering into the back of a 3 ton truck in a straight skirt!

Reaching El Biar we couldn't say which way our billet was, we only knew it was called 'Chateau Neuf'.

They thought they knew where it was and drove on; soon the driver stopped, pointed to a distant light saying he thought that was our house. He couldn't take us any further as he was already late and would be in trouble.

We thanked him, set off for the light only to find it was the wrong house.

Now we were in a foreign country with pitch darkness and completely lost when we heard footsteps coming towards us.

We were panic stricken but then saw 3 American soldiers emerging out of the darkness. We all flung ourselves into their arms with relief!

After explanations they informed us they lived in the house opposite. Both houses had grounds around them and we had not known there was another house there, so they escorted us home.

We got in without being missed, we should not have been out after dark, so we changed our suits and appeared for dinner, we were so thankful to be safe at last that we didn't notice how awful the meal was.

American Hospitality

We did not venture out the next day but after that we got our nerve back and we accepted the invitation the Americans had given us to go into **Algiers** with them in their jeep and were much happier this time.

That evening we all went over to their place and watched a film projected on to the side of their house. The house was painted white like ours and made an excellent screen.

The film we saw was "Cover Girl" with Rita Hayworth in the lead role.

Our food was very poor so the Americans invited **Joan** and I to eat with them. We got mess cans and stood in the queue and nobody seemed to mind even though we were not in uniform.

It was very cold at this time and we were taking lemonade bottles full of hot water to bed trying to get warm. Then suddenly, on January 3rd the sun came out and it was even warm enough to sunbathe.

Giving a show in every place was rather a challenge!

We were working hard, well - travelling hard!

One day our truck - we always travelled in the back of a 3-tonner - came for us at 2.45 p.m. We had a very rough ride, did two shows, then had a very rough ride back, arriving at our billet at 2.30 a.m. We had nothing to eat or drink and had to appear at 10 a.m. for breakfast that morning or go without until lunchtime. Life was very hap-hazard!

We never knew what time the truck would come or how long a journey we would have to make - nor indeed what sort of place we would be working in when we got there, or when or with what we would be fed - but we were very glad to be working.

Giving a show in every place we found was rather a challenge, especially for us dancers!

We would tumble out of the truck feeling anything but glamorous but the troops were marvellous and would always rustle up a cup of tea to welcome us, after which we would unpack our make-up and costumes and work a transformation.

Rarely did we have a proper dressing room, any corner with army blankets to curtain it off would do.

Sometimes they would fix us up with a mirror if one could be found but more often than not we made do with our small travelling mirrors.

I never remember any bad feelings or short tempers being shown no matter how we got in each others way whilst dressing and changing. Of course we would have a grumble at times as we got very tired and we ached all over from the long truck journeys.

Stages were often a real hazard for us dancers and routines sometimes had to be altered according to the size of stage we were given or no stage at all but we got used to adjusting to each one for a different show amazingly quickly.

On one occasion we only had table tops for a stage to dance on, and sometimes the lights would fail. The doors were opened to let in the light which resulted in us shivering with cold as we danced. Another time we only had 2 oil lamps, one each side of the stage. In one camp in Holland we thought the show would have to be abandoned on a dark night when the lights failed until the troops saved the day. Mustering all their torches they shined them on to the stage. The show went on.

Tommy Trinder
North Africa 1944

Tommy, and the familiarity is justified because he was always 'Tommy', a friend to everyone in the company, he was that sort of chap.

I first worked with Tommy in **"Band Waggon"** at the **London Palladium** in 1939 - then again later - touring the London Moss Empire Theatre circuit in **'Variety'**

- A show of different acts with a troop of dancing girls opening and closing the first and, (after the interval), the second halves of the show.
- We did one dance with large balloons, no not the famous titillating burlesque one of Bubbles Devine fame, but sparkling all the same.

Tommy usually threatened to stick a pin in mine but never did. He was always cheerful and full of fun.

Now if it had been the **'Crazy Gang'** in the same circumstances our balloons might have been popped every night!

The next time Tommy and I met was18 months or so later and it was near Algiers. I was dancing with **E.N.S.A**. and Tommy was on a visit doing concerts for the troops. I recall we all had to change in the same room with a sheet hung down the middle separating the girls from the men.

I note after one of our dances Tommy bounced on to the stage and called us 4 dancers back on. Completely unrehearsed he asked our names and a few other details getting laughs all the time but without embarrassing us too much.

To my answering I came from West Hampstead he slotted in his familiar Golders Greenburg jibe used quite often throughout his career, Golders Green being the district next to West Hampstead.

Dancers were not used to speaking on stage and we were therefore quite nervous but we need not have worried, the way Tommy drew the answers from us giving him a chance to be funny was a lesson in his complete professionalism. He then went on to do his full act.

The troops loved Tommy Trinder and so did we.

Algiers to Italy

We were only in and around **Algiers** entertaining the troops for 3 short weeks after we left **England**, when we were given the choice of moving on to **Egypt** or **Italy**. Both were continuing war zones of which we were aware but we chose the latter.

I was still recovering from a nasty bout of dysentery but on January 17th 1944 we boarded the vessel **"Neuralia"**.

In considerable pain from what was suspected to be appendicitis we were up at 6.30 am to board the SS Neuralia for our journey from Algiers to Naples.

Although a smaller ship than the **"Maloja"** on which we had sailed from **Liverpool**, we were not so overcrowded. **Joan Lane, Evelyn Eckott** and I shared a nice little cabin.

Not feeling fully recovered I asked to see the Medical Officer. He put me on a diet.

I seem to recall his name was **Bill O'Meara**, a very good-looking and charming young Irishman.

Result was for lunch I was served in my cabin with the biggest glass beaker I have ever seen filled to the brim with Ovaltine. The same turned up for dinner but this time Bill had his meal served in my cabin, to *"keep me company"* he said. I said *"More likely to show what I was missing"*. I could only muster a wan laugh at my own joke.

Next day feeling much better I was allowed to join my friends in the dining room for a proper meal. In the morning at breakfast we heard some noises and saw the Stewards exchanging worried looks.

We later found out that they were depth-charges fired from a destroyer escort as there was a German submarine about. All the same we enjoyed our 3 days on board, good regular food and a lovely rest from truck journeys.

Arriving in **Naples** was exciting except it was very cold and we had to travel in an open air truck again to our hostel.

19th Jan Wednesday

Had a lovely breakfast during which we heard funny noises & saw the stewards look worried. Found out later they were torpedoes fired from a destroyer there was a submarine about. Maybe I would only like the navy in peace time! Ted felt well so sat on deck writing letters, it is very hard to say only what will pass the censor. Bill sent a note to say "whats Cookin"? I wrote back "Rice puddin". Spent most of the day with him, he is very good looking & I should think he will break a lot of hearts but not mine. He seems to have cured my pain.

Naples

20th Jan Thursday.

We overslept & Bill came & woke us, we don't take kindly to breakfast at 8:00. It was lovely on deck, what a pity it took a war to give me this chance to see some of the world.

Naples looked very beautiful but it is not so beautiful when you are in it & can smell it.

We disembarked & came in an open truck to the hostel. It is called Hotel Rubicino & is just off Gariboldi Square.

Talking as well as Dancing

On our first Sunday in Italy we were all invited to a party. I was embarrassed when a young soldier took me into a corner of the room and began to cry.

Mine was the first English girl's voice he had heard for 2 years.

I talked to him until the tears stopped and we had a good laugh. I realised I had to get over my own shyness, talking to the troops was as important to them as dancing for them.

E.N.S.A. in Italy - 1944

We had no radio or newspapers to keep us in touch with the war. The battles at **Anzio** and later **Monte Casino** had been raging and although not caught up in them we had heard the gunfire.

The places we stayed in were varied. Usually a large house run by an army sergeant with local staff.

Little allowance was made for our 'Theatrical Hours'. Our evening meal was provided in the Officer's Mess after the show. This ranged from a small sandwich to a nice spread. Everyone did their best for us with what they had. Often we still had a long journey in the back of a truck arriving back at the hostel in the early hours of the morning.

The kitchen would be closed so there was no hope of a cup of tea or even a glass of water.

With our late-night return from a show we often overslept and missed breakfast. Food shops were out of bounds because of typhoid so we were not able to supplement meals in any way and we didn't get N.A.A.F.F.I. rations.

Reading my diary I seem to have been hungry most of the time.

As for the hostels, to find one with all its windows intact, electric light and running hot water was a rarity.

'FANCY MEETING YOU' - 1944

Dancing Programme

After the opening song and dance

Mary, Betty, **Mona** and I had 4 other dances.

- A Tap routine; a Ballet; a Spanish routine and a full company around countries ensemble;
- We also danced as 'children' in school, background to comedienne **Evelyn Eckotts** big number 'Awful Child'; plus the finale.

Our Spanish costumes were quite splendid! Halfway through the dance we pulled off the skirt with a flourish leaving us in shorts, *('Bucks Fizz'- this was 1944 – long before the Eurovision Song Contest!).*

The skirts became capes each lined with a different bright colour. We did a slick routine moving the capes in a variety of patterns. They were very heavy and it was hard work.

The ballet was danced to 'Autumn Leaves' and in the pretty apricot coloured dresses in very light 'floaty' material - must have looked effective as it usually drew spontaneous appreciation.

The colourful Full Company item was acted and danced by each dancer wearing a different costume to our soubrette Madelayne Arnold's singing –

"I'm one eighth Hawaiian, with skin like gold,"
"I'm one eighth Antarctic, and oh so cold"
"I'm one eighth from Chile, and that's pretty hot"
"I'm one eighth from Paris, so I know what's what"
"Part of me is Mexican, oh boy that's bad"
"My Irish particle is, slightly mad"
"My Chinese fraction is, just too sweet"
"But my Russian remainder's got them all beat"
"I'm a great exception from nature's laws
"I'm one eighth of everything but yet all yours.

- **Mona** dances in wearing a sarong
- **Barbara** in white skating dress fur hood
- **Betty** in frilly lace blouse and coloured skirt
- **Evelyn** in smart short dress, carrying a hat box
- **Mary**, trousers, poncho and sombrero
- **Joan** dressed in green,
- non-dancing 6 ft **Chipps Saunders**, comedian in dainty little steps
- Actor/Manager **Cyril Wakefield** in superb Cossack costume
- We all then danced and sang the Finale.

THE FOUR DANCERS each had 6 costumes with matching hats or headdresses and 3 or 4 pairs of shoes. It was often a tight fit getting them all in tiny dressing rooms in the camps we visited.

Then there were Evelyn's, Madelayne's and Joan's dresses and accessories, (Joan had a beautiful white full crinoline dress). Then there were all the men's costumes etc. Everything - including all our make-up was packed in two large skips.

Some afternoons we gave a show in a hospital after which everything was packed up and moved with us on to our evening venue. That show over - it was everything back in the skips again.

We mostly did two shows a day, sometimes in the same place, which was a relief, but not always.

Once or twice we stayed a few days in one place which we just loved. Even then we sometimes packed up and went to a hospital for an afternoon show.

The excellent quality of our costumes meant they survived spending so much time in and out of skips and always looked good.

Salerno

Salerno is fondly remembered in some respects.

After a long truck journey wrapped in blankets to keep out the cold, we arrived at a very nice hotel. It was run as usual by an army sergeant with local staff and more surprises were to come when we found we would be working in a nice big theatre.

It was such a treat to have a real dressing room to change in.

We unpacked our costumes and enjoyed the luxury of being able to hang them up especially as we had so many of them. We four dancers had 7 costumes each and our soubrette and singer also had several dresses.

After a meal and a rest we went back to the theatre to do the show. What a surprise when we found that a soldier had beautifully pressed all our costumes.

When we thanked him he told us he worked in a dry-cleaners in civvy street and was used to pressing evening gowns; he said he had enjoyed working on our dresses as a change from pressing uniforms.

The next day we had to pack all our costumes back in our skips. As well as the dresses we had head-dresses, three or four pairs of shoes each so you have some idea of the packing and unpacking we did.

In the afternoon we did a show in a hospital with a very tiny stage, contrasting with our show in the theatre in the evening.

We repeated this the next day, two shows and two lots of packing and unpacking.

During the morning the Town Major had taken us to see the recent battlefield; it was now a cemetery and we saw so many soldiers graves there it really upset us.

We were used to seeing buildings with the marks of bullets on them and constantly travelling over rough mortar bomb damaged roads, but this battlefield and cemetery truly brought home to us what a shocking waste of young lives war is.

After three days in Salerno we packed up our personal things as well as our costumes and were taken by truck back to the E.N.S.A. hostel in Naples.

We didn't usually work on Sundays so Joan and I went with some friends to the Officer's Club in Naples for some tea.

When we got back to the hostel we found that the others had gone off to do a show on a ship. We didn't know what to do. No show had been planned for that day but then a truck came back for us and rushed us down to the docks and we joined the rest.

We did a show for the survivors of **H.M.S. Spartan** which had been torpedoed, the survivors being rescued by the ship we were on.

We were singing and dancing for these brave men and it was a very humbling experience seeing them singing and laughing at our show after what they had just been through. They begged us for souvenirs so I gave them the charms from my bracelet

ITALY - diary entries - 1944

Feb 1

Staying in a nice big house in **Santa Maria**, - no electricity, only candlelight. We are performing in a little theatre in **Capua**, half an hours ride away. We can hear the fighting, gunfire etc., and have soldiers from the frontline in our audience.

Feb 3

Bully Beef (Corned beef) for lunch again, we seem to live on the stuff. After matinee we had tea in Sergeants mess - Bully Beef. After the evening show had supper with the officers - yes, more Bully Beef.

Feb 4

There was hot water at the theatre so had a good wash. People who were on the ship from Liverpool to Algiers feel like family and it was great to see **Roy Robins** and **George Smart** (R.E. Officers) in front for second show.

Feb 5

Woken up by a loud bang (see separate story) a big fright we thought fighting had reached us.

Feb 6

Sunday: *We could hear the guns very loudly today.*

Feb 7
After shows we were invited to a dance at an American camp. They cut in during every dance. With only us seven girls there we barely danced two steps with the same man, it was murder.

Feb 8
We were all tired and bruised after the dance last night. The troops are wonderful audiences; the show is a terrific success.

Feb 9
After the matinee Evelyn, Joan and I saw the Medical Officer about the spots on our tummies; we have Scabies - how awful. He painted us with something and told us to come back tomorrow.

Feb 10
Rainy and muddy and we couldn't get a truck to take us to have our spots treated.

Feb 11
Had lift to doctor and had our tummies painted again. We felt really silly.

Feb 12
The 13 days here in **Santa Maria** and working only ½ hours drive away was great. No long journeys, no packing our personal things and only sometimes packing our costumes for a hospital show - Bliss!

Best of all has been making some friends; we usually move on before we get the chance.

At our farewell party in the officers mess - sick of being laughed at for only drinking lemonade I said I would drink level with my escort for the night; John. Luckily he wasn't downing pints but sherry. We had 3 glasses each and I was so determined not to get 'tight', I didn't.

Feb 13
Sunday: An hour and a half in the truck and we were back in **Naples**. Our trunks always stay in this hostel

and we take small cases on our travels. We are glad to have a change of clothes.

Feb 14

Somewhere near Naples, - very small theatre and at first it was freezing cold. There is a stove in the middle of our dressing room, it gradually warmed up. Worst thing is the spiders! Just before the Finale the lights went out, they opened the doors and we worked in shafts of daylight shivering with cold.

Feb 15

Worked in **Portici**, - theatre was so cold we could hardly dance and the stage was bumpy.

Feb 18

We travelled to **Sorrento** in a caravan, the small windows were too high for us to see out and it made us feel sick. Plenty of hot water in our hotel, I have actually had a bath, Heaven.

Feb 19

Amalfi. We are in a nice hotel but have to climb 180 steps up to it. The cliff lift is out of use for the duration of the war. The lights went out during our first show, we just had an oil lamp each side of the stage. They came on half way through the second show.

Feb 20

The pain I have been suffering in my right side for some time is getting really bad. I can't lift my cloak in time with the music and have to stay out of the Spanish dance.

Chipps is ill and in hospital - I don't know what is wrong.

Naples 1944

Arriving in Naples in 1944 was far from romantic! It was the worst winter on record, non-stop rain and mud everywhere.

I had seen how the troops were suffering on the Newsreels before I left home and now we were amongst it. Life was certainly tough, constantly changing hostels ranging from comfortable to extremely uncomfortable, Lack of hot water and electricity I have covered elsewhere along with broken windows and lack of heating and the daily rough journeys.

On the plus side of course were the troops and their enthusiasm for our efforts, very heartening and some visits afterwards to the officer's mess for reasonable food.

Unfortunately the niggling pain in my side was getting worse. After one afternoon show I asked to see the Medical Officer. He examined me and diagnosed sub-acute appendicitis. Then he proceeded to wash his hands and announced *"Let's go in to tea"*. No mention of what I should do about the pain. The attitude was I was there to entertain the troops not be ill. After tea off I went with the others to another camp for the evening show, visit that officers mess and the truck journey back before I could at last fall into bed.

Life took on a surreal feel as I tried to battle on.

Our Spanish dance involved turning our skirts into capes for simulating a bull fight. They were heavy and gave me a great amount of trouble with the pain in my side. To my shame a special rehearsal was called to "bring me up to scratch". I had sympathy and support from the girls but **Charlie**, our manager, said I had a convenient pain and was just lazy

When, in the officer's mess after the show I seemed a bit 'washed out', and was asked what was wrong, telling them I had sub-acute appendicitis produced murmured *"Sorry"*, but it was never possible for me to be taken back to the hostel and bed until everyone was ready to leave.

When **'Chipps'**, our comedian, became ill he was taken into hospital. Next day after our p.m. show **Eve** and I went to the hospital for her to visit Chipps and for me to see a doctor. As we left Charlie said to me *"Even if they want to keep you in you must come back and do the evening show"*

The doctor confirmed sub-acute appendicitis, at last gave me some medicine and said I must rest for three days. If the pain was no better see a Medical Officer again.

Eve and I rejoined the company for the evening show. I did all the dances except the Spanish. In the officer's mess we found they had made a lovely trifle with the name of our show

'Fancy Meeting You'

- piped in cream. I say in my diary *"By the time we got back to the hostel I was so ill, Eve had to put me to bed"*.

A Proposal from John Hanson

There was an R.A.F. **'Gang Show'** staying in our Naples hostel, (Hotel Rubicino).

John Hanson, later to become a singing 'star notable as the 'Red Shadow' in "Desert Song" and other light opera, **Graham Stark** and **Will Hay Jnr.**, fine comedians, were with them.

I was friendly with John and now that I had to rest we had more time together. My show was away most of the day and it was the 'Gang Show' boys who brought me food. One day John brought me some toast and hot milk and then asked me to marry him.

He was charming and I was tempted to say *"Yes"*, instead I said *"maybe when we've got to know each other better"*

It was not to be. We moved off in different directions and were not able to keep in touch.

I did rally for a while and was able to go and see the 'Gang Show' perform in Naples. I loved John Hanson's voice but was disappointed he didn't look at me. When he finished singing he gave me a huge wink and I blew him a kiss.

I was soon back in my hostel bed and this time on a diet of army biscuits and tea which everyone but me thought a big joke.

Visit from a Cousin

Though not able to give away information of my whereabouts, for security reasons, I could say I was appearing in

'Fancy Meeting You'

- when writing to my cousin who I knew was in Italy serving with the Royal Air Force.

Duncan Stewart and the rest of my father's family lived in Lanarkshire, Scotland, and Dad had settled in London with his English wife. We only met the Scottish branch of the family on rare visits and Duncan had never seen me dance.

Armed with the name of the show Duncan somehow located our hostel.

Unfortunately we were still in bed; unbelievably he was shown into our bedroom.

- **Mona** was in the first bed, in the dim light Duncan whispered 'Barbara?' Mona drowsily pointed further into the room,
- same thing with **Betty** in the next bed,
- then **Mary** in the next bed.
- At last Duncan arrived at my bed I had a horribly drippy cold and looked far from a glamorous looking dancer he would have expected.

104

In later years Duncan, very amusingly, used to enact the scene detail by detail, even up to the 'told in de dose' bit.

Shortly after this I was confined to bed with appendicitis. Duncan caught up with **'Fancy Meeting You'** at **Castlemara** and saw the show - minus me of course.

The name of *"that law"* springs to mind.

After my appendix operation in the 65th General Military Hospital in **Naples**, I wrote to Duncan knowing he was in the area. So many miles from home I really looked forward to a visit from a member of the family.

It was not to be, my letter took nine days to reach Duncan and by the time he managed to get to the hospital I was convalescing in **Sorrento**. *"That law"* again!

Duncan was not able to get to Sorrento and our paths did not cross again until we were both back in the UK. When we were once more able to make our rare visits to Scotland for holidays and family get-togethers we at last met up with **Duncan** and **Betty** his wife.

SAD POSTSCRIPT

After I scribed the above story for this book I telephoned cousins **Duncan** and **Betty** for a chat, hoping for a laugh about his visit to me in the ENSA hostel in Naples, only to hear Duncan, then 92, was in hospital needing 24 hour care.

Next day Wally printed a copy of the story, I quickly wrote a letter and went straight out to post them. Only a few minutes after I returned home Betty phoned to say

"Duncan died this morning!"

65th General Hospital, Naples

March 4th, **Joan** and **Eve** came in the ambulance with me. We were taken to the 92nd General hospital first, where I had to climb to the top of the building to see Matron. She was quite adamant that she had nowhere to put a girl! So it was back down to the ambulance and on to the 65th General Hospital; the unreal feeling returning as I thought, *"How different it would have been had I been at home"*.

The Matron here was also not keen on a girl patient! One could sympathise with her - the wounded from the Anzio battlefield were more important than a girl with appendicitis.

It was pretty miserable for me though. Trouble was I could not be flown home and if my condition suddenly became acute on board ship that would be a problem.

As it happened there were two girls from the Palestinian ATS - **Irene** and **Yanke** - already there but they were due to leave in a day or two.

March 6th, had the operation. I was carried down so many stairs, from the 3rd floor, I felt as if I would slide off the stretcher.

The surgeon said he was *"Sorry he couldn't make the ether smell nice"* for me.

Waking up wasn't much fun, sickness and soreness, then came the cough. I lay awake all night longing for a drink of water and every now and then the agony of the 'cough'; no pain-killers available.

A chap brought Irene and I some cakes and cigarettes, we didn't tell him neither of us smoked. He said he specially wanted to see me because ENSA had done so much for him and his pals.

Yanke had gone and with the nurses busy it fell to Irene to feed me. Then she too left, and I was alone! The only girl in the hospital, apart from nurses.

The building had been a school and my ward was large with beds down the sides and mine at the top furthest from the door facing it.

A strapping 6ft West African soldier walked in. As I lay there he looked HUGE! I wondered what language he would speak? He spoke English beautifully. He was a school teacher before the War. His name was **Alex.** I rarely saw a nurse during the day and Alex did everything for me, and I do mean everything. Watching him walk the length of the ward carrying my used bed-pan was acutely embarrassing for us both but he was charmingly dignified, helping me to be the same.

Food was served in mess cans all mixed together and tea in a large pudding bowl; the latter was heavy and hard for me to handle. The Night Sister brought me a little pink cup but if the orderly brought it into me the Day Nurses made him get it back and give me the bowl. It was the same with bread, if he cut 2 thin slices for me the orderly was sent to get them back and give me a thick slice.

I felt very unwanted!

I know the troops were more important but I reasoned I couldn't help being ill. With no wireless, no magazines or papers and no one to talk to, time passed very slowly.

One day Harry, a medical orderly, came in with a gramophone he had found in a cupboard, *"But there is only one record"* he said.

I didn't know whether to laugh or cry when he announced it was a selection from **'No, No, Nanette'**.

I told him it was the show I was in before joining E.N.S.A., and I sang along with all the songs.

Joan and **Eve** came to see me with some lovely flowers, I noted Joan was wearing my coat. I had brought only a few things into hospital, my trunk and big case were in one of the hostels. Suddenly I longed to get dressed again.

I may sound as if I was sorry for myself but there were high-lights.

For instance the surprise when the ward door opened and a soldier walked in holding aloft a bakers tray in which were about two dozen chocolate éclairs.

They were a present from the camp where I had enthusiastically eaten several after the show one night.

What a marvelous treat after the very dull hospital food. I ate several, of course, but shared with the orderlies and my favourite nurse, (the one who brought me a dainty pink cup after seeing me struggle with a pudding basin of tea).

The incision of my operation was quite long and in those days meant 10 days in bed, then out in a chair for 10 minutes, up longer the next day and then at last able to get dressed. Even after all this my wound was not completely healed and needed dressing for a further few days.

John Hanson and **Laurie** from the R.A.F. 'Gang Show' visited, they brought several bars of chocolate and they had hand-written messages on them.

One day I was surprised when a nurse came in and made my bed. Then I found out why.

My door was opened with a flourish by the Regimental Sergeant Major, he gave me a lovely 'wink' then saluted smartly as in came the Colonel and Matron.

They walked the length of the room to the foot of my bed. I felt ridiculous sitting next to my orange-box 'bed-side table', the division making a shelf where my few toilet things were laid out in a row.

"Good morning, how are you?" Sir enquired.

"Good morning, very well thank you" I replied.

They turned and walked back to the door which seemed to take ages. Another 'wink' from the R.S.M. and that was that.

That night there was a bad air-raid and with uncurtained windows on three sides of the ward on the top floor of the hospital, and not able to get up, I felt scared. When a nurse came and said *"You'll be alright here"*, I had to swallow my pride and say *"No, I am frightened"*.

A stretcher was brought and I was carried down stairs to the basement. Going through an adjoining ward I noted only men who were too ill to be moved were left there.

The basement was crowded, a lot of people standing. My stretcher was down on the floor and I was afraid I would be trampled on.

With the 'raid' over, a medical orderly soldier helped me back to bed. I did wonder why these nurses seemed uncaring towards a young girl as I was, so far from home. I was later told some officers had given nurses notes for me to cheer me up but I never received them

Convalescence

After 16 days in hospital, used to the routine, staff and other personnel I was nervous about leaving.

Missing the company of my show friends I found it hard being on my own.

I had gone from being welcome wherever I went, dancing and singing in lovely costumes taking the minds of the troops, and ours, away from the War, to now being a problem who nobody really wanted.

Also Vesuvius was in eruption and I wasn't sure how close we would go to it on our journey.

I sat in the front of the ambulance with the driver, he tried hard to miss the mortar bomb holes in the road but there were so many of them it was very painful from Naples to Sorrento.

On arrival - there was a double row of officers sitting outside the hotel in the sunshine. I felt so embarrassed with all eyes on me until I suddenly saw a familiar face. We had given a show at this unit.

I greeted him like a long lost brother. Eyebrows were raised. I was in civilian clothes as E.N.S.A. personnel were only just starting to get a uniform. His name was Spy, presumably a nick-name.

I hoped Spy would take me into the dining room for lunch but he told me he was meeting a friend. I was so dreading walking in, the only girl in a room full of strangers I insisted Spy took me with him although it was 20 minutes walk away and I being just out of hospital. Fortunately with so few girls around I think it was good for Spy's ego to walk in with a girl on his arm.

Spy escorted me into breakfast and lunch the next day and in the evening we went to another hotel and dined with 5 of his friends. It may sound odd, in the middle of a war but all the hotels available were being used for convalescent cases. Ours, Hotel Tramantano, was full of Army bods, the Cocumellor was for R.A.F. and Americans were at the Vittoria.

I had an uncomfortable feeling being the only girl at dinner with 6 men, 5 of whom I had never met before. Me being a slow eater, they were always finished first but could not be served the next course until I was ready. That made me slower still.

Nowadays a glass of wine would ease things but I didn't drink then. By the time Spy left Sorrento I had made some friends and lost my terror of the dining room.

Vesuvius Erupting

I was convalescing in **Sorrento** after my appendix operation in the 65th General Military Hospital in **Naples**. I had a lovely comfortable room; the window looked out across the bay to Naples. A picture postcard view, only now I could see the red hot lava oozing down the sides of Vesuvius. There was talk that an earthquake or tidal wave would come next!

I looked down at the sea just below my window and shivered.

The entry in my diary reads— *'I feel rather lost, I don't know where my show is, where most of my clothes are,'* (I had only taken a few when I went into hospital), *'or where I will go when my two weeks here are up, worst of all I don't get any mail as it is still addressed to the 'Fancy Meeting You' company, the censor won't allow me to write home giving my present address'.*

Vesuvius started blowing out clouds of ash blotting out the sun and forming a low 'ceiling' over us.

We couldn't resist going out, someone found goggles and we wore scarves over our faces. The ash was inches thick on the ground. It wasn't much fun and we soon went inside again.

Of most consternation was the fact that we could not get enough water to wash our hair and I had hardly been able to get a comb through the stiffness it presented.

Thankfully the wind changed and the ash left us and descended on other poor souls elsewhere.

Danger was not necessarily past and came from other directions. For instance when we ventured out people were sweeping dust off their flat roofs which was most disconcerting.

Next came the rain.

Underfoot became volcanic mud compounded by 'raining mud' through the trees.

We were very relieved when at last Vesuvius quietened down. Later when I returned to England I was given the newspaper cuttings and photos that accompanied the reports of the eruptions I had witnessed.

Convalescence Sorrento

I convalesced at the **Tramantano Hotel** - then a British Red Cross Convalescent Hotel.

BRITISH RED CROSS CONVALESCENT HOTEL TRAMANTANO - for officers.
my room situated here with patio balcony at the side

We nick-named the lounge 'The Morgue'.

My diary at the time recorded -

March 28 1944 –

Gordon and **me**, younger convalescents, found life very dull.

Mostly older officers relaxed and nodded off there.

Jig-saw puzzles helped but if one of us dropped a piece breaking the silence, heads would shoot up and glare at us, like a library or gentlemen's club.

The Y.W.C.A. (Young Women's Christian Association) had a place in **Sorrento**, nurses were able to stay there for a break.

It was run by a lovely lady, **Miss Gunn**. They served teas etc., and when **Val, Gordon** and **me** were enjoying a tea, Gordon suddenly said *"Let's put on a show"*.

Back at the Tramantano for lunch Gordon stood up and announced we were putting on a show, anyone interested meet in the Chapel at 17.00 hours.

First **Johnny** arrived, he had been shot through the heel at **Anzio**, a fearsome battle still raging, his leg in plaster with the customary metal hoop to stand on.

Then **Frank** who said he could play piano a bit.

That Johnny, Val, Gordon and Frank had never been on stage and I couldn't dance did nothing to dampen our spirits.

March 29 –

We heard that **Phillip Ridgeway**, famous for his radio show, was at **Amalfi**. We thought that he may lend us some scripts of sketches.

We borrowed the hotel jeep and with Gordon driving set off but arriving at Amalfi we were told Phillip had moved to **Positano**.

On nearing Positano we came to a bridge that had been blown up so turned back. The round trip had taken 6 hours, we were tired and starving.

After dinner we contacted Phillip by telephone, not only did he agree to send scripts but offered to come and compere the show.

My room became 'headquarters'.

Our spirits were high so we wrote down all kinds of ideas, rewriting topical lyrics to songs we knew. (What copyright breaches I wonder?)

I had twice been in a show called
"Band Waggon"
first at the **London Palladium**
and then the **Opera House Theatre, Blackpool.**

The opening number of the show was called Band Waggon and we, including Arthur and Richard, had trouble remembering the words of the 'middle eight' , we often hummed or la – laard our way through it.

I changed Band Waggon to Con Depot (Convalescence Depot), rewrote the lyrics to open the show.

March 30 –

Although there were still only the five of us we asked if we could do the show on the cinema stage. I had performed there with **"Fancy Meeting You"** before I was taken ill.

I had no suitable dresses as my trunk and big case were still missing. **George Smart**, who had been on the ship from Liverpool and **George Mason**, (Army Officers), tracked me down and came to visit.

Wonder of wonders they had prised some mail for me from the ENSA office in Naples.

At last - a letter from home, my first since before entering hospital. Mummy wrote such lovely letters and this one gave me a few tears, home seemed far away.

March 31 –

A wonderful stroke of luck, - the Con Depot band has joined us. They belong to the 'other ranks' Convalescent Depot in Sorrento.

I agreed to sing with their singer, -

- - 'You and I';
- - 'Aroura" and
- - 'We'll Meet Again', and
- - by myself "Dearly Beloved".

I was terrified as I had never sung on my own before.

April 1st -

Johnny and I went in search of stage make-up. Not able to speak Italian we had a funny time trying to mime what we wanted. The blank looks on the shop people's faces sent us into hysterics.

April 2nd -

Val took me to **Naples** in the jeep and we eventually tracked down my trunk. Unfortunately, **Eve** still had the key 'minding' it for me and I didn't know where she and the show were.

We called into Val's unit before leaving Naples, **Major Sam** asked us to stay for tea.

Back in Sorrento the boys tried unsuccessfully to open my old pirate style trunk. It had been my mother's since she went into service aged 13 in 1911.

April 3rd –

Show Day! We badly needed more rehearsal and I still had no dresses but my 2 weeks convalescence was up and I had to leave Sorrento the next day.

After breakfast Johnny and Gordon managed to open my trunk.

It was marvelous to have my things back including a pink net evening dress. A quick press and it was as good as new.

At the 11th hour a lady at the YWCA loaned me a nice full length cotton house coat giving me the luxury of two dresses for the show.

We called the show –

Twenty men and a Girl

There weren't 20 men but 15 or 16 men and a girl didn't seem right.

A rehearsal was so bad and so long we didn't have time for a dress rehearsal.

Actually we didn't have much in the way of costumes, a couple of white coats for doctors and a white apron with a napkin on my head for a nurse.

Because of this the opening sketch we made a 'send up' of a fashion parade, showing various army garments and equipment, some of the band and soldiers having their arms twisted to join in.

Phillip Ridgeway arrived oozing confidence which rubbed off on us.

We had a 'Full House' - all rather bored lads determined to have a good time and our efforts were enthusiastically rewarded.

The band's singer, (sadly I cannot recall his name) knowing how nervous I was - held my hand all through our songs.

With Phillip Ridgeway's professionalism holding it together the show was a success.

Afterwards I kept my pink evening dress on and Phillip his dress suit and with Johnny, Val and Gordon we all went to the **Vittoria Hotel** to celebrate.

They were so pleased with the show I was given another few days at the **Hotel Tramantano**.

The **Con. Depot Band** asked me to be in their show. I did more in that show than I did in our original one.

It really was time for me to leave but we managed to get our head waiter to supply some sandwiches and held a party in the room we used for rehearsals.

Gordon got a gramophone from somewhere and we danced, Johnny managing a great quickstep in spite of his leg in plaster.

It was a farewell party and we were all sad and sentimental, wondering if and where we would meet again.

Back in my room I felt as if the end of the world had come, the show was over, where would I go now?

Hotel Tramantano
Sorrento

Other incidents during my stay -
One evening soon after my arrival I sat in the bar listening to some of the officers singing. They then started going round getting people to sing individually, pointedly saying 'lady' and gentlemen so and so will now sing.

I dreaded it coming round to my turn but knew I would have to brave it out.

I sang **"She had to go and lose it at the Astor"**, a popular if somewhat risqué song of the time. I completely surprised myself as I hadn't realised I knew all the words but it went down well all the same.

Val, who was recovering from diphtheria, asked me to marry him 15 minutes after we met and became my special escort. We lunched together, walked round the pretty Sorrento village and then he took me to the Y.W.C.A. (Young Women's' Christian Association) where they served teas and always had lovely cakes, a sure way to my heart.

Although I was the only girl in a hotel full of men I felt perfectly safe and never locked my room door. To illustrate this one morning I awoke to find a stone cold cup of tea by my bed, I had been so fast asleep I didn't hear whoever brought it. You could be excused for thinking I was sleeping off an evening of debauchery but I was teetotal then.

Before my inconvenient appendicitis operation our show toured round various army camps and after the performance we were invited to the officer's mess. I felt embarrassed every time I asked only for orange squash and also for the fact that I didn't smoke either.

Thankfully my present friends were aware of this and I wasn't pressed either to drink or smoke.

From Battle Dress to Evening Dress

I had some convalescence in **Sorrento** following my appendix operation and was then back in **Naples** at the main ENSA hostel, the **Hotel Rubicino**, just off Garibaldi Square.

Still not able to dance and rejoin my show I was alone and when a group of young soldiers came to stay in the hostel I was glad to have their cheerful company.

Madge Elliot and **Cyril Richard**, West End stars, had been appearing in the **Merry Widow**, Franz Lehar's musical, in the U.K. Now they and some of the company were in **Naples** to perform for the troops. With them was **Diana Gould** the ballerina, singer and actress who would later marry the violinist Yehudi Menuhin.

My new soldier friends had been recruited for the chorus and had a wonderful time 'swanning' about in white tie and tails, - a welcome change from battle dress and army life. Of course I went to see the show and told them how splendid they looked in their evening dress and got their autographs for the programme.

It would be interesting to know if any are still going strong, especially the overseas ones from New Zealand and South Africa.

One afternoon the lads asked me out for a walk, they had something funny to show me. Without hesitation in those days, unlike today, off we went and I was puzzled when we arrived at a cemetery.

I was led to where a wall had been damaged in an air raid revealing rows of skeletons on shelves. They all had long hair obviously preserved. It was a macabre sight and not a bit 'funny' to me;

Brr-rrr, it gives me the shivers just thinking of it!

'THE MERRY WIDOW'

Seeing the show in **Naples**, when they came to entertain the troops, was not the first time I had seen **The Merry Widow**.

At Christmas, 1942/43 I was dancing in '**Jack & Jill**' pantomime at **His** (now Her) **Majesty's Theatre** in the **Haymarket**, London,

(My contract for that show was very interesting! Written into my contract was a clause that if there was an air-raid and the show had to be abandoned I would not be paid!) Luckily although there were air-raids during shows we always carried on.

When 'Jack & Jill' finished after quite a long run,

'**The Merry Widow**'- choreographed by Robert Helpman, followed us into the theatre. We were all given 2 tickets each for their dress rehearsal. My mother came with me and we were enthralled by the lovely glamorous show.

Afterwards we hurried to the underground station in the blackout anxious to get home. The Underground Stations were a safe haven for many people for they acted as deep Air Raid Shelters and many families spent the night on the platforms. Sometimes things did go wrong and next day we sadly heard of a bad accident at Bethnal Green Station. The air-raid siren had sounded and people were rushing down to the safety of the underground; some fell in their rush and others tripped over them and a whole crowd ended on top of each other. There were several deaths and injuries.

It was a sad way to remember their show but many years later I appeared in two '**Merry Widow**' amateur productions.

Santa Maria

Arriving in **Santa Maria**, we were billeted in a most lovely large house - full of large rooms with high ceilings and walls, all painted with beautiful scenes.

We actually stayed-put here for two weeks.

No long journeys or packing and unpacking of costumes or personal things, just luxury.

There was a drawback of course.

With no lighting or gas even, it was a bit eerie after dark to move around just with small candles.

My journals show that I recorded washing my hair, going down with jug and candle for water (cold) and going upstairs again between rinses!

Why I didn't just rinse my hair downstairs as would appear logical I just can't imagine some sixty odd years later.

The Theatre was only about 30 minutes ride away, a real one with proper dressing rooms.

We could hear the fighting most of the time and the troops came straight from the front to our shows. At this theatre the first rows were not reserved for officers.

It was a full house as were every afternoon and evening performance.

On one occasion in the middle of a night back in our lovely house I was suddenly awoken by an **almighty BANG!**

We feared the worst and I looked up bleary-eyed in panic at the painted ceiling, waiting for it to come crashing down on me. Although relieved when it didn't we were still confused to know what was happening.

Being so near the 'front' we feared the army was retreating and we hadn't been warned!

Then came a flash of lightning and an even greater thunder clap. *Phew! What a relief!*

Muddy Meeting

One of our dancers, **Betty**, knew her fiancée **Richard** was in **Italy** and she hoped she would meet him as we travelled about entertaining the troops.

In a war zone they had not been able to exchange addresses. She knew he rode a motor cycle as a dispatch rider.

As we travelled about in trucks, every time we saw a soldier on a motor bike she called out to him.

It gave the motor cyclist a surprise of course, but a disappointment to Betty as it never turned out to be her fellow.

Incredible as it may seem one day it really was him!

The dispatch rider stopped, we hammered on the side of the truck to get our driver to stop, and like all good Hollywood movies of that era Betty got down and they ran towards each other, hugged and kissed in ecstasy.

However there had been very heavy rain, the ground was very muddy as was Dick after riding his motor bike so when they parted both appeared covered in mud; but did they mind?

What do you think!

Seeing Spots

Quite often arriving back in the small hours at our hostel, after a truck journey from a camp where we had given a show, we often slept through breakfast.

This was a trifle difficult as all the shops were 'out of bounds' due to a risk of typhoid - so we couldn't buy biscuits or buns.

Lunch was mainly in the hostel before we went to the show venue in the back of a 3 ton truck. We were generally given supper in the officer's mess after a show but this could vary from very little to a feast.

We never gave a thought to this life style and missing out on vitamins etc., until some of us developed some nasty looking spots, mainly on our tummies.

We were shocked when the M.O. (Medical Officer) told us it was 'Scabies'.

We had the indignity of baring our tummies for them to be painted with some antiseptic and waiting for it to dry. This was repeated several times daily.

With no adjustment to our diet or vitamin supplement given the spots cleared up, more importantly they never came back.

Meeting a CAD!

I heard my show company was somewhere near **Bari**. The soldier boys were going back there now their stint in **"The Merry Widow"** was over - so I hitched a ride in their coach. We were all rather fed up but managed to sing to bolster our spirits on the long journey. It took 11 hours with a break for lunch. I was sad saying goodbye to the lads. I wondered how their other mates would treat them having it so 'cushy' for the last couple of weeks, and I bet they'd be in for a lot of leg-pulling.

I made my way to the E.N.S.A. office which I knew was run by a friend of my elder brother **Jimmy**. He had written me a very nice letter when I was in hospital saying he hoped to meet me.

Luckily **John**, (not his actual name) was still there although it was 7.30 p.m. He gave me a warm welcome when I introduced myself. I was hoping the E.N.S.A. hostel would find me a bed and left it to him to arrange. When John had finished the last of his jobs I was grateful when he offered to take me to his flat and cook us dinner. I knew it was too late to get any food at the hostel and I was famished not having eaten for several hours.

John fussed about - taking ages to get the meal, I was afraid he would hear my tummy rumbling. It was a nice meal when it finally came and I tucked in hungrily.

I began to feel uneasy! There was no mention of taking me to the hostel. I felt it must be getting late. I had no watch and there wasn't a clock in the room.

Suddenly the penny dropped, the one man I had not been on my guard with, he being a friend of my brother, had designs on me. I watched my moment, ran into the only bedroom, luckily there was a key in the lock so locked the door and stayed there 'till morning. The next morning I found my own way to the hostel and booked myself in.

The search for my **"Fancy Meeting You"** company failed, sorry to say, they were apparently some 50 miles away I was told.

Before I had time to wonder how I was going to get back to **Naples** a message came from the E.N.S.A. office there that *I was to be sent home on a ship leaving in 3 days time.* I would be flown back to Naples meanwhile.

My first flight. I was very excited. The only girl on board I was allowed into the crew's cabin and had a lovely view, especially when we flew over Vesuvius.

Very thrilling!

H.M.T. Strathnaver

The homeward journey from **Italy** aboard H.M.T. Strathnaver saw 10 of us in a cabin which should only have held 2 people - only this time I had not met any of them before.

- **Kathleen Harrison** was one;
-also **Dianna Gould**, (who later married Yehudi Menuhin).

I had very mixed feelings about leaving **Italy**!

I had made so many friends but of course it was very exciting to be going home, nearly six months after I left.

The "**Merry Widow**" company were also on board and once we were under way they began to give concerts to entertain the troops. I was still not able to dance and there was not anything I could do to join in this.

There were a group of troops trying to hold a sing-song on deck one evening and of course they were stopped as noise carries over water.

They were not allowed up on deck after 8 o'clock in the evening and it was very hot and stuffy down on the mess-deck. So I went down and we had a sing-song there.

Most had been away almost 5 years and were very excited naturally to be going home.

I continued to go down and sing with the troops after dinner every evening until I was sent for by the Commanding Officer. He said he simply could not allow a single girl to go down among all those troops!

Rather funny I thought, I don't know what aboard ship they were likely to do. So I didn't go the next night and the following day people kept coming up to me and saying they thought it was a disgrace that I had been stopped, which surprised me as I hadn't realised anybody else knew I was doing it .

Once again I was sent for by the C.O. and he said he would let me go if I would take an escort with me. Well I was friendly with a Petty Officer called **David** and he very sportingly came and sat just inside the door while I was there singing with the troops.

During the day I was sewing some lovely white material which I had bought in Italy, without clothing coupons may I add, and I was making a dress to wear. I was getting on quite well with it until I came to look for the second sleeve which I couldn't find. So I told the cabin steward who said he had thrown a piece of white material out of the port-hole the other day! Oh dear!

I managed to sew 3 oddments of material together, cut a new sleeve out from it and finished the dress, which I proudly wore when I went down to dinner.

On the last night on board I said to the troops I had been singing with, "*If you do ever see me and recognize me I do hope you will come up and speak as I will never remember all your faces* ".

Monday, May 29th, 1944.

First we saw the **Scottish Coast**, then **England** and we finally docked in **Liverpool**. We were all very excited and looked forward to landing the following day.

Tuesday, 30th May

We were told it would be Friday before we would be allowed off the ship. The weather was bad and we were all miserable with the time passing very slowly.

Thursday, 1st June

The ship moved nearer the shore and we could see people going in and out of a public house, very tantalizing.

Friday, June 2nd

We at last set foot on dry land!

We quickly got through Customs but 'missed' the 2.00 p.m. train to London, and the next one wasn't until 5.20 p.m. Another girl and I took a tram into the town and went to the 'pictures' to pass the time. Sadly I don't record what film we saw.

It was 10.30 p.m. by the time I reached **home** in West Hampstead, surprising my parents and brother Roy.

Looking back now I think how strange it was, there we were, aboard ship, lounging on deck - well sitting on the deck as there weren't any loungers aboard a troopship, - with our lifejackets, which had to be carried everywhere we went, we used for pillows and we just lazed in the sun as if all was well with the world.

Some time later I was walking along the **Strand** in **London**, when somebody hailed me from the other side of the road. He came over and true enough it was one of the soldiers I had been singing with on the ship. He said

"I thought it was you, I recognized the dress ".

I must admit it wasn't the white dress but a Stewart tartan one I sometimes wore.

'From the Dancer's Pool' A New SISTER ACT

Instead of the usual 'resting' period between shows, when we were with E.N.S.A. we had a 'Dancers Pool'.

We spent every weekday morning in the rehearsal room at the **'Theatre Royal', Drury Lane**, exercising and learning practice routines. For this we received 'half pay'.

I can't recall now how long I had been in the 'Pool' when one morning the choreographer asked if anyone was interested in being part of a 'SisterAct', and if so to step forward.

Keen to be working again I went forward and so did another girl whose name I found out afterwards was **Audrey Pritchard** from Herefordshire who later moved to Findon in Sussex.

We were given some steps to do together, passed the test and we became a 'Sister Act'.

Meeting for the first time on that day Audrey and I became very good friends and shared many adventures.

We had three dances to do,

- one a tap-dance with a snappy fast bit in the middle and for this we were kitted out with pale green blouses with dark green shorts; this was done to a popular song of the day '*It had to be You*'.

- the second dance was a 'pointe' ballet, part classical and part modern. For this we wore midnight blue ballet length dresses, more like evening dresses than ballet, and danced to the George Gershwin classic, '*Night and Day*'.

- the third dance was Hungarian, done to a *Slavonic rhapsody*. This costume was the usual native one consisting of frilly white panties and petticoat topped with brightly coloured dresses and floral headdresses with gaily coloured ribbons flowing from each side and red boots completing the outfit.

Audrey and I were well pleased with our costumes and the dances we had to do.

To make sure our arm movements exactly matched, the 'hallmark' of a good sister act; we spent hours practising in front of a mirror.

We became 'established' as a really good 'Sister Act' and were placed for short periods in various companies touring Britain.

'Bhandaries Indian Players'.

One group we were 'placed' with were the 'Bhandaries Indian Players'. We found ourselves as the only English members of the company working to purely Indian audiences including the famous Ghurkhas.

They quite liked our tap-dance - not having seen this type of dancing before, and were mystified where the beats came from.

The ballet was not so popular, Indian music being more to their taste than 'Night and Day'. Our hand movements were meaningless as opposed to the stories their dancers told with their beautiful hands and eyes. We didn't have these stories interpreted for us, more's the pity.

Thankfully the Hungarian dance was a great success; they liked the colourful costumes and the bright and exciting twists and turns.

After the show we had a meal in the Officers Mess as we usually did but this was different, it was entirely Indian food we ate with our fingers.

Large bowls of curry were placed in the centre of the tables and lots of little dishes with extra things in between. We helped ourselves from them picking the food up with chapattis. I had never eaten curry before but to my relief I liked it very much.

Dessert was like a soggy suet pudding but the sog was something very sweet and I loved it and had a second helping. I also liked their very sweet tea.

The meal over Audrey and I were invited to go and see the kitchen and meet the cooks, a compliment for what I suspect was their first non-Indian guests. We hoped we said all the right things as neither of us had done any real cooking. They seemed to be very pleased with us anyway.

Our two musicians were young but they were quite at home with both kinds of music playing for our dances and their own dancers and singers.

When we arrived for the show after a ride in a coach that did not have any kind of heating our feet were frozen and they massaged them back to life for us to dance.

We often got very cold on some of the long journeys to various camps and hungry too.

We didn't handle our ration books and in those days there was very little we could buy without them.

One day Audrey and I discovered Radio Malt, which was not rationed. We bought a loaf of bread and visited Woolworth's to buy a knife, managing to cut slices and spread it with Radio Malt which had a lovely toffeeish taste and was quite thick.

The Indians watched us doing this on the coach, with some amusement. Audrey and I had told them of feeling thin when we got very cold so this life-saver was dubbed 'Thickening Mixture'.

Europe - The Lucky Six

As the name suggests there were six of us appearing in this show that was put together to entertain the troops -

- - **Don Gray** ; Manager/Entertainer
- - **George Andee** - Comedian,
- - **Pat Doherty** - Soubrette.
- - **Sadie Silverman** – Pianist/Singer
- - **Audrey Pritchard** - Dancer.
- - **Barbara Stewart** (me) – Dancer

By now E.N.S.A. had its own uniform -

and kit including -

A tin plate; eating irons; a mug

A tin hat (steel helmet if you prefer)

After a few days on 'stand by' the call came and we reported at the **Theatre Royal, Drury Lane** – E.N.S.A. headquarters

We left there in a coach at about 10 pm

My mother came to see me off and it was only later that: I realised we were waving the Geneva Convention cards we had just been given.

These stated that in the event of our being taken prisoner we have officer's status and should be treated as such! Poor Mummy.

We were driven to **Tilbury Dock** where we boarded 'The Duke of York', *a* small boat that was not a ship.

After a while a 'crazy' meal was served.

We had our tin plates and were given a chunk of corned beef, a chunk of bread plus 3 boiled sweets.

There were no seats but I managed to perch on a small table.

The cabins were tiny.

We were instructed not to undress, keep our Mae West lifejackets on, and not to close the door as it might 'jam' if we were torpedoed!

Surprisingly I did get some sleep as we had a peaceful journey.

There was another crazy meal in the morning but being hungry we didn't care as long as we got something.

Having left Tilbury at 4.00 am we arrived at **Ostend, Belgium** at 12 noon.

So began my –

second tour of duty on active service!

The enemy near by!
WALCHEREN ISLANDS
The Netherlands

One day whilst staying in a hostel in **Goes** (pronounced 'Hoose') in Holland we had to climb up into the back of a 3 ton truck, rather than our usual more sedate 15 cwt with seats. After a bumpy journey we found we had to climb down to a launch. This was difficult as we were dressed in battledress and greatcoats that we were wearing against the bitter cold. Clambering in we found we were destined for one of the **Walcheren Islands,**

I never did find out which one.

Their theatre was very small and all the floor boards were loose.

It was awful for **Audrey Pritchard** and I performing our dances.

One floor board went down one end and up the other as it was trodden on.   Pointe work was extremely exacting and risky.

As usual though, the audience of troops was very enthusiastic, making it all worthwhile.

The Enemy was just 3 miles away!

Enjoying our supper in the Officer's Mess after the show, we were told they were preparing to capture the next island. It was still in German hands only 3 or 4 miles away.

Of course that meant the Germans could be planning to capture our island whilst we were on it, scary!!!

Aboard the launch back we shivered not only from the cold but also knowing the enemy was so near.

After a tiring show we still had to climb back up from the launch and up into the back of the truck journeying back to **Goes** before our day was over.

Whilst in the Officer's Mess a **Lieutenant Hughes** noticed we were using toilet paper from our bags as handkerchiefs, Audrey especially as she was suffering a cold and runny nose. We explained there was no heating, no hot water and only cold water at certain times during the day in the hostel we were in so we couldn't do any worthwhile washing. He promised to send us some handkerchiefs and the very next day they arrived.

Wartime comradeship at its very best!

oh! my aching back!

Whilst touring in **Belgium**, **Holland**, and **Germany** with **E.N.S.A.** (Entertainments National Service Association), the long rough journeys in the back of trucks took their toll.

For some time I had been suffering severe pain in my back.

Medical Officers' advice ranged from

"Nothing wrong with you, get some exercise" and

"the base of your spine is damaged you must give up dancing and not travel in trucks."

When I was offered an injection that would deaden the pain for several weeks, I agreed, but it was pointed out that without the pain I could still be doing more damage to my back.

I was desperate to finish the tour of duty and there was still months to go.

After 24 hours of really severe pain the injection worked. The freedom from pain was wonderful and I put it out of my mind that it would only be for a short time.

The twinges began again after only three weeks and by four weeks the pain was back.

I knew I shouldn't be doing the rough journeys but I was not ready to give up and go home again.

I was told to travel lying on my tummy to protect my back so I lay on our costume baskets, which was not very comfortable and made me feel sick.

I was able to perform my dances although sharp observers might have realised that the smile concealed gritted teeth.

The pain was getting worse and the provision of a vehicle with enough room for me to lie down in was getting difficult.

Sister from Shimmy

My elder brother **Jimmy** was with the Green Howards Regiment when he was 'called up' at the end of 1939. Serving in France he was a lucky survivor at the Dunkirk rescue when all the little boats and ships so gallantly went over the English Channel to evacuate our forces.

He then went to the Middle East for a two and a half year stint during which he joined the TT Army Concert Party as pianist and general entertainer.

Stringer Davis, the actor, was their Commanding Officer, and married that great comedy actress **Margaret Rutherford.**

In 1944 Jimmy was in Holland, near Nijmegen; (yes he did get around - he served in South Africa, Egypt, Palestine, Cyprus, Jordan, Lebanon, Syria, Iraq, Libya, Tunisia, Italy, Sicily, France, Belgium, Holland and Norway). When in Holland he had made friends with **Mardo** - a little Dutch girl - and then her family, **Mr** and **Mrs Bresters** and brother **Jan.**

He learned they were forced to leave their home in Oosterbach and were trying to reach a relative in Eindhoven. Waiting until it was dark, Jimmy hid the family in the back of the 3 ton truck he drove for the Concert Party, - safely getting them to Eindhoven - then getting himself back to camp.

When I was leaving for my second tour overseas to Belgium, Holland and Germany (known as **BLA,** British Land Armies), Jimmy, now back in England, gave me the Bresters family address and map to find their house, in the hope I may call on them.

Touring with **'The Lucky Six'** show we seldom knew where we were going in advance so I couldn't plan a visit to my brother's friends but I knew I was near to them when we reached **Hellmond.**

Audrey, my dancing partner friend in the show, and I set off and hitched a ride in a truck to Eindhoven. We had a bit of trouble finding the house as I had left Jimmy's map behind! Mrs Bresters recognized me at once, *"You are sister from Shimmy"* she said.

Mardo was there but Mr Bresters and Jan were out.

Jimmy had suggested taking them some tins of cocoa and they seemed to be a welcome gift.

Our hopes of calling on the Bresters again were dashed when we moved on to Goes, pronounced 'Hoose', and that is another story.

E.N.S.A. CONVOY

Travelling from **Enscede** in **Holland** to **Celle** and **Lubeck** in **Germany** we had a German coach for the journey, more comfortable than the back of an open ended truck, our usual transport. Because of my painful back, I had to lie across the back seat.

Our convoy was one of 7 vehicles but who were in the other trucks we never found out. A normal 2 hour journey to **Osnabruck** took 4 hours; trucks kept breaking down in turn.

Eventually we left 4 trucks behind, and did not reach **Celle** until 3.00 am. the following day. We had taken lemonade bottles filled with water to drink and keep us cool but they were taken from us when the radiator nearly boiled over.

We parted from the rest of the convoy when we came to a humped back bridge which our low slung coach couldn't go over; we had to go a long way round. It was a nightmare journey with few comfort stops and no food. Arriving at the **E.N.S.A.** hostel in **Celle** at 3.00 am everyone was in bed asleep.

It took some hammering on the door to awake the Sergeant in charge. He sleepily told us we shouldn't be at his hostel but one a further hour's drive away. However he found some camp beds for us. **Audrey Pritchard,** my dancing partner, and I finally got to bed, in the kitchen, at nearly 5.00am.

Some 6 hours on, about 11.00 am, we were on our way again - arriving in **Lubeck** a further 7 hours later.

The 14 hours journey to **Celle** and then 7 hours to **Lubeck** finally finished my back.

When the **M.O.** said if I continued travelling in trucks and dancing I would do serious and permanent damage to my back - I gave up the fight and agreed to be sent home.

I was flown to **Brussels** in a troop-carrying **Dakota**

There were just metal benches along the sides of the plane but once we were air-born I was allowed to sit in the co-pilots seat.

He actually let me fly the plane, what a thrill!

CLAN STEWART - War Service

Father, **JAMES STEWART**

Joined the 2nd Battalion Scots Guards, before the start of World War 1. Dad served throughout the war mainly in the trenches in France earning the **Military Medal** for conspicuous bravery in the field. He was also awarded Oak Leaves and was Mentioned in Despatches.

> **Seventh Division.**
>
> No. *8640,*
>
> Name. *Pte J. Stewart.*
>
> Regt. *2/ Scots Guards.*
>
> Your C.O. and Brigade Commander have informed me that you have distinguished your-self by conspicuous bravery in the field on *16th Aug 1915.* I have read their reports and have forwarded them to higher authority for recognition.
>
> Promotion and decorations cannot be given in every case, but I should like you to know that your gallant action is recognised and how greatly it is appreciated.
>
> Major-General,
> Commanding 7th Division.
>
> Date. *27th Aug 1915.*

In World War II Dad, now a Metropolitan Police Constable, patrolled the streets of Kilburn and West Hampstead, in London, often during air-raids with only the added protection of a steel helmet.

Mother, **MAY STEWART** (Clements) had possibly the most difficult job of all. Often on her own in air-raids with dad out on duty and her three children away from home; brother Jimmy in the Army early in the war, mostly on active service- She kept up a stream of cheerful letters to us. Struggling with food rationing and always finding an extra dinner when I sometimes went home for a Sunday while touring

Barbara!

The Siblings! Between us, brothers Roy and Jimmy and I visited 22 *different* countries.

- 16 of these were notched up by Jimmy, Roy was in 6 countries and I was in 5,'

Daughter, **BARBARA STEWART**, dancing with E.N.S.A. took me to North Africa, Algiers, Italy, Belgium, Holland and Germany.

Son, **ROY STEWART**, when he was 18 in 1944 applied to join the R.A.F. (having been a member of the ATC, Air Training Cadets), volunteering to join as air crew.

Roy had a medical, written exams, was enrolled as A.C.2, given a service number and put on 'deferred service'. The Air Force did this with air crew being uncertain of the number of new recruits needed (How many planes lost in battle?) - They could be called upon in a hurry. Roy had a letter of welcome from Sir Archibald Sinclair. Not long afterwards came another letter explaining the War circumstances had changed and he was no longer required by the R.A.F. He was called up by the Army in the Royal Army Service Corps.

Before he was demobbed in 1947 he had been to Egypt, Iraq, Kuwait, Hong-Kong, Singapore and Keure, Japan. The latter was not far from Hiroshima, and at times Roy took visiting officers to see what the Atom Bomb had done!

Son, **JAMES** (Jimmy) **STEWART**, was 20 in 1939, - the conscription age then. Called up in December 1939 he wasn't demobbed until March 1946.

Jimmy served in - South Africa, Egypt, Palestine, Cyprus, Jordan, Lebanon, Syria, Iraq, Libya, Tunisia, Italy, Sicily, France, Belgium, Holland and Norway.

His first post was with the York and Lancaster Regiment. After only two days the R.S.M. (Regimental Sergeant Major) asked if anyone played the piano. Jimmy stepped forward.

He was needed to accompany a girl singer at the Sergeants Dance. Armed with the address he called on the young lady for a rehearsal and, as he put it, had a built-in girl friend while training in Plymouth for two months.

After training Jimmy joined the Green Howards Regiment. Then his overseas service began, starting in France. A friend wrote and told me how Jimmy played his piano accordion in the open air every night as troops appeared from all directions to listen; the friend likened him to the Pied Piper of Hamlin. The accordion was lost when Jimmy was rescued from Dunkirk.

A few days after arriving in Egypt, calling at Durban, South Africa for a spell on the way as ships couldn't use the Suez Canal, another accordion was found for Jimmy. His open air evening recitals started again

When the Army Padre held a church service Jimmy played the hymns, after which the accordion was put in the Padre's truck

Twice they were surrounded by the enemy - Field Marshall Rommel's Afrika Corps - and had to break out. The Padre was captured during the second 'break out' and Jimmy lost another instrument.

Life changed for Jimmy once more when he became a member of an Army Concert Party,

It was run by **Lieutenant Stringer Davis**, an actor who later married the actress Margaret Rutherford, and appeared in several of her "Miss Marples" films.

Concert Party members did get home for some leave, borne out by 5 of them becoming fathers for the first time - 4 boys and Jimmy's daughter Sandra.

Stringer Davis sent each of the mothers £5, almost a month's pay for a soldier.

In May1945, after performing at 52 venues on the Continent the concert Party was back in the U.K. They were to perform at Strensall Army Depot, where Roy was stationed. Jimmy telephoned to see if I could go up and see his show.

I was just back from Germany. Roy and I enjoyed the show and although well acquainted with his piano playing we had never seen Jimmy in a show. We were surprised to see that he now played the double bass, sang and did comedy sketches.

Very impressive!

This was the first time we had all been together since 1939. It was a few more years before our next re-union. Jimmy and Roy went off on their travels abroad with the army.

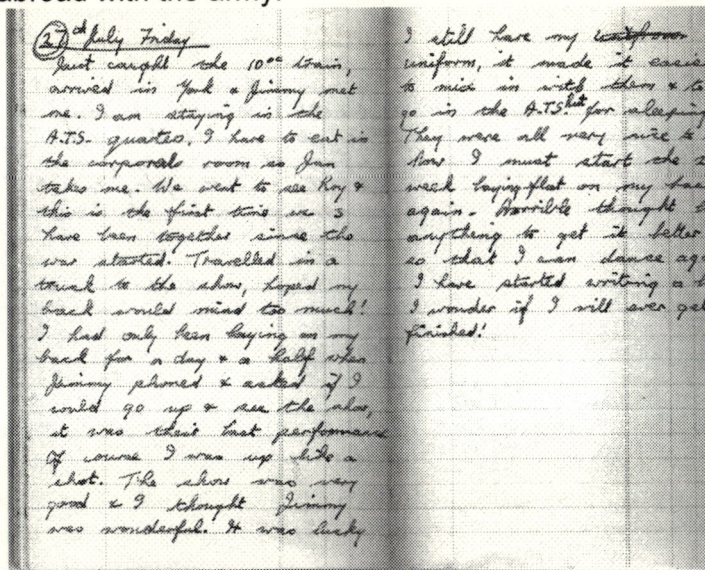

My diary entry at that time outlines our visit to Jimmy's show. The last 3 lines are also interesting! I wondered if I would ever finish the book I had started to write and now –here 62 years later – I have!

I married in 1946 and to my great sadness neither of my brothers were able to be present at my wedding.

Missing the comforts of Home

Moving from Belgium, through Holland and into Germany we spent varying times in each place ranging from one, two or three nights to sometimes when we were lucky - seven.

We stayed in hostels staffed by local people but run by an army sergeant. Although they had been starved and suffering from being occupied by German forces they did their best to look after us.

We met some Dutch people in the street and they said *"Germans"* pointing to their eyes and mimed 'crying'! Then said "English" and put a finger each side of their mouths indicating a broad smile. They couldn't speak English and we couldn't speak Dutch.

We did have a particularly nasty time in a place named **Hoose, Holland**. There was no heating although it was bitterly cold, no hot water and the cold water only turned on for two short periods a day. It was a rush for all of us to fit in a wash. We mostly missed the evening water turn on, which meant going to bed unwashed; not nice after doing a show.

We wore gloves and scarves and battle-dress and stayed in bed most of the day to keep warm. No doubt the kitchen also suffered from the water shortage, the food was dreadful and before long we all suffered from dysentery. Tablets prescribed by the doctor eased the symptoms but made us all feel very sick. It was no fun giving a show, especially Audrey and I doing dances.

Returning to the hostel one night from a show, Audrey and I were allowed to sit with the driver because we were so ill. This proved very lucky as part of our route was along a narrow road that had water one side and the white tapes that indicated 'MINES' on the other.

In the pitch dark it took our three pairs of eyes to keep us on the road, - a nightmare journey!

We were very happy when it came time to move on to Arnhem.

Buckets of Embarrassment!

With few exceptions we did our show in a different place or camp each time, never knowing what to expect at the end of our truck journey. At one camp in Germany we found a quite reasonable stage had been built, a space on either side of it was curtained off from the audience, one side a dressing room for the ladies and the other side for the men.

As we were unpacking our costumes, arranging them on some chairs thoughtfully supplied by our hosts, we suddenly realised we had no access to a toilet. The only way out was into the 'auditorium', not an option in the middle of a show.

Always ready to oblige the 'Army' produced a galvanized bucket, a soldier carrying it shoulder high through the assembled noisy audience, like the cup at the Cup Final at Wembley, they knowing full well what it was for. This of course not only produced howls of raucous comments but also another dilemma.

Galvanized buckets are noisy and we were only a curtain away from the troops!

We timed its use to perfection, however, during the thunderous applause given to the other acts, thus covering any embarrassment we may have felt.

The Bresters

While staying in **Arnhem** during another part of this tour an Officer called **Doc**, (I'm not sure if he was an actual Doctor) took me back to **Oosterbach** on the back of his motorbike.

I had promised the **Bresters** I would try to find their house. We met a solitary man walking in the deserted village and he <u>was</u> the Doctor, and knew which house was the Bresters. It was badly damaged and had a big concrete shelter built in the basement by Germans. I found a photograph album in the debris and took a picture out of it to show I had found the right house.

Now I think, why didn't I take all their precious photographs? All the front gardens there had trenches in them. Doc and I went down into one, it was horrible. I got a 'telling off' when I returned to our hostel for going on a motorbike.

Arnhem Zoo

A truly sorry sight!

We arrived here to see the entrance damaged and the noise of gunfire and fighting had left the animals jumpy' and nervy. They also seemed hungry; we wished we had some food for them.

The parrots were still very perky though. Some soldiers told us they swore like troopers in English, unless ladies were present. A tall story we thought.

Although Audrey and I were in uniform the birds knew we were ladies and didn't swear

When we moved away they had the men laughing at their strong language so we tried gradually moving nearer again but the cheeky birds were not fooled, they clammed up!

Audrey and Barbara learn to shoot

May, 1945 Lingen, Germany

Sadie Silverman our pianist hurt her wrist, so we "**The Lucky Six**" were unable to give our show. I went with **Don Gray**, our manager, to the camp where we were to have performed that evening to explain, without our pianist we could not give a show.

I was invited to stay and go shooting with them. To my surprise Don agreed and left me there. My hosts found the smallest pair of gumboots and **Bill, Tommy** and **Teddy** took me to a tank trap where a spade was set up for a target.

I had never held a pistol before but I soon got the hang of it, surprising us all by hitting the spade a number of times, (get me!). Afterwards I had the distinction of being the first girl to join them for tea.

A party had been laid on for us for after the show and it seemed a pity to waste it so we went back for the rest of the company and all had a lovely time.

The following day, Sunday, was a day off. When Bill, Tommy and Teddy came to take Audrey and I back to their camp for some more shooting, we told Don we were going for a walk. Their truck was round the corner out of sight ready to drive us away.

We went to the tank trap again and this time we learned how to fire rifles, properly, lying on our fronts propped up on our elbows, butt against our right shoulder and we were warned about the kickback so knew what to expect. Unbelievably both Audrey and I hit the target nearly every time, (get us!). Then we changed to pistols again and thoroughly enjoyed ourselves.

My father was a crack shot, a Lewis machine gun Instructor during World War 1, when he was awarded the Military Medal in one battle. Later he won a cup and several medals for shooting with the Police team when he was a London 'Bobby'.

Naturally left handed, Dad had been 'made' to use his right hand at school. There were still some things he did with his left hand and I thought shooting might be one of them so I fired some shots with my left hand. I did well and was really pleased. Like father like daughter I suppose.

After tea we were shown how to clean our guns, before being taken back to our billet.

Our skill at shooting surprised everybody including ourselves!

My VE-DAY
(VICTORY IN EUROPE 1945)

On May 7th, 1945, we performed in a small theatre near Arnhem.

There were six of us in the company, Audrey and I being the two dancers.

Just as we were to go on the stage that night to perform a Hungarian dance an Army Officer asked us to wait while he made an announcement.

I can't remember all he said but it ended with -

"The War in Europe is over".

A packed audience of service men erupted in cheers, clapping and whistling, - the noise was deafening.

When at last it began to subside, the cry began, **"Bring on the Dancing Girls!"**

Right on cue Audrey and I ran on stage and began our most colourful and energetic Hungarian dance with flying frilly petticoats and beribboned headdresses.

The cheers and shouting continued all through the dance carrying us along on the warmth and excitement.

When the show was over we went in the Sergeants mess for some refreshments.

It was hardly a party and we weren't sure what to do to mark the special occasion but somehow we found ourselves singing,

"There'll always be an England",

"Land of Hope and Glory" and

"God Save the King".

Although the general announcement was not made until the next day, May 8th, when the anniversary is remembered,

VE Day for me was May 7th 1945!

Fraternisation,
June 1945 Papenburg

Less than three weeks after we arrived in Germany and only four since VE Day, my dance partner Audrey and I were billeted in a private house for a night.

The people didn't seem to mind but we felt very uncomfortable, especially as the Non-Fraternization Order issued by letter from **Field Marshal Montgomery** was still in operation.

Shortly after this another letter was issued relaxing the rule in respect of children; -

'British troops could now talk to and play with children'.

When we left our hostel the following morning there were several children greeting us, all smiling and shouting *'Hello'.*

How did they know the rule had been relaxed?

Canadian Mac

Audrey Pritchard and I were dancing together as a 'Sister Act' in "**The Lucky Six**" show with **E.N.S.A.** in early 1945 in **Arnhem**, Holland.

We met **Mac**, a Canadian Army Officer, when we did our show at his unit. He came to see the show whenever he could after that and we all liked seeing his smiling face in the audience.

Although we were young we found life hard, on the move all the time, the rough truck journeys, all kinds of places to live in and to perform in and for me there was no relief from my aching back.

Sitting in Mac's jeep one day, Audrey and I chatted and told him our troubles with which he sympathised. He told us that coincidentally he had sisters-in-law named Audrey and Barbara and would never forget us.

We moved on and lost touch with **Mac** until he suddenly turned up at **Aurich**, Germany, having driven 200 miles to say 'good-bye', he was going home to Canada.

For a while he was going to be in London so I gave him my parents' telephone number and asked him to ring my mother and father with news of me.

Three weeks later I was unexpectedly sent home, after being told my back problems made truck journeys and dancing dangerous. Mac was still in London, he had telephoned my home and been invited over for tea, taking his cousin **Mary** with him.

Mac hoped we could be friends with Mary and her husband **Jack** and he was delighted to be able to introduce us before returning to Canada.

Back Home -
with a chronic aching back!

It was lovely to be home but now I really had to face up to my back problem.

- What if I had to give up dancing?
- How could I bear it?
- What on earth would I do instead?

My "Oh My Aching Back " story tells of the treatments I tried and my eventual return to **"The Lucky Six"** company after they came home and were touring in the U.K.

When November and my birthday came round the show had been disbanded and I was "resting".

A birthday party seemed a good idea, Mary and Jack, (Mac's cousins) were invited and they brought with them a tall, dark, good looking young man called **Desmond Lewis**.

By the end of the evening he and I 'had a date'.

The search for a cure.

Home again; I began to search for a cure for my back.

The first doctor said -

"You must lie on your back for three weeks!"

At the end of the three weeks I was so stiff I could hardly move.

A Harley Street specialist said –

"You must allow me to graft bone taken from somewhere else in your body to make your lower back rigid!" - not much help to a dancer.

I had manipulation under anaesthetic in hospital, but then heard of an osteopathic clinic that treated people at a much reduced fee if they couldn't afford the full rate. My mother came with me to the clinic just off Baker Street, in London, and at that time I had no idea what **Osteopathy** was.

A very good looking man with a most attractive speaking voice treated me. My problem was 'slipped disc', generally unheard of in those days.

I went regularly to the clinic for treatment and was often taken out to lunch afterwards.

The pain gradually eased and when my show company came home I was able to rejoin them giving shows around the United Kingdom.

Some years later there was an awful scandal concerning a politician with some call-girls. He was married to a beautiful film star; but also involved was my osteopath who I always found to be a perfect gentleman. When he was sent to prison I felt he had been made a scape-goat and I was shocked and very sad when I heard he had committed suicide.

His name was **Stephen Ward**.

Having it cushy!

Dancing with E.N.S.A. in Britain was very different from serving overseas.

We stayed in small hotels or country houses made into E.N.S.A. Hostels and run by an Army Sergeant with local staff. Hostels abroad were run similarly but the difference being in Britain houses had no war damage. Windows were intact; there was no shortage of electricity, heating or hot water. Baths and washing hair were readily available, rare luxuries overseas.

On one occasion **Audrey Pritchard**, (my Sister Act dancing partner), and I stayed with a family in a private house. There was mother and two teenage daughters, father was in the army.

The elder girl **Kay,** had her hair in a bubble cut, trimmed to 2 inches all over her head making a 'cap' of curls. **Audrey** also had her hair in this style.

The sisters spent all the time we stayed there trying to persuade me to have my shoulder length hair cut into the bubble cut style. Kay was persistent and offered to cut my hair herself - I was constantly afraid then, she might creep in one night while I was asleep and cut a chunk of my hair off forcing me to have the rest cut short.

I was very relieved to leave there with a full head of hair.

Journeys were a lot more comfortable in the U.K. – in coaches over good roads, with comfortable seats, no having to squat on the floor. True the coaches had no heating but at least they were not open to the elements one end. Also dressing rooms were more comfortable and the stages good.

We journeyed, sometimes quite a long way, to different camps each day to give our shows. We never really knew just where they were, sign posts being removed for war time security, and our drive back was in the blackout. As I haven't recorded names of camps it could not have seemed important at the time.

We did work a wide area around Kings Lynn in Norfolk and also the Colchester area, which of course has been a garrison town for many years.

Our costumes and make-up had to be packed after each show but we stayed longer in each place saving us from constantly having to pack our personal things as we did overseas.

We enjoyed a stay in a holiday-camp style complex on one occasion near Chelmsford. A good theatre being part of the set-up meant our costumes had the luxury of hanging in the dressing room instead of spending every night in a skip. The same with our personal clothes. Another bonus was an escape from the daily journeys to camps.

This lasted from two to three weeks. Audiences were just as enthusiastic; we always had 'full houses'. I felt lucky dancing became my war-work and I know we did a good job cheering up the troops.

Most of the above activity was between returning from **Italy** and going overseas again to **Belgium, Holland** and **Germany**.

After 'The Lucky Six' company completed their tour abroad I rejoined them in this country for their short tour before the company was disbanded.

The War being over I was free to leave EN.S.A.

E.N.S.A. brought down 'the curtain' in July 1946 and was succeeded by C.S.E., Combined Services Entertainment – **without Barbara Stewart.**

MEDALS GALORE 1994

Talking with cousin **Frank Piercy**, a member of the *Royal British Legion*, about our war days he said I must be entitled to medals for my overseas service with **E.N.S.A.** (Entertainments National Service Association) during World War II.

I thought no more about it until Frank persisted and gave me the War Office address and persuaded me to write.

I was surprised and thrilled at the age of 70 to receive 4 medals in time for the 50th anniversary of the D-Day landings.

They were –

- **'The Italy Star'**,
- **'France-Germany Star**,
- **'39/45 Star'** and
- **'The War Medal'**.

I had also done shows in Algiers, North Africa, but I was not there long enough to qualify for a medal.

More excitement came when I was asked to pose for photographs with my medals. Fitting into an old dancing costume and fish-net tights, I couldn't resist doing a few 'high kicks'.

Making the front page of our local newspaper" The Bognor Regis Observer ", followed by a feature with picture in "Yours" magazine gave me quite a fillip.

Thanks Frank!

Barbara - 1945 - 1980
Back to Civilian Life

The Boy Friend

After years of dancing in shows in London and all around the U.K and on E.N.S.A. tours in -
- North Africa,
- Italy,
- Belgium,
- Holland
- and Germany,

My future husband walks through the door of my parents' home where I was born, in West Hampstead, London.

After meeting at my 22nd birthday party I regularly went out with **Desmond**.

He lived in a Polygon Club in town (London).

His home and parents were in **Fishguard**, Pembrokeshire.

A qualified pharmaceutical chemist, Desmond worked for Glaxo Laboratories.

Having been away in shows so much of the time I had lost touch with most of my friends and Desmond knew few people in London. We sometimes visited Mary and Jack who had introduced us and Desmond's aunt and uncle but mostly we met in town. We walked in the parks and occasionally saw a show.

The time spent entertaining the troops with E.N.S.A. meant I had lost touch also with agents and was still "resting" in 1946.

Enjoying the comforts of home and being courted by Desmond I must confess that I wasn't trying very hard to find work.

To tide me over I started earning some money trimming lampshades at home. Mum joined me, both quick with our fingers we did quite well. We found carrying several bulky lampshades a half hour walk back to the works was awkward especially if it was windy. Then there was the return walk with the next set of lampshades to be trimmed.

I did a dancing audition for what I thought was a London Show. My joy at landing the job turned to concern as it turned out to be a tour!

Desmond had proposed marriage and we were newly engaged so I actually turned the job down!

Desmond spent some evenings with me at home planning our wedding, not on the scale of present day weddings, (I am 'wedding steward' with my United Reformed Church in Bognor Regis), but with my own forthcoming wedding. With food, clothes, dress material, curtains and bed linen all rationed it was very much make, do and mend.

I borrowed my long white dress, veil and headdress from my school friend **Doris**.

She and my cousin **Gwen** were my Matrons of Honour (not bridesmaids as they were both married).

I made their dresses and hats but where the coupons for the material came from I cannot remember!

Desmond's young cousin **Margaret** and my cousin **Pat** were bridesmaids.

I unpicked the pink net evening dress I took with me to Italy, (see '20 Men and a Girl'), and made the children bridesmaid's dresses from it.

Friends saved rations for the Cake and Wedding Breakfast, and the reception was held at home, quite usual in those days.

Goodbye dancing shoes -
Hello MARRIAGE

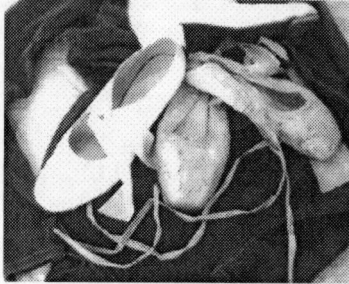

After a night in a London hotel and 2 in Cardiff we 'honeymooned' with Desmond's parents; before settling back home with mine, while - as I thought, looking for a home of our own.

So many people were flooding back to 'civvy' street that flats were almost impossible to find.

After we were married **Desmond** told me he had applied to be a representative for Glaxo Laboratories, which entailed travelling away and we would be living out of London - a shock to me.

Soon he was away all week and home at weekends. Although we were still living with my Mum and Dad, I felt left 'high and dry'. I had always been happy at home helping with the chores but with no Shows to look forward to or home of my own to care for I became miserable and depressed.

When Desmond was given a territory around Leicester he found us a home in two unfurnished rooms. I was happy to join him and really begin our married life. We had a front room on the ground floor and the one above it was our bedroom, also use of the landlady's kitchen.

In our living room was a small gas fire with a trivet in front of it and one gas ring in the hearth. This was how I did my first real cooking.

My drill was to bring the potatoes to the boil on the gas ring, then transfer them to the trivet near the gas fire. It was the same with the second vegetable - and then fry sausages on the gas ring. Somewhere in between the gravy fitted –

All on my hands and knees of course!

I can't recall how I coped with other meat except a Sunday joint went into the landlady's oven.

The butcher was kind to me at first but then the landlady complained I was getting better meat than her!

In theory I was supposed to share the kitchen.

I tried making a sponge cake with precious rationed ingredients but when the oven door was opened *"to see if it was done"*, causing my cake to flop, I gave up!

Our washing up was carried up to the bathroom where, with no heating upstairs, our face flannels usually had ice in them.

It was January 1947, the worst winter on record. Coal was still rationed and the gas pressure reduced which meant I could not have our fire full on.

Desmond was out all day and worked most of the evening so we never made any friends.

I was lonely, bored and hated being in Leicester.

I quickly lost a stone, (6¼ kilograms) in weight.

A highlight was finding the repertory theatre, I loved it. The play changed mid-week and I used to go to both matinees. I got to know the actors and liked picking them out in each different play, sometimes with different make-ups.

Imagine my joy when Desmond was recalled to Headquarters in time for our first wedding anniversary, 13th July, 1947.

I cheerfully packed up and arranged for our furniture to go into store until we found a new home. Until then my Mum and Dad housed us again, they were so lovely; always ready to help me, and brothers **Jimmy** and **Roy** when homes were difficult to find.

At that time there were so many leaving the services and war-work and they needed new homes.

In 1947 our next home was only a street away from Mum and Dad and came just in time as I had put our winter clothes in store with the furniture.

Now we had a ground floor flat a 'front room', bedroom, minute living room with a black 'kitchen range', a kitchen, outside loo but no bathroom. I at last had some scope for home making.

I cleaned the front step every morning and learnt how to clean the kitchen range flues.

It was very hard for Desmond, he came from a comfortable background, an only child he never wanted for much. Now he was, through no fault of his own, unable to provide me with a suitable home.

I was different, enjoyed the challenge of making a wooden crate into a bedside table, a pelmet out of some left over linoleum, painting and decorating it.

This only served to make Desmond feel inadequate. However the flat was not as comfortable or convenient as it sounds and we continued to look for somewhere better.

It eventually came in 1948, a top flat near Paddington Recreation Ground, in Maida Vale.

The house next door had been bombed and we were now the end house with cracks in the walls where the missing house should have joined on. It was pretty scary when the wind blew, we were four stories up. But we did have the use of a 'bathroom'.

Here in early pregnancy, I lost my first baby -

- then Desmond told me he was going to study 'law' in his spare time.

Tailoring

In the late 1940's I took a position as a receptionist for **Morrie Simmonds**, a 'bespoke' tailor in London's Edgware Road.

The room where clients chose their materials, styles and had their fittings was quite small.

I answered the phone, greeted clients, called Mr. Simmonds down from the work-room, ran messages and so on.

One customer I particularly remember was a petite lady who was always immaculately dressed.

One day it would be a black perfectly fitted fur coat over a smart black suit, patent leather hand-bag and high heeled court shoes, I was impressed with how they shone. Black kid gloves completed the ensemble. Another day our client would be in brown, all matching as before topped with a brown fur coat.

My own wardrobe was rather sparse and certainly no fur coat, and wartime clothing rationing not yet fully lifted.

After a while Mr. Simmonds realised I often had little to do so I was taught how to stitch 'Sprats Heads', triangular shapes worked by hand with matching buttonhole thread and mostly used at the top of pleats on tailored skirts. I like sewing and was pleased to be occupied.

On the floor above the workroom two men ran a Millinery business. When attending a Show they fussed over a large case of hats calling it 'The Collection', emphasizing COLLection.

Because I often took messages for them they offered to make me a hat.

What would I like I pondered?

I only owned one hat and seldom wore that so I asked for a soft pill-box, like a pink marshmallow.

The result was a great disappointment, poor material, wrong shade of pink, too stiff and without a lining.

I accepted the hat graciously naturally but I'm afraid I never wore it.

Hello Heartache -

I had lost touch with my show friends, partly because they were on the move, partly because it upset me hearing their show news now that I was "grounded" so to speak - and lastly because **Desmond** didn't like me talking about my theatrical past.

Round about now I joined the **Women's League of Health and Beauty.**

During this time, among other displays, I was in the International Display at the Albert Hall.

Six ladies from about 80 classes from all over the world. I can't remember all the countries, made up the display.

Each group had learned the sequences in their own class in their own country leading up to the event.

It was quite impressive when we assembled on the day and worked as one gigantic team.

When later all the lights were switched off we held small lights in the air and nearly 500 of us trotted round forming different patterns - the applause was deafening – very exciting.

1951 – Desmond and I finally found a really nice self-contained flat in Maida Vale.

Desmond still studying, we spent our evenings in separate rooms, him reading law and me knitting and watching TV, with an occasional visit to a cinema.

It was obvious I needed to find a job, and found one with -

DICKENS & JONES

Just as I had started learning to type with a view to getting an office job, my first husband's uncle **Vincent**, who was a Buyer in the material department of **Dickens & Jones,** the famous London department store in Regent Street, announced he had arranged a job for me in the shop selling dresses.

I should have jumped for joy at such tremendous news, - but I didn't. I wasn't keen as I knew it meant standing all day and with my recent 'slipped disc' problem in mind was very apprehensive. However uncle had committed me and I had to take the job.

I was introduced to **Miss Fenton** -the Buyer of the 'Young Londoner' dress section

Not surprisingly Miss Fenton gave me a frosty welcome. Uncle had 'pulled strings' and she and I had to get on with it.

It is very hard to imagine nowadays but there were –
- 9 sales staff,
- 2 apprentices and
- 2 supervisors just in the one department.

Each customer had the attention of an assistant in one of a row of fitting rooms, helping her into and out of each dress tried on.

I was not a good 'Sales', the term for sales assistant, often the last to 'open my book', make my first sale.

The following are some anecdotes which stand out in my mind –

THE PEARLS - A customer tried on a dress that was high in the front and low at the back, quite unusual in the 50's. She was very undecided.

I was wearing a long rope of pearls, a knot at the throat with the loop hanging down the front. A flash of inspiration saw me taking it off, putting it on my customer with the knot and the long loop at the back.

She turned this way and that looking in the mirrors and looked good, it really 'sold' the dress. I like to think I was first to arrange a necklace in this way.

THE LIP-STICK - At this time dresses were pulled on over the head and fastened at the side.

We used a scarf to cover ladies faces avoiding the garment being smeared with make-up.

One Saturday morning it was nearly closing time (all shops closed on Saturday afternoons); a couple, I surmised probably from Jamaica, started looking at evening dresses. She picked out a lovely full skirted long white net evening dress to try on.

'Madam' looked stunning and loved the dress. I got excited, it was rare to sell an evening dress and I could see in my mind's eye my commission 'rocketing'. Before I could produce my scarf a second time she pulled the dress over her head leaving a bright red patch of lip-stick on the front of the neck.

I panicked. To lose such a good 'sale' was unthinkable. I dived into the packing room and tried to clean the lip-stick off, it didn't budge. I rushed past my customers and upstairs to the work room where alterations are done and thankfully some staff were still there. They tried all their methods, the lip-stick lessened but was still showing. Back I rushed to the showroom,

I showed the stain to my customers who were wondering what all the 'Whitehall Farce' was about. To my amazement they still wanted the dress.

With trembling fingers I carefully packed it with tissue paper and placed it in a box. The Bill paid, the man held out his hand to shake mine saying "Thank you!" I felt he knew what I had been going through.

I was <u>sure</u> he did when I found a folded 10/- note (50p) pressed into my hand. A handsome tip when you consider my weekly wage was only the equivalent of £4.50 per week in today's money!

THE 'STAR' - A separate **Bridal Room** was part of the **'Young Londoner'** dress department. It was all white flounces and very pretty.

'Young Londoner' assistants took it in turns to have a week serving there. One bonus was being allowed to sit down in between serving brides-to-be.

Mothers usually came with the 'bride' and often expected a plain awkwardly built girl to be 'transformed' into a vision in a wedding dress, which we certainly did our level best to achieve, not always easy.

One such was a dainty small girl who looked lovely in floaty white dresses but insisted trying on an elegant gold brocade gown. It swamped her and did nothing for her pale colouring. We tried hard to steer her on to the more flattering materials and styles.

It was no use, she explained the groom and best man were army officers and the gold brocade would 'blend in' with their uniforms.

Useless to tell this dainty little girl the Bride doesn't 'Blend In' with anyone, she is *'The STAR'*.

OOPS! Fussy and dominating mothers accompanying brides-to-be were quite numerous unsurprisingly, and could be hard work.

One such fell to me to serve and working hard to please I managed to find a dress the girl loved and to which mother agreed.

I sent for **Miss Delves,** our Fitter and **Mrs. Fraser** the store's Fashion Advisor.

First the dress was fitted, the hem pinned to the correct length, then some tweaks to the bodice, all under mother's dominant and eagle eye.

Head dresses and veiling arrived from the millinery workroom. Mrs. Fraser fluttered and fussed about trying the bridal tiaras on our customer, then arranging yards of tulle veiling none of which seemed satisfactory but eventually choices were made and a fitting date agreed.

Some time later mother phoned and asked if the fitting could be put nearest to the date of the wedding as possible.

When the bride came for the fitting, mother was in a very different mood actually being profusely grateful for our help.

It turned out the dress needed an **extra 8"** (25 cms), let into the waist !!!

OUR GIRL - When a gorgeous 'Pink' wedding dress arrived in the Bridal Room it caused quite a stir. To that point we had only stocked white, silver or gold brocade.

This was a vision in pink satin, lace and net!

Our own young, engaged to be married **Miss Woods** fell in love with it. Permission was given for her to try the dress on after the store closed.

Usually eager to get off home we all stayed behind while our buyer Miss Fenton saw to Miss Woods as she slipped it on. It was almost a perfect fit just the length needing adjustment.

Even with store discount the price was a bit high but Miss Fenton agreed to reserve this **'Vision in Pink'**

Needless to say Miss Woods mother was won over when she saw her starry eyed daughter looking so beautiful.

So the Pink Wedding dress was sold before it went into stock and I don't remember there ever being another one like it.

More Heartache

Three years later I left Dickens & Jones shortly after I had become pregnant again.

Sadly at 3 months - I had a very nasty miscarriage which took me a long time to get over.

I was weak and very depressed.

It was hard for Desmond,

Desmond was now Assistant Registrar at the Pharmaceutical Society, only one behind the top job that he had set his heart on and for which he needed his Barrister at Law qualification.

When my health was finally restored I took a job with

John Lewis
Oxford Street

Applying for a job with the **John Lewis Partnership** was the first time I had had to fill in a job application form.

Posters were on the wall of the office I was shown to warning of instant dismissal if any untruths were put down. It was a dilemma for me because of my inexperience when starting work at Dickens & Jones in Regent Street I was on a very low salary. I was not prepared to work for so little money again. I enhanced the figure in the past-salary box.

I was engaged to work in the dress department. This time the Buyer was very kind and the other assistants were very friendly and helpful. Happily I settled in, then came a summons to appear before the manager.

Ushered into an impressive office I faced a stern looking man sitting at a large desk from which he never moved. Questioned about my fib on the application form, my heart sank and I explained about my low pay at Dickens & Jones, weakly continuing I was sure I heard from friends it was customary to stretch the truth when it came to other positions' pay levels.

I added that my previous experience was in the Theatre where accuracy in giving ones age, experience and ability was at a premium, especially if you wanted the best chance of getting a job, - obviously not the case in the world of retail stores.

He looked at me, then said he thought I was basically honest but had been led astray by my friends.

Back in the shop my Buyer said, *"Silly girl, I would have paid what you asked anyway"*.

A few days later a very short man walked through the store, I recognized the man who looked so important behind his grand desk. *'No wonder he didn't stand up'* I thought mischievously.

Fishguard.

My job at John Lewis was cut short when my mother-in-law had 3 coronary heart attacks in 2 days.

I went to nurse her at home in Fishguard. I was very fond of **Mrs. Lewis** and she was a good patient. Father-in-law was different!

His trait was to build up the fire with 'slack before going to work' which meant little heat coming out and I used to shiver all day and was sometimes reduced to crying with cold. In the evening 'Dad' poked the fire into lovely warm flames.

Why did I put up with it I have often asked myself? Mainly because I didn't want my invalid up-set.

With no telephone in the house I used to go into a neighbour twice a week to phone Desmond.

I had asked him to use our time apart to study hard and get his exams over, but when I spoke to him he said he wasn't getting any work done as he couldn't study when I wasn't there.

I used to go to bed and cry myself to sleep.

When his Mum was finally well enough - I took her home with me. There I continued to cherish her, she gradually blossomed, I encouraged her to change her hair style and wear pretty colours.

After 3 months I took Mum back to Fishguard, stayed a week then left for home. It was heart-breaking leaving her to a dull lonely life with a very selfish man.

Back home at Maida Vale I decorated the whole flat; I really enjoyed papering and painting; made new curtains etc., and kept myself busy.

1959. My third attempt at motherhood.

Out of luck again!

At 5½ months it all went wrong.

I was taken into hospital where they tried hard to save my baby but eventually she was born dead.

'Can you act, dance or sing?'

When I was fit again I happened to see a poster in our library, -*'Can you act, dance or sing?'*

It advertised, an Amateur Operatic Society called **British European Leprosy Relief Association, BELRA** for short.

It had been 13 years since I had danced, could I still do it I wondered?

I nervously went along; after all I was 35 now.

The welcome was warm and I soon found myself rehearsing for

'Oklahoma'

That was when I met –
- **Bertha Peek** (Evans),
- **Tony Alexander** and
- **Jill Sander**, (now Gasking).

Meanwhile Desmond passed his exams and was called to the Bar

Sadly - it was too late, we didn't share any interests whatsoever, and in 1963 we parted.

Parted from Desmond I started working in the **Public Relations** Office of **London Transport -** and lived alone in a furnished flat-let.
I found neither of them easy.

*Approaching my **40th** birthday my life was in ruins!*

Dancing my way back to happiness!

Thank goodness I had my dancing and over the next few years I appeared in many amateur productions at the Scala and Wimbledon Theatres in London.
After a year of living alone Mum and Dad made a flat for me upstairs in their house at number '67' . I was back in the fold again and very happy to be there.
Bertha Peek (Evans), for many years our producer and choreographer for London Transport Players, also filled the same roles with other amateur companies. She had the inspired habit of persuading members of one company to appear in productions for other of her companies. This habit brought me and my husband **Wally** together, hence the use of the word 'inspired'.
Another of her companies was **The Beaumont (amateur) Operatic Group, Stepney Jewish (B'nai B'rith) Clubs & Settlement**. They were to perform Oscar Hammerstein II and Jerome Kern's
'Show Boat'.
Bertha asked me if I would be Assistant Choreographer and also perform as Principal Dancer. It was quite a journey from my home in West

Hampstead to Stepney in East London, but Bertha could charm birds from a tree.

When I arrived for my first rehearsal with them I found they knew most of the steps Bertha wanted better almost than I did. That didn't stop me fitting in to a very warm and happy atmosphere and I soon befriended the likes of **Sid** and **Irene Caplan** and family, **Sylvia** and **Lawrence Cohen** and family, the sisters **Myra, Adele, Joyce**, the **Kirsch's, Audrey, Cyril, Michelle** and **Clive, Rhoda, Spencer Simmons** and the **Lebby** family. and so many more too numerous to mention.

The intervening 35 years or so have meant that a number of my friends from Stepney have joined the Great Producer in the Sky but what a rehearsal and show they must be putting on up there.

Some years later '**Fiddler on the Roof'** was chosen and a number of London Transport Players were asked to augment their company. Some of Stepney's members having helped out **London Transport Players**, and the **Commercial Union Company,** in other of Bertha's productions. My husband **Wally** was cast as Lazar Woolf the Butcher, and with everyone joking about his kosher credentials etc., mirth was never far away at rehearsals.

Rehearsals under way, both our Mother's became ill. My mother and father already lived with Wally and me. Wally's Mum and Dad came to stay with us so we could look after both Mums. The next time we went to rehearsal we were late but as we walked in everyone stopped rehearsing and all came over to hear how Mum Stewart and Mum Vanner were. That's the caring and concerned nature of these Stepney Jewish company friends. Happily both Mums recovered soon after.

We did a number of other shows with 'Stepney Jewish' as we affectionately called them, notably

"Viva Mexico" adapted and arranged by Ronald Hanmer. Wally had a hilarious time playing an American Senator. He lost his trousers in the process, cleverly choreographed by Bertha so as not to be embarrassing to anyone. I was cast as the back end of a bull with our member John Williams playing the front. Doing a comic dance, sometimes dislocated was great fun. I still look back on those days as some of the best of my life.

Many shows with amateur companies and so many of my friends included –

'Calamity Jane'

'Half a Sixpence'

'The Merry Widow'

Kismet

Barbara!

Barbara

Top Left **MY FAIR LADY**   Top Right **GLAMOROUS NIGHT**
Lower Left **BITTER SWEET**   Lower Right **MY FAIR LADY**

'SHOWBOAT'

CAST

Windy	Albert Thompson
Steve	. Terry Gasking
Pete	Mark Henderson
Queenie	Yvonne Nicholls
Parthy Ann	Madge Royston
Capt. Andy	Michael Guerin
Ellie	Gloria Spanswick
Frank	Stephen Marshall
Rubberface	. Fred Watkins
Julie	. Micky Vince
Gaylord Ravenal	John Barry
Vallon	Frank Bell
Magnolia	Christine Mullord
Joe	. Frank Doran
Backwoodsman	Peter Engeham
Job	. John Reid
Landlady	. Paula Penzer
Kim	. Pamela Payne
Jake	. Nigel Pratt
Max	. Jimmy Lynch
Pianist	Bill Bishop
Lottie	. Helena Bekhor
Ethel	Dorothy Thomas
Seth	. Alan Shave
Doorman	. Frank Davis
Announcer	Ray Perry
Barkers	. Ernie Engeham, Ron Veness

MEN'S CHORUS: Blair Blenman, Barry Bowling, Frank Davis, Tony Earle, Ernie Engeham, Peter Engeham, Fred Fallon, Brian Gordon, Charles Gowlett, Ken Hall, Keith Hicks, Basil Hunt, James Lynch, James Nelson, Walter Peasley, Ray Perry, Eddie Pontyfix, Nigel Pratt, Terry Raymond, Alan Sanders, Herbert Wheatley, Ron Veness.

LADIES' CHORUS: Helena Bekhor, Lisa Braithwaite, Barbara Callow, Penelope Davey, Renee Forder, Hilda Golby, Joan Hardie, Frances Holmes, Di Hudson, Yvette Hughes, Kathleen Jopson, Maria Julien, Shirley Knight, Doris Leeds, June Marsom, Julie Murphy, Vera Ody, Yvonne Olivant, Pamela Payne, Paula Penzer, Marion Percival, Nina Perry, Ivy Rochford, Jenny Rodbard, Beryl Smith, Dorothy Thomas, Dylis Thomas.

MEN DANCERS: Tony Alexander, Reginald Bundy, Peter Eveleigh, Brian Lindsey, Charles Lowe.

GIRL DANCERS: Evelyn Bragg, Susan Brydon, Barbara Lewis, Jill Sander, Claire Scudder, Helena Bekhor, Yvette Hughes, Shirley Knight, June Marsom, Vera Ody, Pamela Payne, Marion Percival, Jenny Rodbard, Dylis Thomas.

' CALAMITY JANE'   'WIZARD OF OZ'

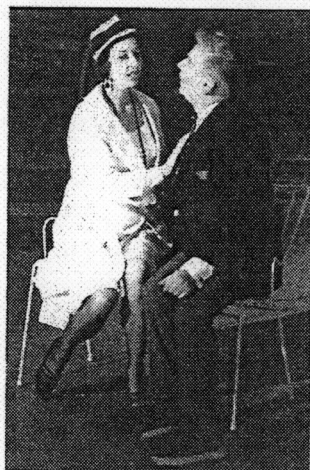 

' NO, NO, NANETTE '   ' BELLE OF NEW YORK '

-    and many, many more!
-    They brought tremendous pleasure to audience
and casts; and to me.

My Many Jobs
(jobs galore!)

In the 1960s I escaped the boredom of working as a clerk in a large office and became a 'Jill' of All Trades with a self drive Car Hire firm.

I answered the phone, booked hires and checked cars 'out' and 'in', I also made the coffee and typed letters with five fingers. I even pushed the Hoover round when the cleaner was on holiday. I delivered cars and collected them back.

My own car was an old Renault Dauphine but my employer wouldn't allow me to park it too close in case customers thought it was one of his fleet. When I was asked to pick up a new part for one of the cars at a garage at Brent Cross fly-over, on the A406 (London's North Circular Road), I set off with confidence. However after a time I worried, there was no sign of the fly-over. I had been under it many times; it was a very large structure impossible to miss.

My unease turned to panic when I found myself joining the M1 motorway. I put my foot down thinking it would be Luton before I could get off. When Watford came into view and a way out I gratefully took it but still had to drive back and find the garage.

I realized I had driven over the top of the fly-over without recognizing it. I located the garage, quickly collected the car part and on my return said I had been kept waiting at the garage. Our mechanic would have known I had driven further by the amount of petrol I had used but he did not give me away.

When I was suddenly 'sacked' as my employer had sold the premises for re-development.

I was shocked and wondered what to do next. All my dancing training and the years spent in the theatre was no help now in job seeking.

Mini-cab

To tied me over I tried my hand at mini-cabbing.

By now I had a presentable Ford Cortina and unbelievably my very first 'job' was to pick up Her Majesty the Queen's Stamp Collector and drive him to Buckingham Palace.

What a thrill to be waved through the gates of Buckingham Palace by the police guard when they recognized my passenger.

It was before the age of mobile phones and the drill was to find a phone box and 'ring' in for the next 'pick-up'. Trouble was I didn't know my way about all that well so by the time I had reached the place another driver had beaten me to it.

Insured!

I made enquiries about training to teach 'Cake Decoration' - a hobby of mine. A Technical College said they would accept me for training one day a week. Next question 'how was I to support myself?'

I saw an advertisement for collecting insurance.

Not by any means ideal but would mean I could have a day free to attend college.

Summertime would have been more ideal but it was November and winter conditions which found me trudging around.

One evening the car 'packed up' on me. It was parked while I made a call but on returning it just would not start again. A man came along and helped me by giving me a 'jump start' then warned me not to stop the engine until I got home.

I had just one more call to make and then I would not need to go out the next day so I risked it, drove there mindful of the advice I had been given, and left the keys in the ignition with the engine running. I picked up my money bag and book, got out of the car, pressed the button down and shut the door realizing too late that I had locked it. It was a really panicky feeling. Luckily my father had my spare keys and I phoned home, told him where I was and he drove to my rescue.

My very poor arithmetic was stretched to the limit when I was given 1s/6d (pre-decimalisation) to be divided among two or three separate insurance policies or more.

I was always out longer than I had hoped, having to call back when people were out. I also often had to go back the next day.

I would get home frozen and exhausted, tip the money out on the floor and start counting. Every time I counted it came to a different amount but I was never brave enough to present the first answer it came to and hope for the best. Then there was this enormous ledger where every insurance policy had to be updated.

All hopes for a clear day for cookery training went 'out of the window '.

The Post Office

I therefore applied to join the Post Office which included the telephone service then. They had an office block near to my home.

I was terrified I would fail the entrance examination, having left school one month after I was 14 and I was thrilled when I passed.

Soon after starting work, glad to be in a bright and warm office after traipsing the streets in the cold and dark.

I got talking to a colleague and found he had done my insurance round before me and left after he was 'mugged'.

A look into the Past

In the middle 1960's **Bertha Peak**, choreographer and producer of the amateur operatic company I had joined asked me if I would go with her to unpack an old trunk.

The depository that had housed it since about 1911 was closing.

Descendants of the family to whom the trunk belonged had been contacted and they did not want it.

Someone suggested Bertha might be able to use the old clothes in shows. She often saved the theatre company large hire fees by making and altering costumes helped by members who liked to sew.

As Bertha and I stood looking at the trunk knowing it had been packed long before we were born, we were excited, nervous and awestruck in turn.

The lid was raised; there between tissue paper was a family story.

Beautiful baby clothes, obviously treasured by the mother,
- several long white skirts we felt would have been worn on a cruise. Each had a name on the 20" waistband. We decided one belonged to mother but I don't recall why it was the same tiny waist as the others;
- a motoring coat with a telegram in the pocket requesting the son pay back the 5 shillings (25p) had been loaned.
- A pierrot suit father had worn at a fancy dress party we surmised, with raffle tickets in the pocket.
- Mother hadn't kept her fancy dress except for a necklace of red velvet hearts which I took as a souvenir which I still have.
- One dress and 2 blouses had expanding waists and fronts, mother's maternity wear we presumed;

- A beautiful Edwardian Dress in pale turquoise and white with tiny pleats. Every pleat was hand sewn with the tiniest of stitches that covered the whole of the dress.
- A riding habit also with a 20" waist; a lovely lace dress which fastened down the front with tiny hooks and eyes, there was an inner lining set and then the outer set on the lace, at least 50 hooks and eyes in all.

Many of the things found their way into our shows and Bertha dyed the white skirts all different colours.

The baby clothes and more delicate things were given to a Museum.

I have often pondered over how the trunk could have lain in the Depository, unclaimed and unopened for so long.

Did the 1914 -1918 World War change their lives? Did they leave the country and is that why their descendents did not collect the trunk?

Who paid the Depository charges for all those years?

The way to a girl's Heart

I was at a low ebb and my dear friend **Tony Alexander** kindly took charge of my social life now that my first marriage had ended.

Tony had been a professional dancer and appeared in the original productions of:
- **Annie Get Your Gun**
- **Call Me Madam**.

He also played in many other productions including
- the title name in **"The Winslow Boy"**
- and the **Young Ptolemy II** in **Elizabeth Taylor** and **Richard Burton's "Cleopatra'**.

Barbara!

Nowadays he is a volunteer for the Variety Club and has just been voted 'Volunteer of the Year'.

In 1960s Tony had been dancing in shows at the **Scala Theatre**, London, and **Wimbledon Theatre** in **London Transport Players'** shows, - the amateur operatic group I had joined.

In 1970 Tony, his lovely mother **Lena**, his partner **Colin** and I flew to Mojacar, Spain, on holiday.

Wally (another member of London Transport Players) and I had been getting fond of each other but I didn't expect him to telephone me.

The call went out all round the hotel for "Barbara Lewis" (my married name).

I was impressed and when Wally made a second call to Mojacar - I was thrilled.

My hero was at the airport to meet me on my return and escorted me home.

Aah!

Violins please maestro.

Dancing a Dream to Wedding Bells

London Transport Players put on two full-blown musicals a year at Wimbledon Theatre in London.

Our producer, **Bertha Peek**, was also a wonderful choreographer and we did many lovely dances at a high standard. Although there had been several years gap since I last danced due to a severe back injury, expertly manipulated into functioning by **Stephen Ward** the osteopath, I very soon worked myself back to form.

When our producer asked if some of us would dance for another company for whom she produced I was reluctant as working full time and rehearsing twice a week already was fine but learning two different shows and rehearsing 4 or 5 times a week would be hard going for this not so young dancer.

When I heard the show was -

'Oklahoma'

- and I would be doing the Can-Can, my favourite dance, I gave in.

I was given the role of Chief Postcard Girl in the 'Dream Ballet' sequence and partnered **Wally** - the man who was to dance the part of the villain, Judd Fry.

Rehearsals for both shows progressed and so did my tiredness. Wally, my dancing partner, often asked me to go for a drink after rehearsal but the answer was always "*no*" as I was the taxi home for fellow dancers.

Such was my tiredness that I was completely unaware of Wally's interest in me. I later learned that he had said he would marry me the first time I walked into rehearsal.

With both shows over I revived and Wally joined my other operatic company.

After a rehearsal I dropped Wally off at Westminster Underground station. He kissed me for the first time. I looked up and we were at the foot of Big Ben.

Quite by chance when Wally asked me to marry him we were at Marble Arch.

When, one Saturday, Wally said we were going shopping and we boarded a bus to Trafalgar Square, I was puzzled. On arrival I was steered into Bravington's the jewellers to choose an engagement ring.

Well after that there was only one place to buy our wedding rings, Piccadilly Circus with Eros looking on!

We were both in our 40's, me rather further in than Wally, so I was thinking a small wedding, nice suit and little hat. But my fiancée had other ideas.

O.K. I thought a dressy frock and a biggish hat. When it was suggested that Wally's two little nieces could be bridesmaids and I saw how the invitation list was growing, I bought a pattern and yards of beautiful satin and lace in rose pink and got sewing.

The nice suit became a wedding dress but I did have a little hat and a short veil.

The Plum Pudding

Leading up to our marriage **Wally** and I stayed in my flat in my parent's house, at West Hampstead, during the week as it was nearer to our jobs. Week-ends we stayed in Wally's house in Cranham, Upminster.

Having invited our respective parents and Wally's brother and his family, to spend Christmas Day with us, we had a grand total of 11, we decided to make a good old fashioned round Plum Pudding, often seen on Christmas cards.

We found a recipe in an old Cookery Book, (not Mrs. Beaton's), and obtained all the ingredients except 'Lemebos', which to this day we have not tracked down. Wally was working at the Royal Lancaster Hotel in Bayswater, and had top Chefs to advise him but none had heard of 'Lemebos'.

Assembling it all, it was tied up in a floured cloth and ready for cooking. It was then that I realised I didn't have a saucepan large enough for such a monster.

I popped downstairs and borrowed Mum's jam saucepan.

The requisite 14 hours boiling had made it just right for eating but when we tried to lift it out of the pot, it wouldn't budge! The rounded sides of Mum's saucepan which had gone unnoticed had now filled up with swollen pudding.

We tugged! No. We heaved! No. We shoved! No.

Down on the floor went the pan, Wally's foot on one handle, me holding the other and a hand each on the pudding cloth pulling. Suddenly with a Whoosh! It plopped out but instead of a lovely round shape it was elongated.

To our relief and joy it settled into the lovely round shape intended as it cooled.

A larger saucepan from Wally's Mum worked well when it was reheated on Christmas Day.

Whew!

Our Wedding Cake

By the time I met my husband to be - **Wally** - I had made many celebration iced cakes, birthdays, christening, anniversaries etc., for family and friends.

I naturally had to think of my own wedding cake. We knew we wanted it special. *"How about we forget round or square"* Wally said, *"and make it in the shape of kisses?"* - Aaaah!!!

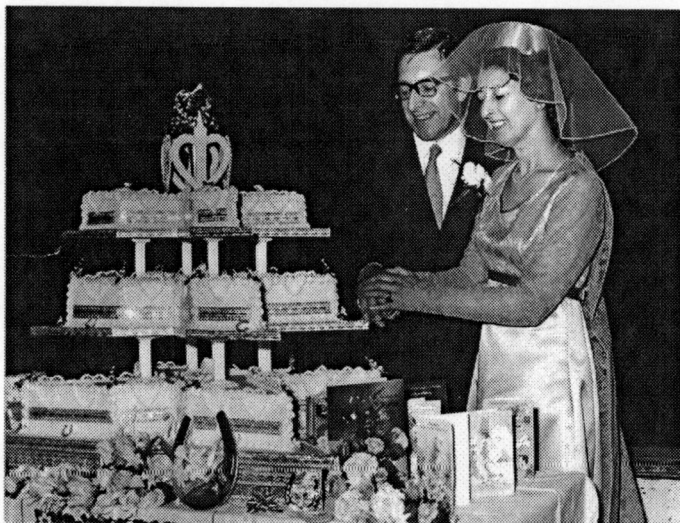

Wally drew the plans. We obviously needed several square cakes we could cut to shape. 3 cake boards would have to be especially made in plywood, (oh yes, it had to be 3 tiers), but that was to prove not too difficult as Wally was working at the Royal Lancaster Hotel in Bayswater, London, and **Clarence**, the head carpenter from Barbados, was a genius.

The second and third tier shapes were easy but the first tier would be a problem, no possibility of hiring a cake-stand so a 4" deep plinth was fashioned.

We fixed ordinary cake-boards to the ply and measured 20 yards of 1" deep silver trimming which we bought, together with the 16 silver shoes, 16 horseshoes, ring with a dove and a silver cupid.

The assistant asked how many cakes we were making, on replying *"One"*, her face was a picture.

We were staying in my flat in Mum and Dad's house in West Hampstead during the week and at week ends in Wally's house in Cranham, Upminster, where the cake was created, rather than just made.

It was almost a building project! Once the fruit cakes were on the boards I could only lift the top tier!

Wally had to move the middle one for me, the bottom was on a coffee table and I worked around it on my knees. About 70 trellis-work hearts in three sizes I designed to go round showing just above the cake edge and over 100 tiny roses.

An icing model chef's hat I placed in the centre of the first tier, Wally's love of cooking, and icing crossed ballet shoes centre of the second tier for me.

Making other symbols, a kiss and a heart; buying a cheap replica of my ring and the doved wedding ring. I placed them on sugar cushions in order on the top tier.

Wally made a box of four hearts with the landmarks of Big Ben (1st kiss); Marble Arch (Proposal); Nelson's Column (Engagement Ring) Eros at Piccadilly Circus (Wedding Rings).

I iced the hearts and the detail of the buildings were picked out in pale blue. A vase of flowers inside topped by a cupid completed the assembly.

We built the cake on its pillars, then proudly showed our neighbour who promptly said *"Will you get it through the door? "*

We gasped, it hadn't crossed our minds - but after we removed the door and with about 1½ inch to spare either side, we did!

We had a wonderful wedding which included Wally singing a song he had written especially for me, notated and played by my brother **Jimmy** and his band as we started off the dancing

The Moving Game

After we married in June, 1971, I joined Wally in his house in Cranham, Essex.

Soon we were back to rehearsing with the **London Transport Players** just off Edgware Road in London.

The show was –

'Wizard of Oz'

to be performed at **Wimbledon Theatre**.

Wally's work was in Kensington. Mum and Dad's house in West Hampstead was nearer to Kensington and the Edgware Road so we spent at least two days a week with them.

We decided to move closer and asked family friend **Fred Hill**, who worked for an Estate Agent in Willesden, to find a suitable house.

We had disappointments, not the least being one on which we had agreed a price, only for the vendor to be told it would be compulsory purchased to make way for a new police station to be built in Queens Park.

Not that long afterwards we settled on another large corner property in Queens Park hoping to let the upper flat to supplement Wally's salary. I had given up my job at the Post Office - it was too far from Cranham.

In January 1972 we moved to our new house on a very wild stormy day.

We excitedly talked of how we could make two self-contained flats. Wally drew up the plans and filed the necessary planning permission papers, without architects or other professionals, and they were passed by the local planning office.

We commenced decorating the upstairs first; our part could wait until the rent started to come in.

Our friends pitched in and helped as well as Dad and Wally's Mum and Dad.

My Dad joked –

"Don't go and see Barbara and Wally, you'll only get a paint brush put in your hand".

At week-ends I made large stews to feed all our volunteers.

Tony Alexander painted a whole long hall way and he and **Colin Gillert** came round on other occasions rubbing down and painting, there was a lot to do.

Charles Lowe, and **Dani Townsend** (Trzos) from America, were also well to the fore. Dani even helped sort out my filing system.

My friend **Eileen** from Cork, Ireland, whom I had met working at London Transport, and who had the downstairs flat with Mum and Dad, was a great decorator. We had contemplated starting a business together at one point so she was very useful.

Brother Jimmy's wife **Kathleen** helped finish off the hall painting with Tony. An all round team effort I'm pleased to say.

It was then we realised how bad my mother's arthritis had become. She had it in both hips. Replacement surgery was in the experimental stage then. Back to the drawing board!

We persuaded Mum and Dad to come and share our house and then let the other two flats in their house to give us the much needed extra income.

Now we had to leave upstairs and prepare the ground floor.

Two sisters had shared the house before us and there was a bathroom off the downstairs kitchen.

There was a step down into the kitchen from the living room and then immediately a step up to the bathroom.

With Mum in mind Wally, although he was working long hours on the project team building a new hotel for the Rank Organisation, put in a completely new kitchen floor making it level with the living room and the bathroom.

Underneath the kitchen sink water had leaked for years it seemed for everything was soaked and rotten. So a new sink unit was put in.

Our friend **Alan Huggett** designed a Central Heating system for the whole house and with his, and another friend **Alex Girvan's** help Wally installed it, all 18 radiators of different sizes. With pipes running up under the stairs and floor boards needing to be taken up chaos nearly reigned, but not quite.

Mum and Dad had lived in their house, known by its number '67', for 54 years. Brother Roy and I had both been born there but, in the way they had always faced life without any fuss, they moved house.

Although Mum and Dad's sitting room still needed decorating we had to start on '67', making it ready for letting. We could accommodate a couple in 'my' top flat at '67' and 4 people in the middle floor, as mentioned before the ground floor was let to my friend **Eileen Baker.**

None of the lettings were self contained and all used the one front door. Although we had not done all the decorating we had intended, Wally came home from the hotel which was nearing completion and said the hotel were employing staff who needed accommodation.

Thinking of the money we might make we let four young men have the middle flat.

Things seemed fine for a short time but they suddenly left the hotel and us. What's more they left the flat in a terrible mess and owing us three weeks rent. Wally wasn't able to trace where they went. We could have been put off the whole idea of renting again but needs must, as the saying goes.

When everything was ready again we advertised in the local paper. A couple of people viewed but left.

We had by now spent most of our available cash and the money that was left over when we sold Wally's house fixing up both houses.

Family Bliss

Mum and Dad shared the bills and we were all very happy together in our house and had a lot of laughs. Dad, a stoic Scot, not given to showing much excitement and exuberant Wally were very different. Dad never betted, Wally loves horse racing and would have a bet most days.

When racing was on TV Mum soon began shouting *"Come on Wally's horse, come on Wally's horse".*

Dad couldn't hide a smile. Then when football was on, a goal was scored and Wally shouted *"Goal"*, Mummy, who was always knitting, would drop it with the shock, sometimes losing a few stitches.

Yes there were certain adjustments. Before long they loved Wally and he loved them, lucky all of us.

We spent most of our time down with Mum and Dad, sharing all our meals. It was a good thing as we never did get time to finish off the upstairs. Not that it stopped us using our big room for a dinner party at New Year; one year having 18 of us at the table.

Tenants

At last we let my top flat in '67' to a couple.

Four fellows came after the middle flat but we were reluctant to let after the experience with the previous male tenants.

When no one else came along we agonised should we accept the four men? We went to see them where they were supposedly staying with a sister of one of them. It was a nice flat and they all seemed a very presentable Irish family. We agreed for them to become our tenants.

For a time we thought we had 'cracked it'. I got on and finished decorating Mum and Dad's sitting room in our house with Wally's help. We had chosen a nice gold shield patterned wallpaper. I started one side from the window and Wally the other. Everything went swimmingly and we had the wallpaper up in no time.

Wally stepped back to admire the work and then, *Oops!* He pointed out that as mine was perfectly level across the shields his had taken a slight slope to the south, hardly visible but to his trained eye as a sign-writer very real. We decided it was too slight and costly to remove it all and do again.

At "67" the couple were the first to play up, getting behind with the rent. I hated rent collecting. After some time I naively accepted a cheque. Presenting it at the bank the next morning I found the account had been closed. I rushed to "67", the couple had flown. Also the electric meter had been broken into and the money stolen.

It wasn't long after that the four chaps began to fall behind with their rent. We hoped they would eventually 'cough up' but no such luck. We gave them notice to leave.

Back to square one.

Back to worry, worry, worry. Even worse - as with our other non-paying tenants - the flat was trashed.

The 'Hole'

On moving the bed in the upstairs flat at '67' after we had evicted the 4 Irish lads we found a hole cut in the partition stud wall that had been put up years before by my father.

They had made a hollow between the plaster boards and covered it with a headboard. It contained a number of Irish Republican newspapers; but what else had it stored we wondered?

This was at the time of an active Irish Republic Army waging war on the English and the thought that they might have been using our house and what they might have hidden in this 'hole' was the last straw. We gave up and Dad decided to sell '67'.

More work clearing the rooms out and doing the necessary repairs and preparing for the house to go on the market.

Then a fresh nightmare! At 2.00am one morning a telephone call from Eileen to say there were people moving about upstairs in '67'. Wally called the police, crept out of the house not to disturb Mum and Dad and drove down to '67' as fast as he could.

When he came home again he told me a constable had met him and together went inside and found two Irish men in bed. Apparently they had been told by our erstwhile tenants to climb the drainpipe and get in through a window as the key had been lost!

Another time one afternoon Eileen phoned to say she had come home and found the front door wide open, a large metal jack in the hall and someone moving about upstairs. I made an excuse to Mum and Dad and drove to '67'. Eileen took the jack into her room and I called the police.

We were anxiously waiting for them when we heard the interloper coming down the stairs. I, very bravely, (get me), went out and challenged him, barring the way to the front door. To my relief two policemen arrived at that moment. One came upstairs with me to see if anything had been damaged or stolen. The other policeman hung on to the man.

Finding nothing wrong I was asked if I wanted to prefer charges or settle for them to give him a warning. I opted for the warning not wanting my parents to be worried.

It appeared the chap had been in prison and was looking for some clothes. One of our former tenants was looking after for him. The police gave him a severe warning. They advised me to paint the drainpipe with special paint that never dries and remains slippery to stop it being climbed in the future.

Eileen and I had a cup of tea to settle our nerves. Then Eileen said she was going to stay with a friend and look for another flat. Who could blame her?

'Squatting' was rife at this time and our house was empty so more worry. We started putting empty milk bottles out on the door step, a different number every day. Each week we put rubbish in the dustbin, and sometimes spent time inside having a front window open, all the time not letting Mum and Dad know how worried we were.

This continued for a long time waiting for a buyer to appear.

Eventually '67' was sold for just £6,000 (the price of houses was very much lower in those days). This was a low price but we were all eager to get off this particular hook.

Our efforts at making some worth while money were again a failure but not for want of trying.

It's galling to look back, now this type of house in this location is selling for upwards of £400,000, but no one could visualise house prices rising so dramatically and, I guess, that's life!

Redundancy!

So we settled down to our new found freedom, with Wally and I continually thinking of what next to increase our earnings.

Then in 1977 the Rank Organisation underwent a reconstruction of their various Divisions, and the Hotels were amalgamated with the Leisure Services section removing to Whyteleafe, Surrey.

Wally was made redundant in the July and as happened with the P.L.A. he had his own pension contributions returned with only a little enhancement

Mum said *"Isn't it lovely having Wally at home"*. It certainly was but aged 47; with redundancy increasing everywhere will he get another job?

The 1970s and a variety of jobs for Wally and I

Interspersed with my various phases of dancing I have had a number of jobs, shown under 'My Many Jobs' chapter, including taxi driver; haberdashery counter assistant; personal assistant to a Post Office Personnel Officer; office worker at London Transport; Insurance round collector.

One job I didn't have but which I thought I could tackle was Celebration Cake Decorator and to this end I had a little tuition with **Hartley Smith**, the renowned cake decorating Master, he had made cakes for Prince Charles and Sir Winston Churchill among others. It certainly honed my natural skills and as I always look at the desserts on a menu before the other courses, fitted my persona.

My husband Wally had also had a variety of jobs including laboratory assistant, in essences, perfumes and brewing products; oil; acids and heavy chemicals; stores assistant Royal Navy; cargo checker London Docks; ledger clerk then Auditor London Docks; electrician's mate; procurement officer building the 'Gloucester' Hotel then purchasing officer the 'Gloucester' Hotel; Assistant to Purchasing Controller Rank Hotels; occasional bookmaker's clerk, with my cousin **Lily's** husband **Fred Stevens**.

When Wally and I married we did not know all of each other's backgrounds but I was soon aware of his love of cooking and he of my love of desserts and cake making and Icing. We both love good food and have always prepared from fresh and still do. Dinner parties for family and friends came easily, even 18 x 3-course ones with choices for each course.

However - our world took a resounding 'knock' when Wally was made redundant for the second time, in July 1977.

Shortly afterwards my mother died and two years later my father died. They had been living with us.

We had tried working for ourselves - Blinds, Stretch Covers; Knitting Style Capes; Wally trying Insurance; even designing Board Games but to no lasting effect.

At our ages of Wally (49) and me (56), despite searching, finding no other jobs available, and with a mortgage to pay, -

Where do we go from here?

Grief

Mum and Dad were approaching their Diamond Wedding Anniversary, 18th January, 1978.

We booked a hall, had invitations printed and started planning.

Suddenly my lovely mother, at 82, had a heart attack and after 2 days in hospital died. We were devastated.

I found watching my father's grief harder to bear than my own, he tried to keep it to himself but we could feel it.

Our cat Mitzi had the run of the house but never went into Mum and Dad's bedroom. After Mummy died I noticed Mitzi, who had been looking for Mum, go into the bedroom. Dad was in there and heartbreakingly I heard him say *"She's not coming back, Mitzi"*.

It still brings tears to my eyes.

I was able to spend a lot of time with Dad and we always went shopping together.

Wally worked on a board game he had been developing, about gardening. I thought it very exciting and beautifully presented. Wally took it, together with a 'Show Jumping' game he had already made to one of the leading games people of the day, (now no longer trading). Both games were taken for assessment and Wally was kept waiting for quite a long time.

The 'Show Jumping' game was returned; they were not interested but asked to keep the 'Garden' game for further consideration. As the days passed our hopes grew only to be dashed after 3 months, they returned it - not interested.

When Christmas came brother Jimmy saw almost the identical lay-out of the Show Jumping game on the bottom of a box of crackers in a supermarket.

Again 2 years after this a very similar Garden game was marketed although there were some differences.

To try and cheer Dad, and us up, we planned a holiday to Elgin in Morayshire, Scotland, where Dad was born.

Mum and Dad had made the trip many times linking up with our Scottish family but for the last few years Mum was not able to make the journey and they stayed home.

In 1978 we had booked a stone built 'Gardener's Cottage'. My grandfather was head gardener in some big houses and our earlier holidays were spent with them in their 'Gardener's Cottage'.

Dad booked on Motorail (defunct for some years now) from Olympia Station to Carlisle, then Wally drove to Carluke, Lanarkshire.

After 2 days with cousins **Vitae** and **Jim Stewart** we all five went to Elgin. It was a great success and we repeated the holiday in 1979.

In 1980 we realised Dad was getting weak and though we talked of another trip to Scotland we knew he would not be able to make it. Dad never lacked spirit and was talking of buying a new car, looking at all the magazines and newspaper adverts.

Dad's granddaughter **Janine** was expecting a baby and we felt he hung on until we could tell him her baby girl was safely delivered.

Just a short time later he finally 'slipped away' at 85.

A Saturday Girl

In the late 70's it was not the best time to earn a living! Wally having been made redundant also found turning his hand to something lucrative frustrating.

Tony Alexander worked for a Theatre Ticket Agency based in a gift and card shop in South Moulton Street, off Oxford Street.

This dearest of friends arranged for me to work in the shop on Saturdays on the gift and card side, a change from the haberdashery to which I was first apprenticed.

I really enjoyed the work and reveled in the thought of being a 'Saturday Girl' in my middle 50's. The money of course came in very useful at this time. A highlight was recognizing some of the customers from show business and other spheres who often came in to buy.

After our move to Bognor the connection was maintained as the shop commissioned Wally to make their sign for outside the shop when he started his sign-writing phase.

Dismay!

Now Wally and I were alone in a house we loved but could no longer afford without Dad's help. The money he left was shared between me and my brothers Jimmy and Roy.

My share paid off the overdraft we had built up that we hadn't let Dad know about.

We missed having Dad to look after, both of us grieving and feeling rather lost.

Making some upstairs rooms into flatlets was not an option; we just didn't have the money. We also remembered the trouble we had with tenants in Mum and Dad's house, '67'.

House hunting for a smaller house was depressing. Selling a big house to buy a smaller one should have been easy but with neither of us having jobs, not for want of trying, we would not get another mortgage. After paying off the present mortgage there would not be enough left to buy another house in London.

Deep gloom set in again.

Against our better judgment we decided to take two young men who were friends as lodgers.

This time we had made the right decision. You could not have had better to share your home.

John was living in the road alongside our house in an overcrowded situation with relatives. **Clive** came from Newtown in Wales. Both John and Clive were model lodgers, helpful in the house, always quiet and prompt payers but we understood they would only be temporary.

We did attempt to act as agents for fitting loose covers on furniture and installing blinds but although at first this worked, problems with mis-fitting to our accurate templates crept in and putting things right was a pain and not lucrative, so we stopped.

Our friends **Gwenda** and **Alan Huggett** suggested we look for a house in Leigh-on-Sea near to them in Rayleigh and cheaper than London houses. They helped us house hunt and things seemed more hopeful of buying a house outright.

We cheered up and put our house up for sale. Timing was wrong again. The housing market was flat and we attracted not a single offer.

This is where real despair set in.

One night we had a bottle of wine and talked of all the things we would like to do in the house. A real flight of fancy. We planned on until the early hours, knowing all the time it was never to be.

From then my lively happy-go-lucky Wally sank into depression and took to sifting in a chair staring into space.

Charles Holland from Leeds, a friend I had first met with his wife **Sylvia** on my first honeymoon, sometimes came to London on business and took the opportunity to stay with us.

Worried sick about Wally, I suggested we do a nice dinner while Charles was with us and invite John and Clive as well. Slowly Wally took interest then really came to life as we discussed the menu.

I laid the table beautifully, Wally bustled about cooking, his old self again. We all had a lovely meal and a happy evening.

Soon after this my friend from professional dancing days, **Sylvia Victor**, sent a property page from a Bognor Regis paper.

'Houses are cheaper here', she wrote.

As I scoured the house adverts the business section caught my eye. There was a restaurant with a flat above for sale.

Kill two birds with one stone I thought.

Wally had always wanted a restaurant and remembering how he came out of depression when we had the dinner party and also how wonderful he was to Mum and Dad, I felt he should have his chance. Snag was on enquiry that place had gone.

Another restaurant was on offer but without accommodation. We needed to also buy a house.

We decided to visit Sylvia in Bognor Regis to look around for a suitable house but had one or two abortive viewings before seeing an almost perfect one decoratively speaking but far too small to accommodate our heavy furniture.

Next day we were to return to London, I had had a dreadful sleepless night. Wally went out for a paper and seemed gone rather a long time. When he came back he said *"Don't say no before you see it, but I have arranged a viewing for an end of terrace house in May Close, Bognor Regis, but it doesn't have a downstairs cloakroom"*.

My mother's name was May.

Is this an omen we both wondered?

Bognor Regis

At £29,950 and with the restaurant lease scheduled to cost £12,000 without agents and solicitor's fees, we were over budget for what we thought we could sell our London house.

One of my favourite sayings springs to mind -

"Shall we throw our bonnet over the windmill?"

We asked if the house price was negotiable and reduced it by £150.

A quick consultation, a viewing followed, we loved the house, especially Wally's kitchen and the upstairs extension and the small garden for which we would not have time to attend to anyway.

Offer made for house and restaurant we returned to London on the highest of highs to sort out all the necessary arrangements.

You may be correct in thinking we had come through some awful headaches up to now. Perhaps what was to come just didn't dawn on us at that time.

The so called 'bridging loan' which never actually materialized; - the bank shall remain nameless; fines for parking under lampposts facing the wrong way, unheard of in London, not in Bognor we found to our cost and a myriad of other small niggles.

Our lodger in London - **John** - changed job and moved on but **Clive** stayed and was a great help while Wally was in B&B in Bognor Regis seeing to the refurbishing of 'Vanners', our restaurant.

We had a restaurant a mortgage on a house in Bognor but we hadn't sold our house in London! We had only received one inadequate 'offer'.

Things change however as always. Our asking price of £38,500 was negotiated to £38,000 which we accepted.

The 'Move' to Bognor was 'on'

Moving day - and night!

As well as Clive, cousins **Vitae** and **Jim Stewart** from Carluke, Scotland, then came down to help pack up. What a 'God send' they were. I could never have managed without them.

The removal family firm, Lanes, now run by 'Young Lane' in Iverson Road where Mum and Dad's house was, were unfortunately away on holiday. They were family friends and had moved us without a hitch from Essex to Carlisle Road.

I looked up 'Yellow Pages' and found a local company. They seemed very good when I went to see their premises and vehicles. As they say in sport *'They talked a good game'*.

On the moving day, - August 14th 1981, packing went smoothly, Vitae, Jim and I saw them off and we stayed to do a final 'clean up' before I drove to Bognor to help the unpacking.

Over half-way to Bognor I thought I recognized one of the company's vans which looked broken down.

On arriving in Bognor about 5.00 pm one van was there with Wally waiting to take some things to 'Vanners' (our Restaurant) Wally showed them the way to 'Vanners' and unloaded and came back. While unloading it was noticed the van had a puncture and couldn't move, it had no spare tyre.

Much later that day the other van arrived. It just parked across in front of the garages belonging to neighbours in the Close! It appeared to have mechanical trouble and it was the one I saw broken down beside the road on my journey down to Bognor.

Unloading finished about 3.00am on the 15th August

A most precious family heirloom, a chess board painted by a Scots .uncle on glass, had been smashed causing me to have hysterics.

Mum and Dad's trinket cupboard and bureau were scratched, similarly with one of the pianos and other furniture.

Another disaster for the unsuspecting us.

I tried to claim later for compensation but they would not budge. Suing was out of the question.

We started our life in Bognor Regis in tears but we were here – we had moved into our smaller house and we were about to open our own Restaurant – 'VANNER'S'.

'VANNER'S'

The Restaurant we leased and turned into Vanner's was quite large, 55 seats plus, but seemed in a good position, in an Arcade leading from the High Street to the Theatre and the Sea.

We had employed a business marketing firm to do a prospective suitability survey. We consulted our bank manager, solicitor and accountant. They all said *'Go ahead'*! It was a good prospect.

Before agreeing to this venture I did stipulate we must employ a Chef; Wally cooks with love and not to a timetable, required in a restaurant. Also I did not want to be a waitress at 57, never having done the job before. I was afraid my memory wouldn't cope with all the various orders. I didn't mind what other work I did.

A snag was the property had no accommodation and we had to buy a house. We agreed a price both for this house and restaurant; selling our London house to finance it - and the packing had started.

Wally moved to Bognor Regis staying in bed & breakfast to supervise the re-furbishing, carpeting and equipment updating etc. - that had been his job with Rank Hotels when they built the 'Gloucester' hotel, Kensington.

We decided to use our surname **"Vanner's"** as the restaurant name.

Friends helped; - the restaurant chair loose seats, which we were keeping, needed new covers. I brought them back to London after one of my regular visits to Bognor. Tailor friend **Charles Lowe** cut the material to size but the zigzag pattern proved somewhat of an eye strain for him.

School friend **Doris Davis**, her husband **Ted** and son **Peter** collected the seats, took them home and returned them beautifully fitted.

Charles gave further help with the peach tablecloths I was making.

Telling Doris and Ted how Wally was planning an 'Opening' party I suddenly realised he would expect a 'Cake'.

I always made a cake for a party and here I was tired out and mostly packed up, how could I possibly bake a large cake?

Dear Doris, (not well herself and heartbreakingly to die some 6 months later), at once offered to make a fruit cake if I would ice it.

We decided it would be in the shape of a "V" (for Vanner's). Tiny tables with wine glass decorations and "Good Luck Vanner's" completed our effort. I still occasionally quake at the thought of arriving for the "Grand Opening" without a cake!

Vanner's was open and full of excitement we started life as 'Restaurateurs'

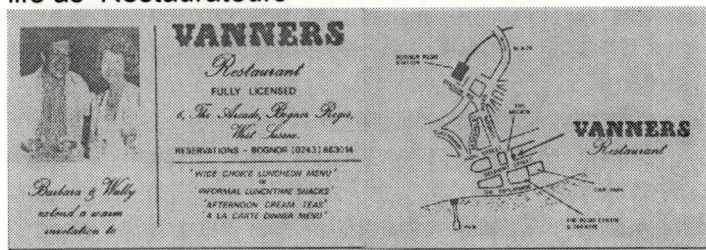

It took some time to sell our London house and buy one in Bognor Regis. Meanwhile Wally remained in the bed & breakfast and I drove to Bognor regularly for the day helping in any way I could; shopping taking washing to the Launderette etc.

We could seat 55 diners so hoped for some 'full-houses' along the way

Our first chef designed dinner menus more elaborate so we could charge higher prices and make more profit.

The 'Sussex Fortnight',

One of the highlights in Sussex surrounds the *'Sussex Fortnight',* horse racing festivals at Goodwood and Brighton.

My cousin **Lily Stevens'** husband, **Fred,** was a bookmaker of note and when he came to the Goodwood festival - the most important meeting of the year - he spread the word and we had a number of his colleagues each night in for dinner.

It was the end of July and this was a good fortnight for us even though I was still in London finalizing our move.

This made our 'books' look a great deal healthier.

14 August 81

Our move from London to Bognor Regis was horrendous! One of the two vans broke down, then the other one 'blew' a tyre. It was 3.00 am before everything was unloaded and it was over. At last I had my smaller house but no time to fully unpack and arrange it.

'Vanner's' naturally came first.

We advertised under the banner *'Vanner's Theatre Restaurant'* being the only restaurant facing the **Alexandra Theatre** opposite the Arcade in which we were situated.

The theatre did not have evening restaurant facilities, only café service during the day.

The theatre was run and funded by the District Council so we thought that a mutually beneficial double Theatre/Dinner ticket, quite popular elsewhere, would benefit us both. We explored the possibility but were turned down flat.

A bigger blow was the refusal to have 'Vanner's' advertise in the concourse of the theatre itself or to allow sandwich boards at both ends of the Arcade.

August/September

For some time on Saturday evenings we employed **Peggy Cochrane**—band leader Jack Payne's widow - to play the piano. She was marvelous and could play anything, moving round the tables asking for requests, rarely being 'stumped'. It always seemed appreciated and no adverse comments.

Pity it couldn't continue when trade tailed off after 'the Season' closed down in mid-September.

Our friends helped where they could, **Mike Castle** and **Ray Bloomfield** came from London for a Sunday lunch on one occasion.

Later, in August, a bus load of our 'London Transport Players' friends came on a day's outing, what a joy to see them. A hilarious lunch time session ensued.

Things got a little fraught when one bright spark turned round our CLOSED notice to OPEN, saying –

"It is the only way to make money".

We had stopped opening for Tea and Cakes a couple of weeks before to concentrate on lunch and dinner. On that day a mass of customers came in and sat down. What panic!

One of our dancers, **Neil Smith**, from Australia, was training to be a chef in Grosvenor House Hotel in London. He promptly 'jumped to the stove' turning out the best omelettes holiday makers in Bognor had ever had, and saved our bacon to boot.

Wally went into overdrive to keep up with chips etc.

If only we could have had that sort of custom continuously! Would we have coped?

Sadly our position deteriorated quickly. Why don't people eat with us? We were never to discover the answer to that question!

One by one we had to let the staff go and take on all the work ourselves.

Wally did the cooking and I waited at table, just the opposite of our intentions.

With Wally slogging in the kitchen I was in charge of 'Front of House'. Never much of a drinker, manning the bar was a headache. I sometimes had to run round from behind the bar and into the kitchen to ask Wally what glass to put certain drinks in.

One evening a couple were having pre-dinner drinks. I understood him perfectly, but her mumbled request "Berls" had me mystified. I tripped to the kitchen but Wally couldn't help except to say we stocked about 6 'Bols' liqueurs. I poured the man's drink playing for time then she pointed to 'Bells' whisky.

We got into a routine whereby Wally went straight down to the restaurant in the mornings whilst I baked apple tarts and bread and butter puddings every day, then took them along in time for lunch. The cold desserts we bought.

My 'dogsbody' duties included shopping, cleaning, changing the table cloths from the red and white check for lunch, to peach ones for the evening dinner session then relaying the 15 tables, then reversing the process after the dinner session for next day's lunch. Oh, and the washing up of course. It was well into the afternoon when we left for home after lunch.

I remember us sitting, with our aching legs up for a short rest, before it was back down to 'Vanner's' for the evening stint.

I brought all the kitchen cloths home to wash each evening and Wally had to be kept in clean whites on a daily basis. I had 3 buckets in which to soak the cloths. The ones used by the waitresses and 2 kinds from the kitchen, i.e. greasy, and very greasy. The dirty table cloths went straight into the washing machine.

If it was fine I hung them in the garden over night, otherwise I filled up the clothes-horses. Then it was off to bed in the early hours. We hadn't expected this venture to be easy but did expect to make some money for our efforts—but sadly it was not so! We were making losses on a weekly basis!

Sunday 27 September '81

Now that the "Season" was over and customer numbers were erratic usually on the low side, we closed so that we could 'dress' the restaurant up.

We decided to go more 'theatre' style by putting up London Transport show posters and photographs, ostrich feather and jewelry clusters, round the walls etc. On a shelf running above the length of the bar we put all our show nick-knacks, after show presents and so on we cleaned and shone everything and were ready to re-open – just!

True it had been 1.00 am when we went home the previous night and rushed straight back after a few hours sleep, but ready we were! The restaurant looked really good.

Tuesday 6 October '81

After we had been open for about half an hour a man walked in and I greeted customer number one after the re-fit quietly confident more would follow now the 'duck' was broken.

"Do you take an Access card?" he asked. Sadly we could not; we were still waiting for Access to send us the required machine. What an anticlimax, we couldn't help seeing the funny side of it. Eventually we had 4 people in for lunch.

The evening was better, 9 for dinner, helped by **Sylvia** 'dragooning' some of her friends in to support our re-opening night. These included **Roy Ewing**, he brought some sound equipment, played his guitar and sang very well, we were impressed.

WEDNESDAY 7 October '81

A better day, Sylvia and her mother came in. **May** gave me a big bunch of blue and white Honesty from her garden. London family friend **Fred Hill** and his friend **Pepe** also had lunch.

Fred was the Estate Agent who had found us our house in Queens Park, London.

This increased in value and so enabled us to start this venture. Pepe, a business man, said he was sure we would be successful in time.

Time was what we didn't have - money was running out fast!

That evening only 2 in for dinner until just before closing when in walked **Ron** and **Joyce**, tenants of the Sussex Hotel just across the High Street from our Arcade. They had had a tough day. Two of their bar staff had gone sick. We were always pleased to see them but it was so late when they came, after they had closed themselves, and they stayed until the early hours of the morning. Ron said how quiet it is for them now Butlins is closed, he reckoned he was loosing £1,000 a week. Our minds reeled at the figure!

One of our biggest disappointments throughout our restaurant venture was the consistent mistakes made to our advertisements by the local newspaper at the time, not surprisingly no longer in business. We have kept the file as memorabilia interest but it was not much fun at the time.

The very first 'ad' for our 'Opening' left off our telephone number and the fact we were licensed.

Some time after when we employed **Peggy Cochrane** at the piano at night and **Roy Ewing** guitar, on another, the 'Live Music' copy was left off. Of course there was always an apology but the damage had been done.

In *October* –
We planned a special Halloween evening, changing the atmosphere by decorating the restaurant with Black Cats, Witches on broomsticks, etc., very professional actually.

Our friends **Manon** and **Ron Jeanes** came for the week-end and were a great help, handing out the leaflets we'd had printed, putting them on all the cars in the theatre car park, we really went to town'. Manon and I dressed up and put green make-up on our faces only to find it didn't show up enough under the restaurant lights. Wally said he had never seen such glamorous witches. Flatterer!

Tony Alexander and his friend **Dolly Woolf** came by train from London supporting us for the evening. We were all geared up for a good night but it fell flat.

After all our effort only a handful of friends came in. Darn it!

We just couldn't find the secret of filling the restaurant.

Our waitress **Liz Birch** asked if she could hold her 21st birthday party in Vanner's. Her parents were coming over from France and naturally it was our pleasure. Another cake to make and ice, seemed like old times.

Friday 6 November 81

The party was a huge success, what a lovely family, **Dad Harry**, **Mum Rita**, **Cathy** and **Sarah**.

According to my diary a wedding was to follow the next day and the groom and best man were in the party, but 'diary' doesn't mention the bride by name, was it also a 'Stag Night' party I ask myself all these years later?

During the evening **Mr. Jackson**, from the Estate Agents with whom we had put Vanner's up for sale, brought 2 prospective buyers to look round which could have upset the 'apple-cart'. At this early stage it wasn't practical to advertise we were thinking of selling, so we had to pretend they were looking for a venue for a function. We need not have bothered for nothing came of it.

Saturday 7th November '81

Mr. Jackson should have come either morning or evening today with his 2 clients and seen us at our best! I rushed around getting down to Vanner's, having washed the cloths, too tired the night before, and as Wally had taken the car I had to walk, collecting the French bread on the way.

We opened dead on 12.00 and customers came in straight away, - unusual to say the least.

Managed to get away home about 4.15 pm, - leaving some jobs but found time for a much needed rest. 6.20 pm soon came round and back to the grind.

Julie our evening waitress came in 6.45pm and **Peggy Cochrane** came in with 2 gentlemen friends **Patrick** and **Peter** at 6.50pm, perfect timing.

She looked marvellous as she walked to the bar - an escort on each arm - and when they ordered 2 crab, and a lobster dinner over drinks we got worried as we thought she was just going to sit and eat. Our worry was unfounded as she immediately went into her routine of superb piano playing and customer liaising and they actually ate later.

Other couples came in after this and had dinner.

Wally had to cook the meals and I served, Julie having gone home. Then we had to swop. Wally looked after the guests and I cleared up in the kitchen. They didn't leave until 3.00am and after switching every thing off we went at 3.20am leaving the clearing up.

What a day and a half!

Tuesday 24 November 81

Mylonie our cook was in this morning so things were a little easier. I still had to work hard as we had no waitress scheduled for the lunch time service, only for evening. We were going to see a London Transport Players' show, **"King's Rhapsody"**, at Wimbledon Theatre to see our friends.

I felt in an awful turmoil as we were waiting for news from Mr. **Jackson** of 'Stevens' our agents re selling 'Vanner's'.

It would have been wonderful to set off with good news that a sale was on. As it was, thinking of being back among all the familiar trappings of putting on a show and not being a part of it, surrounded by all our friends, filled me with trepidation.

During the morning I was close to tears on more than one occasion but we had every confidence in our staff who would 'man' the evening service.

We cleared up quickly from lunch, went home and changed. I so wanted something glamorous to wear but time and money was against me. Wally checked the car, oil, water, tyres etc., we set off at 3.50pm - a lovely day to get away from 'Vanners' and a change.

We were both very quiet - no doubt the worries under the surface having some part in that.

Approaching Dorking, the car suddenly developed a 'clonking' sound. I thought it might be a 'flat' tyre but when Wally pulled over found it wasn't. We were just past a small road so Wally quickly backed into it. A lady drove past and went into a house so we went and asked if we could use her phone to call the AA.

The car had to be towed away!

We were determined to get to Wimbledon so went by taxi, a terrible extravagance in the circumstances but it was the only way. A further disappointment was we were not in time to see our friends in the 'café' where they usually met for a pre-show meal.

We made the opening of the show, which was excellent and enjoyed.

Joe Putnam, a friend and leading actor, found out the last train back to Bognor Regis was 10.36 pm but the show ended at 11.00 pm! Joe insisted we go home to Clapham with him and **Peter Everleigh**, another friend and dancer/actor and stay with them overnight.

They made us so welcome; we sat up talking until 2.30am, mostly about our plight. Both were very sympathetic.

Wednesday 25 November '81

Joe brought us tea at 8.00 am, - it's nice to be pampered - and after breakfast drove us to Clapham Junction station. A change at East Croydon saw us on the Bognor train and we reached 'Vanner's' at 11.30am and found our trust in the staff fully justified, everything was spotless and in order for opening at 12.mid day.

With only 5 for lunch, after clearing up we walked home together and although cold it was dry. Still waiting for news from 'Stevens', agents, about our hoped for 'sale', I glanced at the paper and soon dropped off to sleep

I bustled about preparing for the evening session while Wally was looking at the Lada which had been my father's and which we kept for emergency use - but of course it wouldn't start. Like the last nut or screw, it never does, does it'? So we had to walk.

With only 7 in for dinner, it was a wearisome and seemingly long walk home.

Sunday 22.November '81 – My Birthday

Wally gave me cards in bed and a box of chocolates. My friend **Gwenda Huggett** phoned to wish me a happy birthday and it cheered me up no end.

Had a rush to get down to 'Vanner's' and had to work fast. I had all the table cloths to change, then I did the potatoes getting them on quickly for the roasts.

Liz Birch our waitress came in and when we were almost ready to open **Sue Boarer**, another of our waitresses, and her little girls **Sarah** and **Donna** came in with a card for me and a prettily iced birthday cake. Sue had made and iced it for me and I loved it.

Sunday lunch session over, we closed at 2.00 pm and sat down to our meal, Liz, **Andrew Rawlins** (who sometimes helped Wally in the kitchen) and us.

We had birthday cake for dessert washed down with a glass of wine. Wally then worked on the 'Sandwich Board' he is sign-writing for the 'Sussex Hotel', (later changed name to the 'William Hardwicke'). I got on with the clearing up.

We let Liz and Andrew go, we have to pay them if they stayed to help. There was a mountain of washing-up, food to put away and lastly I washed all the drying up cloths and hung them round the kitchen to dry.

It was 6.45 pm when we got home, Wally made coffee and we sat down exhausted. Later I got a meal while Wally worked on the books. Then I set about clearing up my kitchen, I had no time to wash up this morning. After that I ironed shirts, 11 table cloths and other things finishing at 12.30 am.

I have written this diary entry and it is now 12.40 am. Wally has just put his paperwork away.

Not a bad day's work on my 58th birthday.

How tragic that we are not even breaking even, but losing money.

I had experienced lots of stressful situations in my life – opening nights in some of the top-theatres in the country; dancing through the 'Blitz'; dancing 'close to the front lines' for E.N.S.A; hearing the sound of gunfire from the front often with the enemy a short distance away; laying prone in lorries rattling over wartime roads with a chronic back problem and then going on stage and dancing in agony; the stress in my first marriage; the severe loss in three pregnancies.

All these events had impacted on me but never had I experienced the despair I now felt at the financial plight we were getting into.

The losses we were making at Vanner's were using up all the capital we had from selling Wally's and my Home and all that we had earned in our lifetime. If things did not improve soon we would be broke – everything gone!

27th November, 1981 -

My diary entry reads -

"I feel quite finished, there is no way I can change the table cloths and re-lay the 15 tables. I feel quite done for; I am behind with everything, doubt if I have enough clean cloths for tomorrow evening.

All fight and strength has gone out of me, no matter how I try I just cannot continue to work like this. I am in a muddle at home, never get any cleaning done, never have time for my own shopping (tights etc.) only for the demon 'Vanner's'. I suppose I might somehow get through it if we were at least paying our way but all this only to lose money".

One thing which did help to keep us sane was the support from our friends. **Ray, Tony, Michael, Gwenda** and others who rang up from time to time. It was a great comfort to know we were not forgotten.

Monday, 30th November –

We didn't open on Mondays in line with other restaurants in the area.

Wally told me we had worked so hard cutting expenses, managing with the minimum of staff we had lost £80 less than usual.

We kept up the pretence of having no worries, Wally walked jauntily when out and whistled. I watched myself in shop windows to make sure I had a pleasant unworried face.

'Vanner's' has been 'on the market since the beginning of the month and now it is the last day of November and we have had no offers! It is heartbreaking! We had such high hopes and have worked so hard.

Tuesday 1st December 1981

Against all odds we manage quite well with just the two of us. Wally produces beautiful meals and everybody is pleased.

It was nice to know we were saving on paying a waitress but if just a few more people come in for lunch we would be in trouble. Wally really needs help in the kitchen and we run out of crocks if no washing up is done. We coped very well with 19 lunches, I was very proud of us.

We had a meal and then the phone rang, a man wanted to come and see 'Vanner's' tomorrow.

Unbelievable!

Wednesday 2nd December

Worked very hard at 'Vanner's', made soup, gravy, and custard but no time to do bread and butter puddings.

Surprisingly we had a very busy lunch time, coped although we were stretched to the limit. The thought of a prospective buyer coming to view helped us through.

We had our meal and then slowly began to clear up, let him see we had been busy.

After the crocks were done I left the pots and pans to Wally and began re-laying the tables. I looked at my watch, he was late. I could feel myself growing numb, he wasn't going to come.

Wally came out of the kitchen, *'He's not coming is he?'* he said. *"Oh dear God was I wrong to feel worthy of having my prayers answered?"*

I can't see how we are going to survive, mentally, physically or financially.

I continued to feel numb for the rest of the day which was a blessing. "*I will think about it tomorrow*", I thought, like Scarlet O'Hara in "Gone with the Wind".

One morning a man came into the restaurant while we were preparing before opening for lunch. He said he was from Chichester Crown Court. My mind raced

I thought, *"What had either of us done now?"* We had overlooked paying a Performing Rights bill and will be sued.

When I thought of paying Peggy Cochrane and Roy Ewing to play and getting so few customers and now we have to pay a fine I broke down there and then and cried bitterly. Through my tears I felt so sorry for the man, it wasn't his fault.

"Oh! Dear" he said, *"When I came in I thought how cheerful you looked'.*

I said *"We are normally cheerful people but we are going through a hard time."*

Poor Wally was in the middle of making pastry for pies and he got emotional too.

The man was sympathetic but we still had to pay the fine.

A New Recruit

Our Christmas break had done us good physically and even mentally up to a point.

January was a 'down' period for all catering outlets in Bognor Regis apparently, but we did manage to celebrate Wally's 52nd birthday at the end of February in style, as we always try to do with our birthdays, as opposed to my 58th.

Our bar was at the back of the restaurant facing the door. One morning in early March I was tidying up, making everything ready before we opened when a young girl came in. She walked the 10 metres or so up to me and asked for a job. We were not employing any staff by now and I knew we could not afford her but I was so impressed by her appearance and the way she walked straight up to me I took **Melanie**, (not to be confused with our ex cook **Mylonie**), into the kitchen to Wally and we took her on for a few hours here and there.

It proved a good move for although only 15, Melanie was reliable and helpful. Seeing her unusually flustered one lunch time I asked her what was wrong? Nothing was, the couple Melanie was serving were her parents on a surprise visit. They came to check out 'Vanner's' and us. I smiled, just what my Mum and Dad would have done.

The End of a Dream

When despair was at its worse – hope came in the shape of a prospective buyer. Our financial plight was desperate and we were kept on tenterhooks until the last minute. If contracts were not signed before the end of April we had to pay another month's rent.

The signing happened at 5.00 pm on the 30th March. We had 2 days to pack up.

Melanie and I took down all our nick-knacks and decorations and packed them in boxes, it was a heart-breaking job and I was glad of this cheerful youngster's help.

Saturday and Sunday was spent in packing everything else away and transporting it all to our house. Then we gave Melanie a well deserved 'excellent' reference for when she was old enough to go to college which was her intention.

We met the new owner at 'Vanner's' on Monday, 3rd May at 9.30am as arranged.

Men were already there pulling the place apart. A worker said *"Your things are over there"*, pointing to a cardigan and shoes on a table. I felt very emotional it was all happening so quickly

I now had mixed feelings, 'Vanner's' was very much 'our' place, we had made it really attractive and always kept in perfect order.

There was the sadness at seeing –

'The End'

Wally and I felt a great sense of relief at selling 'Vanner's' but at our age where on earth is life going to lead us now?

We looked at each other and both pondered –

"What on earth do we do now?"

After 'Vanner's'

So 3rd May 1982 was our 'Dunkirk'.

'Vanner's' was sold and we had escaped by the skin of our teeth!

We were sitting at home looking all around us at boxes and belongings everywhere; licking our wounds.

Were we planning our next foray into the big wide world of business? You must be joking! Licking our wounds, certainly, but I was mentally, numb whilst counting the cost!

Our first thought was of course how quickly we could return to London and be among family and friends but with only the money from the sale of the restaurant lease, less the fees, outstanding gas, electric, rates, water and suppliers accounts to settle, even the sale of our home in Bognor would be nowhere near enough to buy in London again.

The economic collapse in the early 1980s which had destroyed some 1,700 businesses on the South Coast alone meant few people were being taken on, even if at 52 (Wally) and 58 (me) we could have found suitable jobs for which we were capable

The people who took over from us were the franchisees of the 'Wimpy Bar' at the entrance of the Arcade.

That operation functioned for a number of years. Since when the site has been a dress shop, bespoke tailors, a sea-side trinket shop etc.

When we cleared 'Vanner's' we had brought a freezer home from the restaurant, which we had brought from London. It was full of a number of our best selling dishes,

- Scampi Newburg,
- Salmon en Croute,
- Hot-Pot,
- Goulash,

- together with a lot of cooked rice and steaks, beef, pork and lamb joints which had not been cooked the week-end of our exit and had to be frozen.

The new owners did not need them so for a short time we were living like Royalty.

Then disaster struck once more, doesn't it always?

That freezer 'packed up' leaving us with the dilemma, do we lose about £200 worth of food or do we buy another freezer which we could not sensibly afford?

We chose the latter, bought a second hand one and continued with the 'high life' in the eating stakes.

As our plight caught up with reality, at one very low point we even flirted with the idea of selling everything, taking a long world cruise and quietly slip out of sight.

Despair, I have found out on more than one occasion, plays havoc with the mind.

I'm pleased to say I am here to tell the tale.

One Door Closes - others Open!

It was not easy to claim any kind of benefit support as you can today although a concession of postponing payment of the interest on our mortgage was very helpful. What on earth are we going to do for a living? Most of our capital is gone – we need to work!

Wally did manage to do a little work for cousin **Fred Stevens** as a bookmaker's clerk but to our relief I was asked to work as Caretaker, Cleaner and Room Letting Officer for our Church, the United Reformed Church and Wally helped me when he could.

Towards the beginning of 1983 our friends **Alan 'Chappie' Shave,** ex Chief Supplies Officer, London Transport, for whom I had worked, and his wife **Evelyn,** suggested that Wally take up the Government's scheme for starting Small Businesses, that had been introduced. An allowance of £40 per week was given but no other unemployment benefits, which we had by now.

Wally was already a natural sign-writer but not experienced. The snag was you had to show you had £1,000 to start. We did not have that much but Alan and Evelyn gave us a 'no interest' loan of £1,000 repayable as and when we could. Good friends!

Wally took the 'Business Course' and commenced sign-writing but competition was strong. Also being in his fifties he was rather slow. The sign-writer who we had to do Vanner's, **Steve Goodheart**, was very helpful though, telling Wally where to get supplies and teaching him to apply gold leaf and gilding. They actually worked together on a couple of jobs.

Steve heads one of the prominent sign companies in Bognor now but Wally had to give up when his eyesight deteriorated.

Part of my Church job was to set out the tables and chairs ready for the users. We soon learned the various patterns needed. It was hard work as some of the tables were the heavy wooden trestle ones some 10 feet long.

On good terms with all the clubs, Blind, Over 55's, Art Club, etc., when filming subsequently came along we asked the Badminton Club to put out tables and chairs for the over 55's before they went home and so on. They all helped each other in my absence. Came the Christmas we were invited to all their parties and had a great time.

The Clowns International is held at Bognor Regis. It is a marvellous event and brings enjoyment to a huge number of people and, as can be seen from our participation below, much needed cheer to my Clown husband Wally and me.

We were still battling but a slight upturn was to come when friend **Sylvia** met the actress **Iris Terry,** known to us as **Tanya**, and her actor husband **Edward Brandon.**

They were semi-retired and *doing a little film 'extra' work*. Sylvia got the names of their agents, - we sent photographs and CVs to both and were put on their books.

Tanya was a descendant of the "Terry" family, show biz legends. Her mother was **Vesta Victoria** the music hail 'star' - the top English performer on 'Broadway' in New York from 1890s thru' 1920s! She was said, by some to have earned a £4,000,000 fortune. Tanya unfortunately did not inherit it.

I was hoping to sing "Poor John" ('John took me round to see his mother') in a revue with our Church group but I had lost the music and could not buy another. I was driving Tanya somewhere and said, "I suppose you don't have the music to "Poor John".

Her reply gave me a tingle down my spine. *"That song was written by my uncle for my mother* she said.

I knew Vesta Victoria sang "Waiting at the Church" and "Daddy wouldn't buy me a Bow-WoW', but I didn't know about "Poor John".

God moving in a mysterious way

The **United Reformed Church** in Linden Road Bognor Regis, had a very thriving theatre group, The **Linden Players**, putting on pantomimes, plays and revues. Our London friend **Peggie Dean** had told me about her friend **Peter Morgan** who produced the shows, the pantomimes written by him including all the songs and music.

This had sunk to the back of my mind when we moved to Bognor Regis to open "Vanner's" restaurant.

Later after we had sold the restaurant, Peggie came to stay with us, she introduced us to Peter. This led to Wally being asked to produce a play for Linden Players.

Peter and his Italian wife Angela were going to Italy for 3 months so he was unable to produce the play,

'Idea for a Play' by Richard Tydeman.

It was quite a tall order for Wally as the roles had already been cast and he didn't know the people or the play. What a lucky break it was for us. We were soon part of a warm, happy group of people. There was no dancing for me to do so I took on the role of prompt.

The play successfully over we started finding our way to Church on Sundays. Having been married in the Congregational Church the year before the United Reformed Church was formed, by the uniting of Congregational and Presbyterian ideals, this was quite natural, but the warm welcome we received was exceptional. Our worries were still ever present as we searched for a way to earn enough to save our home.

The Church came to our rescue when making me Caretaker (Cleaner) and Room Letting Officer.

As well as the Church Sanctuary and large Church Hall there were 4 other rooms, a kitchen a garden and grass surrounds needing care and attention.

The lavatories were antiquated with part of the gents open to all the elements. Certainly not an easy job for me even though Wally did help when he could, but it did keep our heads above water - just!

'My Favourite Role'

When **Angela** and **Peter** moved to Minehead, Somerset, it seemed as if it would be the end of

Linden Players until someone suggested Wally might produce one of Peter's pantomimes,

The Church Hall boasted an excellent stage and there was a wonderful 'wardrobe' of costumes designed and mostly made by **Sheila Gibbons** (now a good friend and my Yoga teacher).

'Sleeping Beauty'

was the pantomime chosen and we were flung into the wonderful world of show rehearsals once again.

Auditions were held and I landed the part of "Fairy Toogood", the Fairy godmother, a role I love as I get to say *"All will be Well"*.

Out came the pointe shoes again and at the age of 60 I made all my entrances on pointe and danced in the ballet.

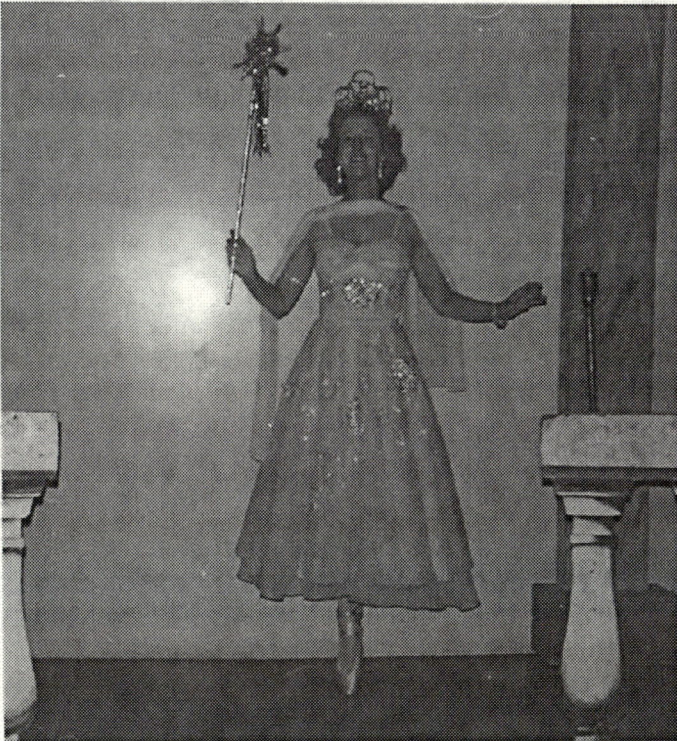

It was marvellous to see how the church congregation and friends all turned to, from painting scenery and backcloths, manning the door, selling programmes and the other numerous tasks needed, even serving tea and biscuits in the interval. The whole place buzzed with activity.

I had a few problems teaching dances to the children, as you would expect especially the boys. With help from the 'Principal Boy', **Christine Simpson**, we managed.

Sheila Gibbons, our wardrobe mistress, produced magnificent costumes for the principals and the large chorus.

It was wonderful how all the church members pitched in during the six performances making a behind the scenes team second to none, even to serving 'cuppas' and cakes to the packed audiences during the intervals - yes they were sell-outs.

I was 60 by now and had a photo and 'spread' in the local paper

'No Retirement for this Fairy Queen'.

As we took our bows at the end of each show I couldn't help thinking to myself -

"I bet I am the only Fairy Queen who will be cleaning the toilets in the morning instead of waving my fairy wand".

Keep Dancing!

As this book reveals - my interest in dancing started at a very early age. I was on stage as a professional dancer at the Hackney Empire and the Shepherd's Bush Empire when I was just 14 years old.

That interest has been with me throughout my life and I really have danced through Life!

One of my latest episodes was at my husband Wally's choir 'dinner' in December 2006 held in our own U.R.C. Church Small Hall.

An entertainment spot after dinner by members of the choir has become a tradition.

I was asked by Wally to fill such a spot, after a 3 - course Christmas dinner, with a 'tap' routine. Wally had said *"don't worry; I'll put you in at no.7 to let your dinner go down'.*

Still dancing at the age of 83 and still thoroughly enjoying doing so!

'Qualifications!'

I have mentioned elsewhere my dancing teacher **Flavia Galli** didn't enter her pupils for examinations.

Fortunately for me qualifications were not called for at professional auditions, only ability.

For over 7 years before and during the war I had earned my living as a professional dancer working at the London Palladium, several other London theatres and touring around the country with various shows.

I had three summer seasons at the Opera House Theatre, Blackpool, the number one 'out of London' venue.

War work with E.N.S.A. meant dancing in North Africa, Italy, Belgium, Holland and Germany.

Aged 36 with my professional career behind me, I joined an amateur Operatic Society as a dancer. Shows were performed at the Scala Theatre, London, the traditional home of J.M. Barrie's Peter Pan', until it was pulled down.

Our company moved to the Wimbledon Theatre, in 1969, our first production being 'Belle of New York', in which I was the lead dancer as Kissie Fitzgarter,

Forward to 1982, now living in Bognor Regis and running our restaurant 'Vanners' with my husband Wally.

I and a young neighbour joined a tap-dancing class. In July of that year I took Grade 1 and Grade 2 examinations in American Tap-Dancing.

As the certificates show I passed with honours - not bad for a 59 year old!

Glorious 60th

When **Fred Hill** - an old family friend left me a little money in his will I knew exactly what to spend it on – petrol.

Since moving to Bognor Regis in 1981 I missed dancing in 2 musical shows a year at Wimbledon Theatre with London Transport Players amateur operatic society. I just longed to be dancing again.

Oscar Hammerstein II and Jerome Kern's

'Show Boat'

- is a show full of dancing and singing and when I heard opening night would be my big "0" birthday I was determined to be there.

What could be more exciting than tapping, high-kicking and singing on Wimbledon Theatre stage as I reached 60 years of age?

I drove from Bognor Regis to London for rehearsals once a week at first then twice a week as the show got nearer.

I usually drove back each night but if there was a November fog about stayed with fellow dancer **Charles Lowe** in Clapham returning home the next morning. Come show week husband Wally joined me staying at Charles' flat.

What a wonderful week!

I had, 'pressies' and flowers every day as the company gradually heard about my birthday.

The new friends we had made, in the United Reformed Church we joined in Bognor, hired a coach and 35 came to the Saturday matinee.

Lucky me, even if my 'cover' had been blown to the rest of the dancing troupe, to many of whom I could have been mother and even grandmother.

Thank you Fred!

WALLY drops a BOMBSHELL

We were staying with Wally's mum in Canning Town, London, for the wedding of Wally's niece **Denise** to **Alan Shepherd**.

A beautiful bride and bridesmaids, handsome groom and all the family present added up to a very happy day.

January 12th 1986 (the next morning)

When I woke up, Wally told me he was going into hospital the following Friday for a major operation for a malignant growth in the bowel.

I was utterly shocked;

(a) He appeared perfectly fit,

(b) How could he have attended hospital appointments without me knowing?

(c) How did my chatter-box Wally keep such a serious thing to himself?

He was determined not to put a damper on his niece's wedding and had even postponed the operation until afterwards.

The original date he was given was 10th January, the day before the wedding.

Why did I not pick up the 'vibes' and notice there was something wrong with Wally? Well I did in one way but put it down to the effort to keep up the mortgage payments on our house and the constant worry that we might lose everything.

I duly delivered Wally to hospital the following Friday and went home lonely, upset and worried.

True to form Wally settled into hospital life, the nurses and doctors gave excellent care and his fellow patients, all suffering with similar ailments, were a cheery lot. My vigil started with the afternoon visit from 2.00pm to 5.00pm then I ate my tea in the car, before going back 6.00pm to 8.00pm.

The support I had from my church friends, family and our other friends was marvelous and really carried me through. The telephone rang all morning with local friends and all evening, once I was home, from further afield friends and family.

Wally himself sailed through the operation, never complaining and visits both for me and friends were easy. He has always said the warmth and support he felt surrounding him was a physically real one. The daily 'Get Well' cards he received from our friends **Tony** & **Colin**, usually humorous, were eagerly looked forward to by the rest of his ward and the nurses. He even received one from their poodle Sacha.

The day before Wally came home, he asked me to take in some Guinness stout, crisps and party bits, they were going to have a ward Party, it was allowed then.

I was ready to cosset my invalid but his recovery was amazing, helped by Tony and Colin inviting us to their home for convalescence.

Wally had auditioned for the part of Alfie Doolittle in
'My Fair Lady'
for London Transport Players,
- a part he had longed to do. With his operation intervening he was afraid he would lose the part. He told the producer but implied the operation was not serious, he wouldn't be absent for long.

Wally complied with doctor's orders to the letter, no lifting; no driving etc. consequently his recovery went really well. Oh and he was wonderful as 'Doolittle'.

I got to play the **Queen** who only walks on says *"Charming"*, *"Charming"*, and walks off. I did have a super bejeweled costume though.

Wally was monitored very carefully by our -
St Richard's Hospital, Chichester
- with regular colonoscopy tests gradually getting further apart until in the year 2000 he was given the 'all clear'.

We cannot thank enough our G.P. at the time -
Dr. Bond, who diagnosed the problem so promptly, **Mr. Ashby**, the consultant/surgeon and his team at St. Richard's Hospital, the **nurses** and **auxiliary staff** and all our concerned family and friends for what has been a further 20 years plus together.

Does that sound like a speech at the 'Oscars'?

Getting my Wally back fit and well - I felt I had won the 'Prize'.

P.A.M.
Physical Activity to Music

On hearing that our local District Council was planning a training course for teaching Movement to Music - I applied.

After an interview I was asked to do a few exercises but fought the temptation to do a couple of cart-wheels and the splits. I was accepted for the course although aged 65.

Then came the bad news - the six months course cost £85.

Commiserating with friends, for I couldn't afford the £85 after the loss of Vanners, **Beryl English,** a church friend who ran a Nursery School at our Church premises said *"Come and work for me and earn the money."*

Although at first it was a means to an end I loved working with the little children, 3 to 5 years old, and stayed until Beryl completed 50 years of teaching, here and abroad, and retired in 1994.

The course was called –

Physical Activities to Music, dubbed **PAM.**

Having left my elementary school two weeks after my 14th birthday it was a shock to find myself studying Anatomy and Physiology and writing essays. Learning how to plan classes I did expect but it still came hard working out charts and depicting exercises with match-stick people.

To obtain the First Aid Certificate I needed I enrolled for a **St. John Ambulance** course.

Next step was to start my own class.

Husband Wally suggested the name **Musifit** and designed posters to advertise.

As a member of the United Reformed Church in Bognor Regis, I was given a favourable rate when booking the Church Hall.

I was terribly nervous, for with all my theatre experience I still had little self confidence off the stage.

I'm pleased to say since doing talks in later years on a number of subjects I have gained in that respect.

Most nerve racking was having my **PAM** instructor sitting in on a class, for a final competence certificate was not issued until examiners had seen a teacher in action.

Getting more comfortable as a teacher I decided to add Relaxation as an addition to the normal class work. *"What if they all lay there rigid"* I thought to myself but went through my relaxation routine in a gentle voice. All seemed well but just as I stopped worrying the comedian of the class gave a loud theatrical 'snore'. To my horror all the heads popped up. *"Now you can all just lie down again"* I said, and they did.

Another time I had the class all relaxed but when I started with "*Now gently open your eyes*" no one moved. I continued *"have a good stretch"*, nothing! I was completely 'thrown', they can't all have gone to sleep I thought. It was then I noticed a certain person laughing - I had been 'set up'!

When my PAM instructor came a second time to watch me I was more confident and passed the test.

I was very proud when presented with my PAM Certificate and although I gave up teaching some years ago I remain friends with a number of my class which includes my helpful friend Beryl and we meet for coffee or a meal for birthdays.

Barbara's maiden Talk

When I was asked to give a talk to our church fellowship meeting my instinct was to say no. I had rarely spoken of my adventures dancing with E.N.S.A. (Entertainment National Service Association) during World War II and certainly never thought of giving a talk on that, or any other subject. However, with a little persuasion, I agreed.

When I asked how long I would be expected to speak and was told *"Twenty minutes"*, I replied *"Oh, I don't think I could do it in only 20 minutes"*.

Mary, the fellowship secretary said *"That's a long time to talk you know "*. I looked through the diaries I had kept during the war and put a talk together.

Came the day I was naturally very nervous and worried that I would only get half way through when 20 minutes were up so I talked very quickly. They obviously liked it for I wasn't stopped after 20 minutes and completed my talk, of almost 40 minutes.

There were even numerous further questions asked. Some time later when the subject came up Mary said *"I could tell you were nervous because you spoke so quickly "*. I feel I answered in my own way as I was booked to give a further talk, ENSA part 2, with all the extra material I still had unspoken.

I have since added to my repertoire with talks on Television film work, dancing in shows at major London and Blackpool Theatres, as well as touring and even Cake Decorating (successes and near disasters I have known). The fees I get for talking are always most welcome!

I really look forward to giving talks now that my book has been published. Please contact my publisher TwigBooks (details on page 2) if you would like me to talk to your group.

REG BUNDY
('Regina Fong')

I first met Reg Bundy in 1963 when he joined The London Transport Players, amateur operatic society.

He was young and starting out as a dancer. I was not so young, having retired from my career as a professional dancer some years before.

The first show Reg appeared in was
'Brigadoon'
- at the **Scala Theatre, London**
(also a first for our dear friend **Jimmy Lynch** and for **Wally Vanner** who some years later became my second husband).

Reg had a wonderful temperament and willingness to learn but at that time had no dancing experience. Our producer **Bertha Peek** appointed Reg to 'lead in' one of the Clans in the 'Entrance of the Clans'. Reg invariably set off on the wrong foot during rehearsals but thankfully 'got it right on the night'.

Reg was looking for lodgings at that time so he could do as many amateur shows as possible and audition for the professional theatre when the chance occurred. For a while he slept at the back of a lock-up shop that sold items that had been collected each day in the 'house clearances' the owner had undertaken.

It was late at night when he got back to the shop after working all day and rehearsing all evening. Reg never knew what he would be sleeping on.

The bed he used the previous night may well have been sold during the day and with no lighting available to see clearly he would 'kip-down' on anything that was soft and available.

Reg would almost immediately drop off to sleep but would awake in the night and stumble to the toilet over all kinds of furniture, stuffed animals, and so on.

He told the hilarious story of waking up one night to jump out of his skin as he found himself face to face with a skeleton, and of another when a giant lifelike stuffed bear seemed to be coming for him.

. The next London Transport Players production was
'Call Me Madam'
and Bertha the Producer made Reg and I partners.

Reg had a great sense of humour, we had so much fun at rehearsals, sometimes doubled up with laughter I like to think the help and encouragement I gave him contributed to Reg finding his feet as a dancer and then going on to become a wonderful entertainer

He did six shows with us. I was grateful for his strength and timing when he hoisted me aloft as the Princess Samaris in

'Kismet'
also at the Scala.

In my capacity as 'Cakemaker' to friends and family, I made him a cake with a big 'Star' emblazoned on the top when he got his first professional job.

Little did I know then how prophetic that was to be. The next summer Reg was in the

'Rolf Harris Show'
in **Yarmouth**, Norfolk

I went with a party of his 'London Transport Players' friends to support him, enjoying a week-end by the sea as well as swelling the Saturday night audience.

Reg landed a super dancing role in the film

'Oh What a Lovely War'.

In 1992 a number of us ex-dancers decided to form an annual "Bertha's Tuesday Class" reunion.

Reg by now was a star in his persona as –

'Regina Fong'

- but found time in his busy schedule one man shows and occasional acting parts to come back and visit his old mates.

His arrival at our reunion was typical Reg Bundy!

Full of smiles and a body language that exuded fun and joy Reg greeted us with –

"Hi folks, have you heard about my hysterectomy?"

It seems that Reg was playing in the pro version of

'Fiddler on the Roof'
in the West End of London
with **Alfie Bass** in the lead

- when Reg was carted off to hospital with severe abdominal pains. The hospital diagnosed acute appendicitis and operated immediately.

Next morning a groggy Reg woke up and almost immediately discharged himself from hospital so that he could get back into 'Fiddler' without delay.

The hospital warned him against it but he was insistent so they made him promise that he would go straight round to his doctor's surgery and let them know that he had just had an Appendectomy operation and that he would need the stitches removed.

Still groggy Reg got to his doctors surgery and reported his operation and the need to have the stitches out in a few days.

The Doctor's receptionist on booking him asked – *"Tell me Mr Bundy what operation did you have?"*

Reg – (making what I think was an 'innocent' mistake') *"I had a Hysterectomy".*

There was an uncanny silence from all the staff and people in the waiting room. The receptionist repeated the question.

*"I'm sorry **MR** Bundy, what did you say you had?"*

"A Hysterectomy' replied Reg in all innocence.

The staff and some of the patients were stifling giggles.

"What's wrong?" asks Reg.

"Well," said the receptionist *"you do realize Mr Bundy you won't ever be able to bear children!"*

Collapse of entire waiting room including Reg in peals of laughter.

Reg really was a super character and a joy to know.

'Regina Fong'-
Reg Bundy's Stage Persona

Sir Ian McKellen one of Britain's greatest actors described **Reg Bundy's** performances as **'Regina Fong'** as

'Scourge of the 'naughty boys' in the front row"
- at the 'Black Cap' pub in Camden Town, London, where he reigned supreme".

Sir Ian placed **Reg** in the 'Top Ten' of female impersonators, along with the likes of –
- Barry Humphries (Dame Edna Everidge),
- Les Dawson and
- Roy Barraclough,
- Danny la Rue, and
- Paul O'Grady (Lily Savage).

It was so sad when we read in 'The Times' Obituary columns that Reg had joined the 'Great Producer in the Sky',

Reg was a naturally funny young man who is missed by all whom he befriended.

A DANCING LIFE

I was just 14 when I danced in my first professional show; the pantomime

'Babes in the Wood'

at **Shepherd's Bush Empire** now B.B.C. Television studios; and at **Hackney Empire**,

- recently brought back to it's former glory and featured by **Griff Rees-Jones** on television.

I little knew what lay in store for me, the colour and excitement dancing would bring to my life; the interesting people and 'stars' I'd meet and work with, wonderful and sometimes bizarre variety of costumes and the many different dances to be learned for each show.

So many places visited while touring in this country and the many adventures I would have during World War II as a member of **E.N.S.A.** (Entertainments National Service Association) touring North Africa, Italy, Belgium, Holland and Germany entertaining the armed forces.

Then the equally wonderful dances and costumes when I later joined amateur companies, principal among which was the London Transport Players, a recreational arm of the old London Transport organisation which ran London's buses and the underground system.

A bonus was making life long friends and meeting my husband Wally.

In my professional days it was hard to keep in touch with other dancers. After rehearsing, working, and on tour living together, when the show ended we mostly went into different shows and eventually lost contact.

Sylvia Victor is the exception - first meeting in **'No, No Nanette'** - in 1943, we were out of touch at times and then our paths would cross again. Now we both live in Bognor Regis.

Sylvia and I could never have imagined that in our late 70's we would audition for and land a job dancing in - **'The All New Harry Hill Show'** - a series of six shows screened on ITV Channel 4

Then after three auditions I was being flown to **Barcelona** to "jive" in a 'Commercial' for the **J.Walter-Thompson Agency**! Incredible!

Who would have thought I would still be 'tapping' away in my 80's? Mostly on the kitchen floor I admit, although I did do a tap dancing 'turn' for Wally's Choir when 83 years old and I still love doing it.

Lucky, lucky me - doing what I love most has given me an amazing and very full life.

In ENSA uniform (1945)

With Audrey on Tommy and Teddy's jeep in Germany (1945)

ENSA ENTERTAINMENTS

PRESENT

(By Arrangement with Jack Hylton)

CYRIL RITCHARD & MADGE ELLIOTT

In

" THE MERRY WIDOW "

with

MARK DALY and full London Company,

Lyrics by ADRIAN ROSS — Music by FRANZ LEHAR

THE CAST

Viconte Camille de Jolidon	JOHN LERA
Marquis de Cascada	BRIAN FAUBERT
M. de St. Brioche	ARTHUR GLEIM
General Novikovich. (Military Attaché) .	JOHN PYGRAM
M. Khadja (Counsellor of Legation) . .	WILLIAM MARCH
Nisch (Messenger to the Legation) . . .	JACK GORDON
Waiter at Maxim's	RAY CAREY
Prince Danilo (Secretary of Legation) . .	CYRIL RITCHARD
Baron Popoff (Marsovian Ambass. in Paris)	MARK DALY
Natalie (Wife of Popoff)	GEORGINA
Olga (Wife of Novikovich)	EDWINA MAY
Sylvaine (Wife of Khadja)	PAMELA JENKINS
Frou - Frou } Girls at Maxim's. .	DIANA GOULD
Lo - Lo	EILEEN HUNTER
Sonia (The Merry Widow)	MADGE ELLIOTT

As performed for the troops in Naples (1944)

As Adelaide Adams in "Calamity Jane" -
LT Players (1977)

As the Queen of
Transylvania in
"My Fair Lady" -
LT Players ((1986)

As a maid who has been at the
sherry! in "Me and My Girl" -
LT Players (1965)

As Kissy Fitzgarter in
"Belle of New York" -
LT Players (1969)

Backstage at Wimbledon Theatre
- age 49 (1969)

A scene from "The Quaker Girl" -
LT Players (1968)

Backstage with husband Wally

With dear friend Ray Bloomfield
In "Bitter Sweet" - LT Players
(1979)

Playing the back end of the bull in "Viva Mexico" -
Beaumont Players (1976)

Our wedding cake (1971)

The beaded ball gown -

and   the birthday cake I made for
myself at my mothers request

Barbara!

With husband Wally outside "Vanners" - our restaurant in Bognor Regis

At the bar in "Vanners" - Peggy Cochrane is on the left

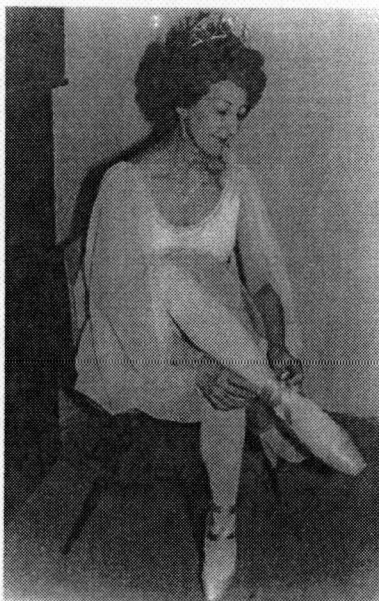

Preparing to weave my fairy magic in "Sleeping Beauty" - Linden Players (1984)

En pointe putting everyone to sleep in "Sleeping Beauty" - Linden Players (1984)

Barbara!

Fixing my tiara before
going on stage to deliver
the happy ending in
"Sleeping Beauty" -
Linden Players (1984)

A couple of publicity shots to send to
agents

Filming John Osborne's "Too Young
To Fight Too Old To Forget" (1984)

In the garden of Wilton House filming
"Mozart" for "Musical Prodigies" -
a TVS series (1988)

With Iris Terry (Tanya) filming
"Howard's Way" (1988)

Aged 78 and dressed as a canary in the
"All New Harry Hill TV Show"

In the middle of Harry Hill's
"Sevenoaks Cerardiac Arrest
Rehabilit ation Centre" dancersl

With Harry Hill and my dear friend Sylvia

Dear ~~Barbara~~,
    Thanks for doing the show with
such great enthusiasm. I hope
you're not too exhausted – there's
    another one next year –
So I hope you'll be able to take
    part.
            love Harry

The card Harry sent me (Sadly the next series didn't happen)

With husband Wally in our Bognor Regis church

Wearing my medals at a
VE anniversaryParty
(1995)

Here I am with Tony, Colin, Jill, Terry (seated) and labrador Saffron's 11 puppies

At the 75th anniversary party of Actors Equity - National Theatre (2006)

Barbara!

A qizzical me in the late 1990's

Barbara 1980 to date

Life as an 'Extra'

The loss of VANNER'S left us looking at a very bleak financial future. Our capital had been tied up in the venture and was now gone; how were we going to pay our way through our older years.

Although I had enjoyed my 'Glorious 60' I still felt young at heart and willing to meet new challenges if only they would present themselves! Then along came the opportunity to become an 'extra' in a TV production.

These days 'Extras' are called background or supporting artistes.

When leading actors are in bars, restaurants, getting out of cars, trains, buses etc., in shops, with shop assistants or other customers, we are the other people.

Colloquially we term ourselves **'the wallpaper'**, missed if we are not there but seldom noticed if we are.

HIGHS & LOWS

Since then I have filmed in –

- Goodwood House,
- Goodwood Race Course,
- Wilton House,
- several other large houses,
- the Albert Hall,
- The Guards Polo Club in Windsor Great Park,
- The Ascot Sales Ring,
- Next to a Hot Air Balloon while it inflated and was then taken up,
- Sat in a German Junkers 52 airplane,
- leant how to play Roulette and Black-jack
- Hours up and down on Owen-Owens escalator,
- worked with Rotweiler dogs,
- the Royal family look-alikes,
- Horses in riot gear,
- Richmond Theatre,
- Arcade Bognor Regis,
- driven my car with a hundred others forming 'a traffic jam', (scary!)
- Worked all night in a Supermarket, (not recommended).
-

And many, many more!

To give a small flavour, appearances include –

- 6 Weddings and 7 Funerals,(no not with **Hugh Grant**)
- 3 'Ruth Rendell' Mysteries,
- 4 Agatha Christie,
- 4 'Only Fools & Horses',
- 6 'Howard's Way',
- 3 'One foot in the Grave'
- etc., etc.

Costume styles as well as period
- 17th, 18th and 19th centuries
- 1920's, '30's, 40's, 50's, 60's, 70's, 80's,
- look like a 50 year-old, 60, 70 and 80 (not difficult).

When you are 'booked' as an 'Extra' the agent will give the location, name of programme, and a vague idea of the scene.

Wardrobe instructions range from –
- 'Full Evening dress and jewels' to
- 'Old Casual',
- once 'Uncombed Hair' for a football match crowd.

It is not easy to know exactly what is meant by
- 'Up market Casual' or
- 'Smart Suit',
- 'Not too Fashionable',

when no colour or style is mentioned.

Comfort is very much in mind and weather.

A chilly morning can become a very hot day and return to chilly come evening.

Mostly we have to remain in the same clothes throughout. Simply wearing plenty underneath to be removed and replaced as necessary is not always practical with so many looking on.

It is then 'grin and bear it' time.

We meet people filming who we never see at any other time, living as we do in locations far apart.

Over the years however we have come to know each others families as photographs and news is exchanged.

It is like stepping into another life.

My first job was easy. It was –

"POTTER"
starring **Robin Bailey**.

We just sat comfortably in a small country Church.

A break out in the sunshine for coffee and biscuits and then by lunch time we were finished.

An experienced friend said *"Don't expect them all to be so easy"*. Years and many jobs later I know what he meant.

'TALES OF THE UNEXPECTED'
Roald Dahl
('A Sad Loss' starring **Haley Mills**)

This was only my second television job and we had 3 days on it. The venue was a lovely big house in Hampshire so not a lot of traveling.

Its main feature was a large swimming pool which we had to lay around on loungers, occasionally shifting, pretending to drink fancy Pimm's type drinks.

"Cushtie", as Del- boy Trotter would say you may think!

It was wonderfully sunny and mostly pleasant but having to stay put at the hottest part of the day with the sun beating down, - not so comfortable.

We costumed ourselves so had to take a number of outfits for wardrobe to check.

Looking out over the Solent off Southampton, seeing the large liners moving in and out was a bonus.

I'm sure the thought must have crossed my mind - *"This 'extra' life's not all bad "*

'TRAINER'

Set in the world of professional horse racing, mixing with owners, jockeys and trainers - gave me the opportunity to experience the Sales Ring at **Ascot** with horses being auctioned just for the story.

We also filmed a further episode at the lovely race course at **Goodwood** - again not far to travel from home.

There I met **Anthea Askey**, daughter of **Arthur Askey** with whom I had worked in -
'Band Waggon'"
at the London Palladium

I also appeared with 'big hearted Arthur' in a summer season in Blackpool at the Opera House Theatre; also in -   **'Jack and Jill'**   - Pantomime
at the Palace Theatre, (Christmas1940/41)

and again in   **'Jack and Jill'** the following year
at His (now Her) Majesty's Theatre.

Sadly by now Arthur had died. Speaking to her about her Dad she told me not long before he died he'd said
"Oh, I do miss Fairy Land,"
- meaning 'Theatre' in general.

Anthea was with her husband **Will Fyfe, Jnr.**, son of the great Scottish comedian and actor, a real favourite of my own Scottish father.

'CAMPIAN'

Filmed at the Richmond Theatre, **Brighton** we were costumed in 1930's style evening dress and given stockings and suspender belts to wear;
"But we are wearing long dresses, our comfortable tights won't show" we pleaded.

Wardrobe would have none of it *"You will walk differently in stockings"* they insisted.

It was a night 'call', fortunately a fine one as I found I was to be a lady arriving at the Theatre, not settled sitting in the auditorium as I expected.

Over and over again I, with my escort, had to go away from the theatre and then be filmed 'arriving'.

In the early hours of the morning 'they' at last decided they had the correct balance of shot.

I was waiting outside the dressing room where the make-up people had taken over. Wigs are expensive and had to be put on and taken off by *the 'experts'.* Alone, I thought how eerie an empty dark theatre is.

On the wall I noticed an illuminated address. Thinking it was rather amateurish – (Wally my husband is a signwriter and artist) - so I looked more closely. The exact wording has faded from memory now but it was from the inmates of the local 'workhouse'.

A 'thank you' for their yearly visit to the pantomime. It was signed by 11 workhouse warders. I pictured the inmates' dull and dreary lives, but enjoying their once a year treat, the colourful pantomime.

I am so grateful for all the colour I have and have had, in my life.

As a corollary my friend **Sylvia Victor** drove me home to Bognor Regis and as we arrived there at about 4 am, in the front window, was a large display saying -

'Happy Anniversary Darling'
It was 26th June.

RUTH RENDELL MYSTERIES
- 'Best Man to Die'

For this episode I was instructed to take night-wear, dressing gown and slippers to St. Mary's Hospital, Southampton. On arrival I joined several others assembled inside the main doors.

The crew, also there with various bulky items of equipment and the 'extras' bags took up a lot of space.

Settled down to await instructions we saw doors at the end pushed open by a bed, in it sat a young woman cuddling a baby. When some time later this was repeated it dawned on us this was for real, a mother with her new born baby being taken back to a ward. When a third girl appeared a spontaneous round of applause rang out from us all.

Certainly an unusual talking point when her folks next visited her.

George Baker was Inspector Wexford in the series. In this story he was visiting his seriously ill 'stage' wife.

We all changed into our night-wear, dressing gowns etc., and moved about on direction as patients.

It speaks volumes for the craft of acting and how hard it must have been for George Baker to act losing a fictional wife when his own real life wife was very seriously ill in hospital fighting for <u>her</u> life.

LOVEJOY

"Lovejoy" was one of my favourite TV series; I tried never to miss watching it. **Ian McShane** was such a lovable rogue in the title role. When working on the programme it was interesting to see his enthusiasm and energy.

When we heard **Linda Evans,** Star of the wonderful American serial **'Dallas',** was to be a guest artiste, we expected her to get the special attention due to such a big 'star'. In fact Linda arrived without fuss and was unaffected and friendly.

In one scene, a large room in a grand house, the director didn't give me a position. Linda overheard me say

"Oh, I don't know where I should be".

"Come over here" she said, *"you can be talking to me until I walk into the middle of the room to say my lines".*

A completely natural and nice 'one of us' type of Star we meet quite often as extras.

MULBERRY

You would think with a husband who watched his first football match at West Ham United in 1936, and has been a supporter ever since, (his sighs of '*Oh dear*' I can feel enveloping me even now) - when I was booked to be a football spectator at a match I would jump at it. Well, not quite.

Having a father who had been 'useful' I believe the term is, on the football field meant I knew a little about the game the emphasis being on <u>little</u>. This 'booking' however had a sting in its tail. I was warned it would be extremely cold with a bitter wind. Taking the advice to 'wrap up' seriously I wore -

- Two vests,
- Two petticoats,
- Blouse,
- Polo necked Sweater,
- Leather Waistcoat,
- Thick Cardigan,
- Ordinary Tights,
- Wool Tights,
- Thick Wool Leggings,
- Trousers,
- Two pairs of Socks,
- Boots,
- Thick Overcoat, Heavy Raincoat,
- Thick Wooly Hat,
- Scarf
- And two pairs of Gloves;
- who mentioned Michelin Girl?

It was lucky I only had to stand and watch the game at a small club ground, not up in the stands of a plush Premiership venue, as so many clothes severely hampered movement. Unfortunately I couldn't wear a mask to help with the stinging eyes and runny nose!

Certainly not one of the better sunbathed, warm, relaxing jobs sometimes encountered.

HOWARD'S WAY

One of my favourite B.B.C. programmes - it was produced by **Gerard Glaister**.

'Howard's Way' gave us quite a good deal of work as it was filmed mainly in the Southern Region.

It had a very strong cast which included
- **Tony Anholt,**
- **Andrew Bicknell,**
- **Ivor Danvers,**
- **Nigel Davenport,**
- **Susan Gilmore,**
- **Dulcie Gray,**
- **Jeff Harding,**
- **Jan Harvey,**
- **Edward Highmoor,**
- **Lana Morris,**
- **Kate O'Mara,**
- **Glyn Owen,**
- **Stephen Yardley**

- and **Maurice Colbourne** whose untimely death at such a young age not only devastated his family and friends, among whom were cast members, but put great strain on the series.

However in true B.B.C. fashion the strength in depth was there and the various series came to a satisfactory conclusion.

My husband Wally and I were in a summer scene in the garden of the 'Jolly Sailor', at Bursledon Marina.

We were set as background to Susan Gilmore and Edward Highmoor, at a table sipping make believe drinks, (i.e. brown water), me in a sleeveless cotton dress and Wally a short sleeved summer shirt.

What's the problem with that? I hear you say.

The problem was that it was cold and raining intermittently.

Nowadays with filters and lighting even these scenes can be made to look like a balmy summer day.

For us then - while the scene was being set up a big umbrella was held over us and coats put round our shoulders which were removed when shooting started. Each time there was an adjustment to the set or camera position back came the umbrella etc.

We laughed, we were quickly very wet especially as the table slanted towards us and the rain slid off into our laps. The shelter of the brolly was rather pointless.

I whispered to Wally wearing a big smile in my best ventriloquist pose as if I was enjoying myself, *"Isn't this lovely; can we come again tomorrow?"*

Wally smiling back through gritted teeth answered *'I was thinking we could find some where wetter!"*.

More of HOWARD'S WAY

When the 'wedding' was filmed with **Tracey Childs** as the 'bride', there was an air of a real wedding being attended. Most of the main characters were there as well as a good helping of assorted 'extras'.

The wedding dress was a closely guarded secret and was continually speculated on in the press up until the moment the 'bride' appeared on the set.

One person was missing however, **Tony Anholt**. The attractive 'villain' in the story, would not have been a welcome guest - but as Tracey and Tony were dating he gave up a day off to take some personal photographs of the 'bride' and wedding.

One early morning, friend **Sylvia** and I set off at 6.00 am, early call, wearing full length evening dresses and all the glittering jewelry to go with it.

We drove to Hythe Marina near Southampton, only to be told, to our alarm, to board a small boat. The weather was not good to say the least, but I am pleased to say one consolation was the boat remained moored to the quay.

During the morning the **Queen Elizabeth II** sailed past in all it's majesty on its way no doubt to docking, but out of our sight.

Rain fell on and off between 'takes' and we ladies had to sit on the deck with a tarpaulin held over our heads between times - not the best treatment for hair, evening dresses and high heeled shoes in which to look like rich guests partying on a houseboat! Our discomfort was compounded by a very chilly wind.

The day wore on, we were tired, cold, disheveled and very fed up.

As darkness fell, having effected its 'turn round ' routine, delivering it's passengers, been cleaned up, taken on fresh supplies and a new set of passengers, the **Queen Elizabeth II** slowly sailed by again on it's way out looking wonderful, with all it's lights ablaze.

After 14 hours we were at last finished, arriving home after 11.00 pm. As for the scenes we filmed - not a clue. No doubt we had lost all sense of feeling even in the brain to this day.

DAVE ALLEN SHOW

I dragged myself out of bed at 5.00am, washed and dressed, had a slice of bread and honey; my usual energy supplement; a cup of tea then collected a few things I thought I might need, raincoat, umbrella, bar of chocolate and a drink.

I called for my friend **Iris Terry** (Tanya), daughter of **Vesta Victoria** the old Music Hall 'Star', and drove to Lyndhurst, in the New Forest, Hampshire, arriving at the hotel where 'wardrobe' and 'make-up' were to be.

We were early for our 8.00 am 'call'.

We sat in the lounge bar joining a myriad of other people - some we knew but not others - and ate the food Iris had prepared as a second breakfast in case we had to hang around waiting. Normally we have a good breakfast served on site but not this time.

Two girls came in and sat on barstools a little apart from the rest of us. Two at a time from our group were called for make-up and wardrobe fitting.

My hair was pinned down and a close fitting wig applied. Dark brown, smoothed straight back on top with bunches of curls each side. The effect was Ugh!

A little later they decided curls were too much, and were combed out, re-arranged and topped with a bonnet.

I was costumed in a long sleeved cotton blouse, a thick petticoat and two heavy wool skirts; a long sleeved black wool bodice, a big white collar, large grey apron and the apparition revealed was a Cromwellian Puritan woman.

By the time it was my turn the shoe bag was practically empty but I found some shoes that were passably comfortable.

The bar stool girls were also in make-up and turned out to be stunt girls.

It was interesting hearing about other jobs they had been involved with, in particular one in which they were hanging upside down on wires - a hair-raising stunt when there had been trouble with a damaged wire and they were told to be perfectly still and not put any further strain on the wires; not easy staring down at a 90 feet drop!

For our 'shoot' they were to be filmed as gossiping women being 'ducked' in a pond for their sins but were still gossiping when they came up again out of the water.

By now we were back in the lounge bar and it was about 11.00 am. Some time later a coach came to take us all to the location in the forest.

Lunch was served and on this very cold bleak day we were grateful for a hot meal. Negotiating with a slippery plastic tray of food while climbing back on the coach and trying to slide back into a seat almost made us stunt girls, and not easy, the wool material of my bulky skirts sticking to the material of the seats.

Make-up girls appeared again to make sure all wigs, and beards and whiskers, the latter on the men, were in place.

Hands inspected, no nail varnish or jewellery allowed, and brown make-up put under our nails.

Did people, even puritans, never wash in those days I wondered?

2.30pm we left the coach and walked to where the scene was set up, a very exposed position, and a strong cold wind was blowing.

I was glad of my skirts and long sleeved thick bodice. Some however had thinner costumes but we all hugged our own coats around us in an effort to keep warm.

There was a pool with **two ducking stools,** nearby some stalls, a sort of Cromwellian 'Mini Market' with cages of chickens and some running loose, pecking away. They seemed happy and oblivious of the cold wind and people in strange clothes milling about. They were obviously very experienced feathered 'extras'.

Dave Allen stood by watching as we were given our positions, he too suffering from the cold but always cheerful and patient.

A flat bottomed boat took the stunt girls along to the ducking stools but they found climbing on to them none too easy as they too wore voluminous skirts. I know they had wet suits underneath but the water was grey and uninviting.

We were given our instructions and direction how to react then off with our own coats, face into the biting wind and grin and bear it.

The ducking had to be done twice and then the girls were hurried off back to the hotel. I hoped they would get a hot shower.

Our misery went on as the camera was positioned for the action to be filmed from where the girls sat, giving their view of things. By this time we were all wrapped in our coats again while we waited. My shoes were thin and my feet were stinging with the cold. Our faces were frozen and our eyes and noses began to run. At 4.15 pm we had a welcome break for tea and sandwiches but there was nowhere to sit or shelter.

The camera man and the director went out in the little boat to take some shots. We all had a laugh when the Director threw the anchor overboard and the chain it was attached to slipped through his frozen fingers following the anchor into the murky deep. With a big grin on his face he shouted *"Cut"*.

By the time we returned to the hotel, had our wigs and costumes removed, oh the joy of having our own warm clothes back again, it was 6.30 pm.

Iris fed me some life-saving chocolate as I drove back to Bognor Regis where I dropped Iris off at her home, then arrived at mine at 8.15 pm, over 14 hours after leaving home in the morning.

Being an 'extra' is not all glamour or even 'beer and skittles' as the saying goes.

HILARY - Marti Caine

Proved to be one of the worst jobs! Not I hasten to add because of Marti.

My husband Wally was just out of hospital after a major operation in 1986, when our agent rang to book **Sylvia Victor, Iris Terry** and **me** for a day's filming the next day.

I was reluctant to leave Wally but needed the work – we needed the money!

The location was a church in **Eastbourne, East Sussex,** the scene a wedding.

So it was up to the loft for suitable clothes and an early-ish night. Sylvia and Iris called for me at 5.00 am, and the nightmare began.

It was February and still dark, - snow was falling and visibility almost nil. After a while we minded to turn back but it was getting lighter so Sylvia, driving the car, bravely battled on.

Arriving at the church we wondered where to park but we need not have worried. **Marti** was in the doorway already costumed in a smart wedding guest suit and hat, looking lovely, albeit very cold, her natural cheerful screen self shining through, so friendly and helpful to everyone, and she directed Sylvia to park just outside the church.

What a 'star'!

We slightly defrosted over a thankfully hot breakfast at the mobile canteen truck, but then taking our seats in the pews with a galaxy of other 'extras' and no heating, our feet and legs soon lost all feeling. Worse, we realised instead of high heeled shoes and skirts we could have worn slacks and boots as our lower halves were not in 'shot'.

By lunch time and stiff with cold we could hardly move. We lined up outside again for our food, snow still falling, and of course on it, as we scuttled back inside.

Commiserating with fellow 'extras' we discovered why we were engaged at such short notice. Four people after a miserable freezing time the day before had refused to come back.

Two hours into 'overtime', some extras were allowed to go. Remembering our difficult journey from Bognor Regis, we were scared the roads may be freezing over and be slippery. We asked, since we had the longest journey and my husband just out of hospital, if we could go but this fell on deaf ears.

Luckily when we were at last released it had stopped snowing, the roads had not frozen over and we had a better journey home.

FORTUNES OF WAR

Starring **Emma Thompson** and **Kenneth Brannagh**
Before they married the episode in which I appeared was filmed at Shoreham airport, a highlight was seeing a **Junkers 52,** a German warplane, flying in to land.

Later we realised this was our job, to be inside as passengers. The original seats had been removed and temporary ones placed in a few rows. We had a fright when suddenly without warning the noisy engine burst into life, aware that our seats were not fixed in place.

Of course it was not taken up but we were still rather glad to climb out of this small elderly aircraft.

EASTENDER'S

My agent phoned to book Wally and me for an episode of this B.B.C. long-running 'Soap' opera.

We were to go on the ferry from Portsmouth to Caen in France and spend 4 nights in Caen filming before returning to Portsmouth.

Our joy at the thought of 4 days work for both of us was short lived. It was cut to just the one day; - over to France and back again.

We left home on the day at 6.30am in plenty of time for our 'call' but with 10 miles to go - just past Emsworth, Hampshire - the car temperature gauge went straight to the top, the engine fluttered and the engine cut-out did just that! Cut the power to the engine. Fortunately Wally was just coming up to a lay-by and managed to steer in.

I phoned the A.A. and then my agent. He gave me the number of the Floor Manager for the 'shoot'. It was some consolation to be told we would be in time if we got to Portsmouth by 8.30 am, the ferry didn't leave until 8.45 am.

We were devastated, me rather tearful. We needed the work and had already seen 4 days reduced to one and now it looked as if we could miss that one.

Although it was very cold - Wally and I stood outside; making sure the A.A. man would see us and not sail by as happened to me on a different occasion.

He came along very promptly. A quick inspection and diagnosis revealed a lack of radiator fluid. We had suffered a similar fate about a year previously but Wally had kept it under control, until now. He had carried water around since the previous stoppage which helped.

Tests had to be done under the car to make sure no damage had been done to the engine but our A.A. saviour, knowing we were tight for time, told us to follow him to Portsmouth; the test could be done in the car park.

This was another lucky break as he knew exactly where to park, absolutely next to the terminal and led us there.

I rushed to Ferry departures to book us in with the floor manager. Wally had to stay until the tests on the car were complete. All was well and he hot-footed it in to join me.

What a relief to board the ferry, and quickly sit down to get our breath back.

It had been many years since we traveled to France on a ferry. The last time we crossed by hovercraft to France and back by ferry. We were impressed by what now resembled a luxury hotel with a variety of restaurants in which to spend our meal allowance.

The story line was **Shane Ritchie**, playing 'Alfie Moon', taking his grandmother 'Nana Moon' (**Hilda Braid**), to France to visit her husband's war-grave.

A widow since WW 2, she had never made the journey to France before.

The first scene was filmed in the tea-shop.

'Nana' and 'Alfie' were sitting at a table opposite each other. At another table with some other extras I was 'in shot' – well ½ of my face to be exact - for most of the scene.

We had a pot of tea to pour out, adding milk and sugar then having a sip. The tea started fresh and hot and the sandwiches fresh. By the time we poured the tea back into the pot to be poured out again for each 'take' it was pretty awful. Pretending to drink we made sure it never touched our lips.

The scene took a long time to 'shoot' as there were difficulties with the dialogue meeting the director's exacting standards.

After almost 25 years of filming, I was still impressed with the patience the crew showed.

Shane Ritchie himself was patience personified, even giving humorous asides during the breaks, his stock-in-trade as one of the country's top comedians.

Wally's contribution was 'background' at table in the scene 'shot' from other angles. Wally had a further scene out on deck as we approached France, walking slowly holding the arm of a young girl, his granddaughter? They had to time the walk past Trevor Peacock to the 'sharp end', the bow, to perfection, which they did each time it was 'shot'; or so Wally told me!!!

The sea was completely calm; we had to look out at it to know we were moving.

On arrival at Caen, passengers disembarked including, **Hilda Braid**, **Shane Ritchie** and **Trevor Peacock**, the crew and some extras. We were at liberty to leave the ferry for the 5 hours or so before it was due to start the return journey.

Wally and I chose to remain on board; the dock area did not look very inviting. Loungers had been booked for us and by now, about 7 hours after we left home, we needed a rest.

When I wasn't dozing I was fascinated to see the stream of the various vehicles driving into the ferry's hold.

The time dragged a bit, we were glad to be on the move again for the return journey.

Arriving back in Portsmouth, at about 9.30pm, we made for the exits but the doors remained closed. We stood crowded together with other passengers unable to leave.

A man had collapsed with a suspected heart attack and they wanted to get him away first and were awaiting an ambulance and the paramedics was the explanation.

It was 10.30 pm by the time we left the ferry and about 11.15 pm when Wally and I arrived home.

A long day but fairly comfortable and interesting with extra pay for the delay.

No we never heard how the man fared.

A DAY TO REMEMBER

George Cole starred in this rather sad story about a family trying to cope with a father suffering from Alzheimer's disease.

Our scene was set in Owens a department store in Southampton.

We spent the whole day going up and down escalators, when 'shooting' some going down and others including George Cole going up.

To 're-shoot' we all had to return to our starting places and it is surprising how long a small scene like this can take.

Up and down, up and down.

It was a wonder no one went down with 'escalator' sickness.

The classic Gerald Hoffnung piece 'the pulley and load of bricks' readily slipped into the mind.

ONLY FOOLS AND HORSES

Being an extra in a market scene was so interesting. It is amazing to see the work that goes into setting it up; arranging the fruit and veg. stall and one full of sweets. They were unwrapped but we were told not to eat them as they had been sprayed to protect them from the cold damp weather. True or not, it worked, none of us risked it.

Our scene was 'Del Boy', **David Jason,** 'flogging' a case of cutlery. 'Rodders', **Nicholas Lyndhurst,** was the 'look out'.

There is a lot of stopping and starting when building up a scene, with people chopping and changing positions and movements until the Director is satisfied.

Outdoors filming quite often has to be stopped for stray dogs barking at a crucial moment or planes flying overhead etc.

We had numerous stoppages and each time 'shooting' restarted, David Jason had to go through his fast spiel again.

Sooner or later actors can make mistakes in delivering their lines, you only have to see the 'out-takes' programmes to appreciate this, but not David, - he was word perfect .

Rain brought filming to a halt and as we could only use the location on a Sunday, we had to wait a week and all go back.

This happened for a second time with rain again to blame. The third Sunday the weather was fine and the scene completed, for us a 'nice little earner'.

A difficult scene for David Jason but he never showed any signs of impatience and never once tripped up on his lines.

I worked in **'Only Fools and Horses'** a few times and although twice miserable and damp, this was my favourite episode, and not only for the money.

A very LONG Commercial Day

When I was 'booked' to do a **'Commercial'** and the meeting point was somewhere near Tottenham Court Road in London, I decided to drive there from Bognor Regis.

I looked up the nearest car park and mapped out the little walk I would have to take to the meeting place. I allowed plenty of time and I parked and I was about to walk away when a man said –

"You do know this is not a 24 hour car park, don't you? It closes round about 7.00 o'clock ".

I had no idea, as usual, what time I would finish so I got back in my car and looked around for a 24 hour car park which I eventually found and again parked.

Then it dawned on me that all the instructions I had written down to the meeting place were from the first garage and now I really was not sure how to get there. I asked a few people on the way and eventually arrived almost late which was very annoying after my very early start.

I changed into the evening dress which I was required to wear and several of us were driven to Finsbury Park where the commercial was to be made in Finsbury Park Town Hall. Frequently a double-decker bus, converted with tables etc., where artistes can eat is used as was the case here and we sat in there chatting away waiting to be needed.

When it came to meal time we had to queue up outside in the road at a mobile canteen van, the usual practice but it did seem very odd in a busy London street all in full evening dress.

It was the middle of the afternoon before we were actually called and we had to cross over a busy road and walk a little way to the Town Hall.

The commercial was an Amstrad 'Ad' depicting a formal dinner with several round tables. The speaker had a foot high pile of paper to get through and all the guests were so bored we all drifted off to sleep all over the tables.

It was getting well into the evening before we finished and allowed back to our bus.

We were driven back to change into our own clothes and then I set out to find my car having made a note of the road the car park was in and I got there without a hitch.

By now it is dark, I am on my own and when I go into the car park my car is the only one in there at the farthest end of the floor. My feet made such a clip clopping noise in this empty space I was very frightened but I swiftly got to the car put my dress and things in the boot, prayed it would start first time, which it did, and I drove out.

I then had to drive all the way home to Bognor Regis, some two and a half to three hours.

A very long commercial day!

Looking at 'the Royal Family?'

Engaged to film in a wedding scene for Sky Television, I arrived at the location presented myself to 'Wardrobe' for them to approve my chosen outfit. Passed by them and 'make-up' - I joined other 'extras' in a coach provided to wait until such time as we were needed.

Still very early morning we were astounded to suddenly see the **Royal Family** arrive *en-masse*.

Of course it was the Royal Family 'look-alikes'.

They were amazingly 'real' and it was a strange feeling to be in the queue for lunch in front of Prince Charles, in full naval uniform, then to have Prince Philip hold a door open for me similarly attired.

All of them were very friendly and had plenty of stories to tell. Especially the Princess Diana who had on occasions acted as a decoy for real Diana!

As in real life, the consensus was the Queen Mother' look-alike was our favourite.

Mozart 'Child Prodigy'

In the TVS television series on child prodigies, 'Mozart' was to prove one of my better jobs.

Filmed in **Wilton House, Dorset**, home of the Earl of Pembroke, it was directed by **David Heather** whose 4 year old son **Freddie** played the 6 year old Wolfgang Amadeus Mozart.

Dressed in his satin and lace outfit, which he donned without fuss, he looked splendid.

Costumed in a lovely period dress and powdered wig, I sat in a gorgeous room on a dainty satin and gilt settee in front of the most elaborate gold fireplace topped with a large ornate mirror. Luxury, utter luxury.

Four year old Freddie needed several cushions to be high enough to reach the spinette key boards.

Between each 'take' he had to be heaved up, as the cushions were rearranged.

I so enjoyed drinking in all the magnificent splendour!

After shooting further scenes walking in the beautiful grounds we finished early and I was sorry when it was over,

Winter and
JOHN OSBORNE

Being 'booked' for filming on Bognor Regis pier, just a mile from home, was enhanced when my husband Wally was asked to stand in for another extra.

The reason was a requirement to have a 40's short haircut which the original bod chosen refused as he had cabaret commitments as a singer.

The programme was
'The John Osborne Story',
later re-titled
'Too Young to Fight, Too Old to Forget'.

Arriving on the worst kind of a December day, cold, rain and a biting wind, Wally and 5 other men duly had their short back and sides haircut (extra fee of course). Everyone then changed into their 40's period 'summer' clothes but shivered as we waited to be called for a 'shoot'.

The 'hair-cut men' were to be fishermen, fishing off the pier. With no let up in the weather, the ASM, (assistant stage manager), suddenly brought round balaclava helmets for the men to wear, bursts of laughter all round as the haircuts were covered up.

Later, with the wind still howling, it was deemed too risky for the men and camera crew to work off the end of the pier so the scene was scrapped.

An end of pier **'Concert Party'** scene was the main theme and a stage had been erected, sheltering the principle actors. This went ahead next day, us extras shivering in deck chairs as the audience. Wally was now with me, on an extra day.

We kept our top coats hugged around us, they being removed by wardrobe personnel between 'takes', us - teeth chattering, laughing and clapping the 'Show'.

What a day!

DR. JOHN BODKIN ADAMS

Timothy West
starred in a Television film of the
'Life of Dr. John Bodkin Adams',
- a doctor whose practice was in Eastbourne, East Sussex in the 1950's.

Within his care was a Ladies Rest-home as well as other surgery patients.

The ladies were very fond of their Doctor, often giving him presents. When some of them left him money in their will, the police became suspicious.

In 1957 Dr. Adams was arrested and accused of murder. His trial was a sensation featured on all Newspaper front pages and lasted many months. Eventually Dr. Adams was acquitted and cleared by the Medical Council to resume his work.

In 1985, with **Sylvia Victor** and **Iris 'Tanya' Terry**, I was booked for 'extra' work on the film. The scene was set in the Retirement Home. At first the 'make-up' people were not very pleased with we three; flatteringly they said we didn't look old enough to be patients from the '50's.

A fellow extra sharply said *"You should know theatre people never look their age"*. However with grey wigs and 1950's old lady clothes we soon looked right.

Some non-Equity elderly ladies joined us, very unusual then. They were authentic locals who knew Dr. Adams at the time of his trial and afterwards. He had always been held in very high regard and they assured us none of his patients, or indeed anyone who knew him, ever thought he was guilty of committing the euthanasia with which he was charged.

CASUALTY

Casualty, the long running BBC serial soap, was and I believe still is filmed in Bristol, Somerset. There is a permanent hospital set up in the studio.

Driving there early morning I got hopelessly lost in Bristol Town, - this despite having family living in and close by this grand old city. Even a milkman I stopped and asked for directions sent me the wrong way.

Oh for sat-nav in the early 1990's!

When I eventually found the studio, I was, for the first and only time, late.

Expecting my efforts to count for nothing and to be told I wasn't wanted, which would have been a great blow to my ego and credibility as a professional, I apologized and explained to the floor manager. He laughed and said *"Don't worry, people always have trouble finding us and arrive late the first time."* I was so relieved.

Off to make-up and wardrobe I was given a great nasty looking bruise down the side of my face and neck, (make-up I hasten to add),

"You're a battered wife" they said.

A Polaroid photo was taken of my make-up and joined others on the wall over the mirrors so that it could be accurately repeated for continuity should it be needed.

That day was spent sitting in the waiting area of Casualty, reading a magazine, fidgeting, waiting to see a doctor (could sound familiar to some looking back to those days).

The Polaroid was required as I was asked to go back the next day and this time did get to walk about in scenes being 'shot'. In some I am quite sure I was filmed on the other side of my profile unblemished by red, orange, purple, black and blue tints.

Mealtimes were fine as far as the food was concerned but with actors wearing all kinds of dressings and bandages and realistically bloody open wounds, not exactly appetizing.

We extras often refer to ourselves as the 'wallpaper' in a scene, rarely noticed but if the background was bare, would be.

I don't recall 'wallpaper' ever being so gruesome and grisly as it was filming '**Casualty**'.

The Arm, Witches & Grinny Gogs

I usually went on filming jobs with friends, sharing a car. The first time I was booked for a job on my own I felt very important.

I drove myself to the studios in Southampton arriving in very good time. Someone from 'Wardrobe' came down and said to me *"Are you the Arm?" "Oh no"* I said, *"I don't think so ". "Well, will you just come and try the costume on?"* he asked.

Well of course I agreed.

The costume turned out to be a sort of blouse made out of lining material with the right hand sleeve being a heavier type of hessian material. So I tried it on and it fitted perfectly. He was satisfied so I left it with him and went downstairs to join the others on the 'shoot' waiting to be told where to go next.

A minibus arrived and a few of us boarded and off to the location which turned out to be a stonemason's yard. We sat about on great lumps of stone and I felt quite alone without my friends as I did not know anyone there.

After some time 'wardrobe' came and put me in the blouse, apparently I was - *'The Arm'.*

I didn't know what an 'Arm' does; my agent had told me to wear a tweed skirt dressed as an 'upper' class lady would for gardening.

They dirtied my hand, put dirt under the finger nails and there I sat feeling very lonely and puzzling what I was going to be asked to do. Then I found out.

Deeper into the yard was a very large truck and on top of it were very large pieces of stone. There was a step-ladder for me to climb but it stopped short from the top of the truck and two men 'yanked' me up the rest of the way, and then I discovered what it was I was going to have to do.

A well had been made in the middle of the stones and I had to crouch down in it and be covered up with a tarpaulin, stretching my one arm out that had been costumed as if I was trying to pull the tarpaulin over me.

Then of course I had to get down when 'shooting' was finished, feeling decidedly embarrassed wearing a straight tweed skirt. Now I knew I would have been far better off dressed in a boiler suit.

I was helped down, the director thanked me, they usually do,

"That's *alright*" I said, "*Anytime you need a hand.....*"

Wrong Directions

Filming jobs with friends are almost always preferable to being on one's own, especially when going to locations or a part of the country that you have not been to before.

Leaving early and once more on my own, I was having a lovely drive through the New Forest , I had the directions my agent had given me and they were quite clear and I had the feeling that I couldn't get lost.

In fact I was going to be rather early and as the night before **Richard Briers** daughter **Katie Briers** who was floor manager had phoned me to say "You *can have an extra half hour in bed Barbara, we won't need you 'till later*". I stopped at a newsagents in Downton and bought a paper.

I sat in my car reading for a while until I decided it was about time to go. Picking up my instructions I read -

'Go to the traffic lights, turn left, over two bridges, turn left again, past the **Wooden Spoon** public house and you will come to a big house, well you will only see the gates, big white gates on the left and the film crew are there!

I carried on and although it seemed a very long way there was no sign of bridges or the Wooden Spoon Public House – I was lost!

Parking my car I asked a man for help, he scratched his head, mystified. Light began to dawn! *"These directions are from Salisbury"* he said. *"You need the opposite from Bognor Regis!"*

I turned the car back to the newspaper shop and reversed the directions and sure enough I found the wardrobe and the make-up people and the mobile food truck.

I presented myself and was put into an apron as I was to be a cleaning lady - and with that the wardrobe people started to move off. *"Where is the house*?" I asked, *"About a mile down the road"* was the reply, so I gathered my things together, they by this time had disappeared, and I started walking. There was no sign of the house but how can you possibly go wrong at this stage?

I asked somebody but they didn't know, I asked someone else, "Oh*, that's the house on the other side of the road"* they said. So the gates that I had first driven to was where the filming was going on. By now it was getting very warm and I was getting worried because I looked like being very late.

It was a long walk back but as I was getting near I saw some people loading a car. I thought *"They must be going to the house"* so I hurried all the while thinking *"If they move off before I get there I'll just cry".* I got there, begged a lift and arrived at the location,

I hadn't been needed so hadn't been missed. When Katie Briers said *'Why don't you go back and have some breakfast, we don't need you yet?".* I almost collapsed - thinking of my recent tribulations, thinking of that long walk again, but help was at hand there was a car to take me so off I went to have some breakfast.

Later on I did my stint, wielding a Hoover in a most gorgeous and very large room and although I had to do it over and over again I didn't mind a bit as I just loved all the beautiful things around me.

I was finished by about 10.30 am but I wasn't allowed to go home as they wanted to do another shot and I spent the whole day sitting on an iron seat in the garden, waiting, and it was 5.00 pm before they said *"We don't want you any more- you can go home"*

Frivilous Mourners
"PULASKI"

Funeral scenes at one time seemed a specialty of mine. I've certainly had my share and one such was in –

'Pulaski'
a detective story starring
David Andrews and **Glynis Barber**.

Four of us made the journey to Hastings, East Sussex, some 55 odd miles, from Bognor Regis.

In the filming we had to walk down a long flight of stone steps, only trouble being we had to walk all the way up again between 'takes'.

It was a full day's work so you can imagine our poor tired legs when we were dismissed.

Next day, -

- **Iris Terry**,
- **Rosemary Croome-Johnson**,
- **Sylvia**, **Victor** and
- **me** –

- were back in our black funeral clothes and this time we were 'arriving' at the Church.

At lunch time, our scene in 'the can', we were released.

It was a warm sunny day and whilst driving through Brighton on our way home, we saw an ice cream van. It was too tempting.

Feeling like kids let out of school we skipped over and with much laughter we made our choices, gleefully carrying them back to the car.

As we sat enjoying our treats it dawned on us - we were all dressed in black from head to toe, including black stockings and hats, obvious funeral attire.

What, we wondered, was the ice-cream seller thinking of our high spirits?

WAITING FOR GOD

I was in three episodes of this popular series; -
- 'Tom' - **Graham Crowden** - attending an exercise class which was great fun in the making;
- A very grand funeral, given to a fellow guest at the retirement home, the centre of most of the action, who had no family ;
- Best was being featured right in the front in a special Christmas Show scene, often repeated on TV, in which the characters in the series were cast in a Nativity Play.
- As you can imagine everything goes wrong and is hilarious, **Stephanie Cole** as the producer, eventually coming to blows with one of the other characters.

When we filmed, the cameras were placed among the audience - us - and we observed the stage set and play being played out. When switched to the stage with the cameras on us it needed no pretence to laugh and react on direction as if we were watching the play,

I just remembered what we had been seeing filmed some time before - and it came naturally.

Meeting the STARS!

One of the good things about being a Television Extra is being involved in favourite programmes and working in popular series with well known 'Stars'.

Among my more notable are the following—

- AFTER HENRY
  with **Prunella Scales.**
- AGATHA CHRISTIE STORIES - several,
  with **Joan Hickson, Geraldine McEwan.**

- <u>CATS EYES</u>
  with **Jill Gascoine.**
- <u>DARLING BUDS OF MAY</u>
  with **David Jason, Pam Ferris,
  Catherine Zeta Jones.**
- <u>DAVE ALLEN SHOW</u>
  with **Dave Allen.**
- <u>EVER DECREASING CIRCLES</u>
  with **Richard Briers.**
- <u>HOWARD'S WAY</u>, several,
  with **Jan Harvey, Stephen Yardley,
  Tony Anholt, Tracey Childs,
  Glyn Owen.**
- <u>LOVE HURTS</u>
  with **Zoe Wanamaker, Adam Faith.**
- <u>LOVEJOY</u>, several,
  with **Ian McShane,**
- <u>ONE FOOT IN THE GRAVE</u>
  with **Annette Crosby, Richard Wilson.**
- <u>ONLY FOOLS & HORSES</u>, several
  with **David Jason, Nicholas Lyndhurst.**
- <u>POIROT</u>
  with **David Suchet.**
- <u>RUMPOLE</u>
  with **Leo McKern.**
- <u>RUTH RENDELL MYSTERIES</u>
  with **George Baker.**
- <u>WAITING FOR GOD</u>
  with **Stephanie Cole, Graham Crowden**

Commercials

'Film extra' work takes in television commercials which are not normally exciting. Some people are under the impression that actors in these make fortunes. Yes top actors do, alas 'extras' do not! Having made quite a number I illustrate with just a few examples –

'Beef Eater Restaurants', - where youngsters were tap-dancing in top hats, tails and canes a-la-Fred Astaire and one girl drops one, *"Oops!"*. Instead of being on the stage I was just in the audience.

'Mumms Champagne', - a number of scenes moving through life from baby, exams, prize giving, to a wedding, the scene in which I was just a wedding guest in picture hat and splendid dress drinking champagne. Unfortunately no free samples were dished out.

'Amstrad', - the setting of my "Long Commercial Day" story, elsewhere. Principal was an after dinner speaker, sheets of paper piled a foot high on his lectern, showing how easy printing is. He's reading from the top page. Us dinner guests in evening dress at usual hotel round tables, gradually falling asleep with boredom. Sir Alan Sugar should have been there with his *"You're Fired"* punch-line.

'Water Privatisation', - Orchestral Concert in the Albert Hall, London, Some of the audience begin to leave gradually then building up to a rush to buy shares.

'Gas Privatisation' - about 50 'extras' doing the conga forming the shape of a graph. This was filmed in a field with rough grass - many inches high. A path wide enough for our feet had been cut short in a zig-zag shape. We did the conga along this path forming the graph pattern. It was alright the first time but when

we were asked to go back for a second 'take' had no room to turn round. We had to shuffle backwards, not at all easy. After several re-takes we were exhausted. There were several *'Gas Commercials'* all preceded by someone calling out to *"Tell Syd"*.

'Peugeot Cars'. - This was an even harder job filmed in Throgmorton Street in London. A crowd of 'extras' were required to walk up one side of the street cross over and walk down the other side then back over to the 1st side, walking non-stop. We had been asked to dress for town, no mention of the walking, so we were not in our comfortable walking shoes. We walked all day; at one point Sylvia and I were exhausted again and we hid in a shop door-way for a rest. Not for long, we were soon found. While we walked a Peugeot car was travelling down the street at about 5 miles per hour. When it was shown on TV it was speeded up, the car going at a normal pace and we looked as if we were rushing about like flies.

'Just One Cornetto' - Although it was filmed in December, outdoors, we were asked to wear summer clothes. I crammed all the undies I could manage plus a thick jumper under my dress and wore two pairs of tights. Still sat and shivered then the opera singer came out with *"Just one Cornetto"* and we threw our red roses at him. Mine missed.

'Nat West Bank',- filmed in Shepperton Studios.

The set was a café with several small round tables. The theme was businesses going 'bust'. I was asked to join a business man at a table. Mechanism under it was primed to go off with a 'Bang!' sending the table up in the air.

I had to sit with my legs to the side while facing the table, and *I was warned to keep my legs well clear or they could be severely injured*. As I picked my cup up ready to drink there was the explosion and the table went up in the air.

277

I did not have to 'act' surprised alarm. The last full frame shot of the commercial was me looking surprised and still holding the cup.

I was told that the pose was not held quite long enough for me to qualify for repeat fees; a pity as this commercial was shown many times over a considerable length of time. There was no 'danger' money forthcoming and the day's work was from 8.00am until 8.25pm to make plus the 5 hours traveling, a total of 17 *1/2* hours. My fee was £128.47, which worked out at £7.34 per hour. It was very welcome but not exactly making a fortune!

An audition for
OLDER DANCERS

It was with excited disbelief my friend **Sylvia** and I boarded the train to Victoria Station from Bognor Regis to attend an audition for 'Older Dancers'. Aged **74** and **77** respectively, with our professional dancing days well behind us, we thought we were pushing our luck.

All the 'older dancers' at this audition learnt a short dance and were videoed dancing five at a time.

Returning home to Bognor Regis we were amazed to be told we were among the 6 ladies and 4 men chosen to be in a pilot recording of
'The All New Harry Hill Show'
for **ITV.**

We fixed 'digs' with Sylvia's friend in Ealing, London, and rehearsals began.

We ten dancers were all ages and shapes especially chosen by **Harry**.

Needless to say Sylvia and I were the eldest.

The show was recorded at Teddington Studios. We eagerly watched out for it to be shown but it was not broadcast and as time went by forgot about it.

The following year there was another audition for 'Older Dancers' commissioned for a
'Commercial'
to be made by The J. Walter Thompson Agency
to be filmed in Barcelona, Spain.
Sylvia and I were off again.
This time we were asked to do any kind of a dance of our choosing.
Both of us opted for a 'tap' routine; - shoes came down from the loft and music taped. We did separate auditions as we had no time to learn a joint routine.
We came back home that afternoon to a message that we had been 'booked' to dance in a series of -
6 'All New Harry Hill Shows',
great excitement as you can imagine.
Unfortunately - after the second audition Sylvia became ill but I was called back to London for a third audition for the - **Barcelona Commercial** - and landed it!
Jiving; - *yes jiving at 78 years of age!!!!,* with **Ray Edwards** who I met at the second audition. What excitement!

'ALL NEW HARRY HILL SHOW'

Sylvia Victor my friend and neighbour danced with me in a pilot recording of the proposed
'All New Harry Hill Show'.
Hoping for a series which we understood was contemplated; we eagerly watched a few months for

the pilot to be shown but when it did not appear we forgot all about it.

Imagine our excitement when a year later our agent phoned booking us for a series of 6 shows. Sylvia and I moved back into the 'digs' in Ealing, West London, where we had stayed before, then travelled to the rehearsal venue in Ladbroke Grove.

A happy reunion followed with the eight other dancers, making up the 9 in the troupe.

- **Ann, Avril, Barbie, Jill, Basil,**
- **Eric, Bob, Malcolm, Barbara** (me)
- Also **Jenny Arnold** our choreographer –
- and of course **Harry Hill.**

In two days of rehearsal we re–capped on the previous year's dance and learned three others, Phew!

On Monday after a Sunday off, we went to Teddington Television Studios. Finding our way between wardrobe, make-up and the 'Greenroom' - not to mention the 'loos' was a puzzle at first.

After a rehearsal on stage we were re-united with the costumes we had for the pilot recording and they all seemed to fit; short white pleated skirts for the ladies and white shorts for the men and the red shirts.

We all bore the initials

S.C.R.C.,
Sevenoaks Cardiac Arrest Rehabilitation Centre,
- a 'dig' at our ages that **Harry** light-heartedly featured after each of our dances for the series.

Sylvia was 75 years old and I was 78! We were by far the eldest, (the youngest being 50 something).

No one warned us of the next five costumes wardrobe produced. Needing a sense of humour was not mentioned at the audition either.

We had hilarious times in the wardrobe room, good job they were so kind and helpful and joined in the fun as each extraordinary costume was produced.

All **Harry Hill's** idea.

It was not like working in a theatre when you would appear from the wings or be on stage in position when the curtain went up. Oh no! Feeling utterly ridiculous we had to enter in full view of the audience and climb onto the stage and walk to our starting positions.

After recording 3 programmes we had nearly two weeks rest at home.

During this time all the girls were called back for one day to record an **Ali G** type number, the all-black costumes of shiny plastic and leather, being somewhat skimpy to say the least.

When handed mine I had to say *"I'll never get into that"* but I did!

Long black wigs and exaggerated lips and eyebrows finished us off. What a sight!

With our rest days over - we had two more days rehearsal in Ladbroke Grove then back to Teddington where we spent quite a time in the Green-room watching television waiting to be needed.

When 'Spinola', trained by Peter Harris, (a horse **Jill** had an owner-ship share in) was running we all had a bet on it. The Cherry Hinton Stakes at Newmarket, a top 2 year old fillies race was going to be televised.

We were in our costumes, various daft 'birds' I seem to recall, in the green-room waiting to do one of our dances. As the time for the race was getting nearer we were on pins hoping not to be called. When it was only 5 minutes away we all got together and decided come what may we wouldn't go until after the race, even though keeping a production team waiting was unheard of in the profession.

Luckily we were not needed at that point and we saw the race.

Actually all of us wound up excitedly shouting at the screen with **Jill** the loudest; *'Spinola'* went into the lead some way out but approaching the last furlong the pack started closing with every stride, we started shouting then holding our breath, it was excruciating but she held on to win by a short head after an incredible ride by Richard Quinn the jockey. Oh boy, did we cheer!

Later, after the filming, in the canteen, Jill bought a bottle and it was bubbly all round—in plastic cups!

Both Wally, my husband, and I had reason to thank Jill again the following year when she arranged for us and another couple of friends to go round the stables and meet another of her investments and other horses; as an ex–bookmaker's clerk for my cousin Fred Stevens, right up Wally's street.

'the Hamilton Challenge'

Christine and **Neil Hamilton** featured in each of the **'ALL NEW HARRY HILL SHOWS'**.

The one I particularly liked was the wrestling match between them with Christine the victor, using very clever photography which we were able to watch.

Of course the surprise sketch after a 'tennis' match when they were undressing in the changing rooms, and Christine suddenly stripped off her top, to expose a manly chest, ran this a pretty good second.

We found both Christine and Neil very friendly and dare I say it in spite of their 'press image', enjoyably cheerful and 'ordinary', although they may not think of themselves as that.

One of the maze of rooms in the studios was empty except for a grand piano complete with candelabra, a la Liberace, and passing through on one occasion, I found Neil playing the piano quite beautifully. Not the sort of scene reported by the normal 'press' headlines.

Costumes

The following tries to get across the fun and even bewilderment we experienced at the hands of –
H.Hill, Esq.
in the
'All New Harry Hill Show' series.

In the first show of the series we dancers wore straightforward shirts just as we did in the pilot show the year before, with short pleated skirts for the 'girls' and shorts for the 'men'.

In large white letters on the backs was
S.C.R.C.

(Sevenoaks Cardiac Arrest Rehabilitation Centre) - which allowed **Harry** to make a joke at our expense as we went off. They were repeated, only smaller, under our own first names on the front pocket.

What Harry Hill had in store for us, costume wise, for the other 5 shows was not explained at any juncture until we turned up for rehearsals and went to 'Wardrobe'.

OLIVER CROMWELL SOLDIERS - Dancing to the tune of "Oliver's Army" was not too exacting as a routine but the costumes? Not light representational 'dancers' fare; Oh No! These had been used by men in a film battle scene and were really heavy. So cumbersome that we were unable to dress ourselves and needed help from wardrobe people.

We should have had breast plates but as it was quite impossible to move our arms, as the dance required, they were left off. To complete the ensemble we had steel helmets and big heavy boots, - a great boon to dancing! When 8 feet tall lances or pikes were brought on for us to hold eyebrows were raised but we were prepared to give them a 'go', with hilarious results, further detail not needed methinks. Thankfully they also were scrapped.

BIRDS - We all looked quite splendid, representing real birds in vibrant colours. I was a canary. With the big bodies we could have been taken as 'pregnant' each and every one, including the men. The sleeves were feathers giving the illusion of wings. Hoods covering our heads with 'beaks' sticking out and matching tights and flipper- like feet made dancing in them great fun, possibly not quite the "Swan Lake" effect the writers and choreographer had in mind. Hold on, Harry is the main writer! Oh well!

BABIES - Another typically Harry inspired outfit.

Flesh body stockings, large nappies with outsize safety pins. The girls wore lacey matinee jackets with bows in their hair. Dummies hung on ribbon around our necks, blue for boys pink for girls.

Harry suggested starting with dummies in our mouths, we did. At least we had trainers laced with blue or pink ribbon, not bare feet.

RASTAS - I'm not too sure how much into 'reggae' all of us were before learning the dance but with the colourful jackets and trousers, thick long black dreadlocks and Rasta style hats we seemed to slip into the idiom quite readily.

HAMLET - Sir Larry would have been proud of us in these with our short straight black wigs with fringes, which surprisingly suited us all, and plush figured satin doublet and hose easy to dance in. Then of course out came the 'Yorrick' skulls to carry, so all our hand movements already learned had to be changed at the last minute. The *"Alas I knew him well"* did not have quite the same ring to them with an energetic dance routine to do.

MY 'STAR' SOLO
(alas - twas cut!)

Before we returned to London for our second stint of filming, (for **the All New Harry Hill Show),** 'Wardrobe' phoned asking me to take my tap shoes to the next rehearsal.

On arrival I was surprised to find no one else had been asked to take theirs. Later, **Steve Brown,** the Musical Director and **Harry Hill** asked me to do 16 bars of tap dancing, 'just like that'.

A very short introduction was played over for me to know when to start. Then played again and I was 'on'. Good old feet didn't let me down, I did a triple 'time step' getting in all the beats I could to make it sound special.

In the studio again we had filmed our opening dance routine in front of an audience as usual. 'Wardrobe' sent for me and I was put in the red shirt and white skirt worn in the opening show, miked—up to enhance my tap beats.

285

Back to the studio I was told to dash on to where Harry was standing, tap for 16 bars and run off again.

I was to move when the Floor Manager gave a signal by dropping her raised arm, repeating this several times; - technology is a wonderful thing!

Ronne Coyles, himself a great tap dancer, and a regular in every show in his guise of a somewhat vertically challenged **'Steve Redgrave'** as he was then, (now **Sir Steve** of course), was so kind helping me down off the stage each time I had to run off. We eventually seemed to get it right for all concerned.

Sadly though all this effort ended up 'on the cutting room floor', my 'Star' Solo was not to be.

POST SCRIPT -

Harry Hill wrote a personal card of thanks to each dancer which was followed by a letter from producer **Nick Symons** saying the **'All New Harry Hill Show'** was awarded the *top prize* in the Comedy Category ,

a Silver Rose, at the **Montreux Film Festival**.

Nice to think I was lucky enough to be part of it.

Jiving in Barcelona

It all started with a phone call from my dancing friend **Sylvia**. She was going for an audition for 'older dancers' in London next day, would I go with her?

We could do any kind of dancing, Sylvia suggested tap. So it was up to the loft for tap shoes then a frantic search through tapes for suitable music.

Next day we went off to the **Pineapple Dance Studio.** In turn we did our best - smiling and making it up as we went along.

A few days later we heard Sylvia and I had made it to the 'Short List' and must go back the next day. If successful we would be flown to **Barcelona** to appear in a Commercial being made by an American Company.

'Vanner's' in the previous section of this book explained how we had lost almost all our capital in a restaurant venture that failed to work. Since then money was always very tight and the cost of auditions in London was using up all we had. However, Wally said the expense gamble (i.e. would I get through the audition and recoup our expenses?), which it was for us, was too good to miss.

This time I was introduced to an actor called **Ray Edwards** and we were asked to 'jive' to '**In the Mood**'. Luckily we got on well and gave it all we had.

Sadly, Sylvia became ill and had to drop out.

Ray and I were called back two days later for a third time and still Wally thought the costs would be worth the gamble. Ray and I were to jive to "**Mack the Knife**" in front of the American production people.

They were very surprised when they heard my age (78 years young) but it didn't put them off for Ray and I got the job! We had seen other people at the auditions but did not know which of them would be with us.

The next day my agent phoned as contracts had to be signed.

Oh dear! Is this going to be another train fare using up our scarce money - but no Wally took it over the internet and I was to take it with me - signed, to Spain.

Another call the day following asking which was my nearest Airport. I told him Gatwick, warning him my passport was in my married name of Vanner,

I work under my single name of **Barbara Stewart** as on my Equity Card.

"No problem" he assured me.

During the flurry of preparations a Spanish man rang from Barcelona giving me my flight time, flight number, and a number to quote when collecting my ticket at the Airport.

He was Charlie, he said and gave me his telephone number. Later he phoned again, said I would be met when I arrived and went through everything again. By then it was Saturday, my flight was on Monday leaving at 8.10 am.

Up at 4 a.m., collected by taxi (they paid) at 5 a.m. and reached Gatwick at 6 a.m.

Armed with Passport and Charlie's flight number off I went to collect my ticket- only to find it was in the name of, - you guessed, - Stewart.

Luckily with my Equity Card I got them to change it to **Vanner.** One other snag though - I was at Gatwick Airport and the flight was for the 8.10 am plane, but from Heathrow!

It *was* now 7 am. *"I can't possibly get to Heathrow for 8.10 am "*. I said. Of course all the others including my partner for the commercial – Ray, live in London and would go from Heathrow.

I must say the airport staff were very helpful and eventually found *me* a seat on the 9.20 a.m. flight from Gatwick to Barcelona.

Comfortably settled in my seat, it occurred to me that there may be no-one to meet me at this later time. Oh for a mobile phone I thought, especially as I had Charles' number, how would I manage a call from a phone box in Euro's?

On arrival at Barcelona I anxiously searched for someone holding my name up when suddenly I heard people calling *"Barbara"* and the next moment I was in the middle of big hugs all round.

Louise and **Brian**, who dance the tango, with **Sally** and **Briggita**, the line dancers, had waited with their Spanish driver for me. The rest had gone to the hotel with another driver. **Laura** and **Barry** were still missing so we waited for a while but then had to move off.

We learned later that Laura, the third Line Dancer, had been caught up in my mix-up. She was told there was no ticket in her name at Heathrow but there was one for Barbara Stewart, so although it was rectified she had missed the 8.10 am flight.

The delay meant there was no time to check in our hotel so we were driven straight to the **Ritz Hotel** where the wardrobe people and Directors were staying.

We were shown into a large room with clothes on rails all around and introduced to Head of Wardrobe. She was a tiny American lady with a very loud voice whom we secretly dubbed *Ruby Wax*.

I tried on at least a dozen dresses each being pronounced *"Gorgeous"* by Ruby.

No mention was made of lunch, it was 3:0 p.m. and my last meal was breakfast on the plane at 10.00 a.m. Luckily I had a bottle of water and some biscuits to keep me going.

Eventually it was down to a choice between a black dress and a brown one for me. I was paraded before the Directors and cameramen first in one costume and then the other and back again

The brown one had to be pulled over my head, my hair felt a mess but there was no mirror about for a tidy up. No decision was made

All this time Louise was also trying on dresses while Sally and Bnggitta were put in jeans - all *"Gorgeous"* to *Ruby Wax*!

Brian and Ray joined us and began trying their things on behind the screens provided, you understand. At last - sometime after 5.00 pm we were driven to our hotel.

I settled into my room and went in search of food. I was starving and to my dismay discovered that the hotel *only* served breakfast.

I enjoyed being out in the warm summer air and sat and watched people including children out walking. I was too tired to go in anywhere to have a meal on my own and to have to work out paying in Euros – it was my first brush with them - so I bought some croissants and buns and had a picnic in my room

I put my feet up and started doing a crossword but was nodding off. It was only 7 30 p m but I had been up since 4.00 a.m.

I put my pyjamas on and took off my make-up but as I was about to sink into my bed the phone rang!

A Spanish voice said -

"You are wanted back at Wardrobe!" I could hardly believe it!

There I am in my pyjamas - no makeup on - and a man downstairs is waiting for me!

"I'll be about 5 or 10 minutes" I said

"5 would be better" came the reply.

I jumped back in my clothes, hastily put a little makeup on my sleepy face, and dashed out.

It was back into the black dress and *'Ruby'* led me to a room for inspection - on the way she said *"Now is the time to scintillate, Barbara"*

"Some hopes" I thought but in the room were all the top people who were paying the bills and had the last say!

I smiled and twirled. They hadn't been able to find Ray my partner at first (he had been on the beach).

Then it was into the brown dress again I smiled and twirled!

Then back into the black. I smiled and twirled again. They still hadn't made their minds up when I was driven back to the hotel and bed, at long, long, last.

Next day **Louise**, **Brian** and I were driven to the location. It was a club with a large ballroom.

A large Spanish lady began making me up - talking non stop to a friend.

Louise was next to me having her hair done - then we changed places

The hairdresser spent a long time on us and made our hair look really special.

We were then shown to a wardrobe van parked along the street where our costumes were. It was the brown dress and it had to go over my head - so it was back to the hairdresser!

Back in the club there was quite a buzz!

About 16 Spanish extras were being costumed; *Ruby* and her staff worked very hard.

My belt needed an adjustment and while she was attending to it she was asked a question to which she replied *"It will have to wait, I am busy with this principal"*.

After all the years spent as an 'extra' myself I thought *"does she mean me?"*

Ray and I were first on the scene - it was a celebration party. The extras grouped round and clapped to the music. We jived and jived and jived.

When there was a break for change of lighting, camera position, or to rearrange the extras' 2 chairs were brought for us and some water to drink.

The filming went on for *nearly 6 hours!*

Then we had a lot of still pictures taken which may be used for magazines or other publications. (I hoped so as it could mean more money!)

There was a buffet of filled rolls, tea, coffee or cold drink available all day so Ray and I then rested and ate.

It was **Louise** and **Brian's** turn next doing their tango with the 'extras' for background.

At about 9.00 p.m. we all sat down to a hot meal which was most welcome and very good - but we had to first change into our own clothes – then back into our filming clothes.

Close on midnight, Ray and I were called back! They wanted a 'wide shot' taken from above.

Off we were again jiving, stopping and starting

After the third bout of jiving I suddenly knew my energy had gone!

I whispered to Ray *"I'm having a problem now!"* Luckily they ware satisfied and we were finished!

My legs would have turned to jelly if I had been asked to dance again.

The extras still around us began clapping us so we went round the circle clapping them. We were thanked by all the crew and directors and were made a great fuss of, with me receiving a great many kisses.

As we, with Louise and Brian left at about 12.30 am., the Line Dancers were just beginning their stint.

We were due to leave for home in the morning so on our way back to our hotel we asked our young Spanish driver, **Mimi** (short for Jemima) if she would take us to see the Gaudi Cathedral on the way back. She readily agreed although she had also been working all day on the set. At almost 1.00 am we could not go inside but we had a good look at this amazing building, our only bit of sight-seeing.

On my homeward flight I had Sally for company, she had changed her ticket as Gatwick suited her better.

She was only 36 and 'mothered' me all the way, fetching me tea when we were waiting, grabbing my case off the luggage carousel when we arrived, etc.

It was a very hectic but exiting 3 days!

Everyone treated me like a 'Star, but the welcome home I had from Wally was even better.

TV Extra's eye-view (behind the scenes)

Working with 'stars' in a variety of locations make working as a television 'extra' unpredictable and interesting.

"**AFTER HENRY**" starring **Prunella Scales** with **Joan Sanderson** was filmed at Teddington Studios in the scene in which I appeared.

By contrast a scene for -

RUMPOLE OF THE 'BAILEY' starring **Leo McKern** was filmed in Chichester Catheral only six miles from my home in Bognor Regis, - a nice job.

'TENKO' the famous series of women in a Japanese prisoner of war camp was somewhat disappointing for me for although several friends were extras my face was thought not 'gaunt' enough. However it passed muster for the scene where, the war over and released from prison, ladies were going home. Filmed at Southampton docks cleverly made to look like Singapore, the first batch of ex-prisoners embarked on a ship taking them to freedom. I was with another batch waving them off and hoping to be aboard the next ship out.

Usually we remain silent whilst filming crowd scenes is underway, miming talking or cheering and a sound track being inserted later. This time we were asked to shout and cheer as we waived the ship away. After rehearsing and then 'shooting' the scene several times I ended up very hoarse.

BOBBY DAVRO SERIES - My scene took place in a small theatre. Extras were the audience filmed from behind. My back view is famous among friends who pick out my red hair sometimes 'seeing' me in things I wasn't in then when I have been 'in shot' missing my front view. Back to the show, -

Bobby on stage doing an act that called for him to put a worm in his mouth. Ugh! that's what we all thought. Bobby worked out a way of faking it but the director wouldn't agree to that. *"The worms have been boiled"* he said *"and are quite clean"*.

Don't ask how far the worm went in Bobby Davro's mouth, my eyes were tightly shut!

'THE BILL' regularly used extras, me included, and an early episode was a funeral filmed in Kensal Green Cemetery, North London near where I used to live. A miserable winter's day - we stood around the grave for a long time. The coffin was lowered into the grave then dragged out again for each re-take. Authentic funeral workers handled the weighted coffin. In between 'takes' they regaled us with stories of real life funeral mishaps, such as a coffin being too large for the prepared grave but modesty and protocol forbids repetition of other examples. When the 'crew' were at last satisfied with that shot we were to move away from the graveside.

The order "Action" was given but our frozen feet were stuck in the mud and we were stumbling about as though drunk. After stamping our feet free of mud and back to life we were filmed leaving in an orderly manner.

Next we were moved into a pub room on the opposite side of the same road for a 'Wake' scene. What bliss to be inside, out of the wind and able to sit down. Our relief was short lived. Smoke was pumped into the room to create a pub atmosphere. Phew ! Talk about Health & Safety.

'BRITTAS EMPIRE' starring **Chris Barrie**, a scene taking place in an elderly persons exercise class. I wore a baggy track suit and had to cover my red hair with a grey wig. Hanging on to 'zimmer' frames we did slow motion movements until **Chris Barrie** bursts in, trips over and slides along the floor clutching an out of control chainsaw, neatly slicing off the front legs of the 'zimmer' frames causing the old people to fall in a heap. Very authentic but I don't recall being paid danger money? Must speak to my agent!

'CAT'S EYES' starring **Jill Gascoine** took us into a Casino. We had a chance to dress up and wear our jewellery this time. The croupiers were the real thing, the punters we 'extras'. I was playing Black-Jack having been 'schooled' by the croupier. Never very quick with figures, before I had time to add my cards up they were snatched away, I had lost. Realizing how much money I would have quickly lost if I had really been gambling I was appalled.

Jill, playing an under cover detective was required to sing. The crew were pleased with how well she did, and the scene was completed very quickly. Jill reminded them that she had done a lot of singing in the past.

'CALLING THE SHOTS' starring **Lynn Redgrave**, saw us filming in a large house in Hampstead just along from 'Jack Straws Castle', an old and famous Inn said to be frequented by Dick Turpin, the highwayman.

In our scene, Lynn was visiting her mother in an old people's home. My lasting memory was tall, elegant

Lynn arriving and shaking hands with each of us extras, already costumed, my red hair covered with a scarf, and in our places and she introducing herself.

A number of hours later, the scene recorded, she thanked each of us before she left. Nice lady.

Barbara the Author

Incredibly to me and with the help and encouragement of a lot of my friends I am now a published author.

I do hope you have enjoyed reading my story and that you will buy a copy as a present to your family and friends.

Give me the opportunity and I still pick up my dancing shoes and continue to 'Dance my way through life!'

Sincerely
Barbara Stewart

Barbara Stewart

Barbara!

Books from *TwigBooks*

- **BARBARA - the Memoirs of a DANCER**
  By Barbara Stewart
  ISBN 9780954723675: First published by *TwigBooks* in 2007

- **Little Nessie, Bedeliah the Witch, & Chester the Cat!**
  By Julia Mowery
  ISBN 9780954723637: First published by *TwigBooks* in Autumn 2007

Books for the Professional Manager –

- **HOW to MASTER FINANCE**
  By Terry Gasking
  ISBN 9780954723613: First published 1991. The rewritten and revised International Edition first Published by *TwigBooks* in 2006

- **PERFECT FINANCIAL RATIOS**
  By Terry Gasking
  ISBN 9780954723644: First published 1993. The rewritten and revised International Edition first Published by *TwigBooks* in 2007

- **GET OUT of DEBT with Terry Gasking**
  By Terry Gasking
  ISBN 9780954723606: First published by *TwigBooks* in 2004

- **CASH & the ART of BUSINESS MANAGEMENT**
  By Terry Gasking
  ISBN 9780954723651: First published by *TwigBooks* in Autumn 2007

All Available from -

TwigBooks (www.twigbooks.com)
1-2 Biggs Lane, DINTON
Aylesbury, Buckinghamshire
UK, England HP17 8UH
0 (or 44 International) 1296 748412
sales@twigbooks.com

Printed in the United Kingdom
by Lightning Source UK Ltd.
121420UK00001B/301-321/A